The La  s

The Last Knight of Flanders

Remy Schrijnen

and his SS-Legion "Flandern"/Sturmbrigade
"Langemarck" Comrades on the Eastern Front
1941-1945

Allen Brandt

Schiffer Military History
Atglen, PA

Book Design by Robert Biondi.

Printed in the United States of America.
ISBN: 0-7643-0588-3

We are interested in hearing from authors with book ideas on military topics.

Published by Schiffer Publishing Ltd.
4880 Lower Valley Road
Atglen, PA 19310
Phone: (610) 593-1777
FAX: (610) 593-2002
E-mail: Schifferbk@aol.com.
Please write for a free catalog.
This book may be purchased from the publisher.
Please include $3.95 postage.
Try your bookstore first.

Contents

Foreword

This book is the authorized biography of Remy Schrijnen. Schrijnen first served as a messenger in the SS foreign volunteer legion (SS-Freiwilligen-Legion) "Flandern" and later as a no. 1 gunner in an anti-tank gun unit of the SS foreign volunteer brigade (SS-Freiwilligen-Sturmbrigade) "Langemarck." Schrijnen was awarded Germany's highest decoration for bravery in battle, the Knight's Cross to the Iron Cross, for actions during the battles in the northern sector of the Eastern Front during the fateful summer of 1944. While the story indeed centers around the life and times of Remy Schrijnen, its primary purpose is to explain and detail the thoughts, motivations and experiences typical of all the Flemish volunteers who fought alongside the Germans against the Soviet Union in the Second World War.

Since the end of the war there have been many books written about the foreign volunteers who fought with the Germans during the war. While all of the foreign legions fought under the German flag and primarily under German leadership, each of these units has a unique history that is specific to the country in question. Not all of the legions fought for the same reason, and within each unit there were a variety of motivations to fight.

It can be generally stated that the Eastern European Legions, most prominently the Latvians, Estonians and Finns, each fought with the Germans in defense of their homeland against the Soviet invasion. Some viewed the Germans as the lesser of two evils, while others held them in high regard. In the beginning, they were considered by many to be liberators. Despite the fact that they fought within the German army, members of each of these countries hoped to obtain complete independence for their homeland after the conclusion of the war. Of the above named countries, only Finland was to remain independent after the war while Estonia and Latvia remained occupied by the Soviets. Even today, more than 50 years after the conclusion of the war and almost a decade after the fall of the Soviet Union, these countries still suffer from the Soviet occupation.[1]

Soldiers from other countries represented amongst the foreign legions within the German Wehrmacht possessed a variety of motivations for joining the war on the side of the Germans. Some were religious, others patriotic, some were purely political. Others believed in final German victory over the Allied Forces, both Eastern and Western, and wanted the blessings of the victor. Some simply admired the Germans and their army and wanted to take part in the adventure of the Second Great War. In almost all cases though, the fear of a "Red" takeover of Europe was among the reasons why men from Western – and even Eastern – nations volunteered. As far as the Flemings are concerned, they fought for very unique reasons as well, the majority of which are discussed in greater detail within the text of this book.

The Flemings had a mixed view of the political situation concerning their unit, but in general the Flemings were devout nationalists who primarily viewed themselves as soldiers fighting for their country within the German army. The political situation concerning their country divided the men into several groups, all of which were united in their struggle, despite members' varying viewpoints. Belgian and Flemish politics were a primary discussion topic amongst the men while not on the front, as was the political situation concerning Germany itself.

The Flemings fought under a primarily German and Austrian[2] leadership corps which enjoyed only a mixed reputation. Negative sentiments developed due to differences in nationality and political disagreements. Political dictates from above also influenced the Fleming's view of their German superiors. It should be stressed that each German and Austrian member had his own unique reputation amongst the men. Many Germans and Austrians were respected and held in very high re-

---

[1] For instance, the city of Narva in eastern Estonia is almost completely Russian. The Russians also play a major role in the Estonian government – mainly due to the large number of Russians who live there.

[2] The Austrians were considered to be Germans by the Flemings during this time, as Austria had been a part of Germany since the Anschluß in 1938. The Austrians are differentiated from the Germans in the text, since they were somewhat different than the Germans and maintained a different reputation amongst the Flemish volunteers.

gard by their men while others were simply despised. Some German and Austrian members held a mixed reputation, being popular with some and unpopular with others.

As for the Flemish officers, there were very few in the early stages of the war. These were primarily ex-officers of the Belgian Army and the political leaders from the homeland who possessed only a very limited military background. Many Flemings considered the Belgian-trained officers to be lacking in comparison to their German and Austrian counterparts. They simply didn't enjoy the disciplined and detailed training being offered by the German Junkerschulen. Later in the war, however, there emerged a strong and capable Flemish officer corps. The majority of these men had suffered through years of battle on the Eastern Front, fighting first in the enlisted ranks and later as non-commissioned officers. These men were recognized for their capabilities and subsequently enrolled at the SS-Junkerschule Bad Tölz by their German superiors. At the officer candidate school in Bad Tölz, specialized courses were conducted for German and non-German SS officer candidates alike. Those that partook in these courses only had very positive things to say about their experiences there.

But it was the backbone of the Flemish units, the dogged Flemish enlisted men, who made the unit so reliable. At first the German leadership considered the Flemings to be simple cannon fodder, but after several difficult battles in brutal weather conditions, the Flemish "Landsers," as the German enlisted men liked to call themselves, earned high respect from their the German and Austrian leaders. A former staff officer of the 6. SS Panzer Armee under Sepp Dietrich recently commented to me that "the Flemings were by far more reliable than their Walloonian counterparts."

While the general history of the multi-national Waffen-SS is far beyond the scope of this book, the topics reported on and discussed herein offer the reader additional insight and background on this topic by reflecting upon the actual experiences of the typical Flemish Waffen-SS soldier, not only from a military standpoint, but from a social and political viewpoint as well. The material used to write this book is based primarily on a variety of personal recollections and opinions of those represented. This material has been inserted into the general framework of the factual history of this time period as it has been reported in military and general history texts.

Allen Brandt
November 1997

Acknowledgements

I would like to express my sincere thanks and gratitude to the following individuals, without whose help this project could never have been completed. Each of the following people graciously offered continuous support and corresponded with me on numerous occasions. Their patience concerning my many questions will never be forgotten. Many of them also allowed me to visit them for the purpose of conducting in-depth interviews, which, on almost every occasion, lasted late into the night. I would like to thank these individuals for their sincere and genuine hospitality during those visits. Finally, I would like to thank the veteran's organization of the Legion "Flandern"/Sturmbrigade "Langemarck" for inviting me to their annual reunion.

Remy Schrijnen
Remy Schrijnen provided the bulk of the story, most of which he carefully recounted from his memory or had recorded with the help of his comrades during his internment in the Belgian Beverloo prison after the war. Remy remained in constant contact with me throughout the preparation of the manuscript and answered each and every one of my letters and questionnaires on the very same day that he received them. He also supplied important photographs from his personal collection and took part in several interviews, both on the telephone and at his home. I wish to sincerely thank Remy and his wife Joanna for their hospitality during my visits.

Georg D'Haese

A hearty thanks to Georg D'Haese, who provided many facts concerning Kampfgruppe "D'Haese" and the battles in the Blue Mountains of Estonia. Georg helped me formulate a more precise chronological representation of the events during that battle by supplementing the general framework of the fight with little-known facts. He also corrected some of the long-standing mistakes concerning the struggle. Heer D'Haese also submitted detailed reports about the motivations of the young Flemish volunteers who served in the Waffen-SS and supplied, confirmed or debated facts concerning the general and political history of his native Belgium. He also was kind enough to supply important photographs from his family albums. I also wish to thank Georg and his wife Ursula for their kind hospitality during my visits.

Anton (Toon) Pauli

Toon Pauli is the chairman of the veteran's administration for the Flemish volunteers, St. Maartensfonds. Heer Pauli, also a veteran of the anti-tank gun company, had a large influence on the outcome of this book. He supplied, confirmed and debated facts concerning the history of this unit and of the general and political history of his native Flanders and Belgium. He coordinated correspondence with other veterans and even arranged to get permission for the use of several photographs previously published in the multi-volume history of the Flemish units written by Jan Vincx. Heer Pauli very patiently translated reports from Flemish to German and maintained contact with several veterans during the preparation of the manuscript. I also with to thank Heer Pauli for his kind hospitality during my first visit of the FLA/FLAK/PAK Treffen in Antwerp.

Jan De Wilde

Jan De Wilde supplied some of the best previously unpublished photos from his personal collection. Heer De Wilde, who started the war as an infantryman and later served as a Schirrmeister (technical sergeant responsible for vehicles, equipment, etc.) for the anti-tank gun company, provided facts concerning the motivation of the volunteers, the general history of the Flemish units and Langemarck's anti-tank gun unit. He also related important information about the political history of Flanders and Belgium as well as other detailed reports concerning the history of the Flemish units. When it came to questions that required further research, he corresponded with other veterans to find missing facts.

Herman Van Gyseghem
Hermann Van Gyseghem served in the 7. (Stg.) Kompanie of the 6. SS-Frw. Sturmbrigade "Langemarck" as well as the SS-Panzerjägerabteilung 27. Herman Van Gyseghem graciously provided excellent information regarding these units. He also offered insight into the motivations of the young Flemish volunteers as well as his own experiences after the war.

Anton Kotlowski
Herr Kotlowski supplied valuable information on the history of his company as well as the SS-Panzerjägerabteilung 27 in which he continued to serve as company commander. He provided important background information concerning the general history of the Waffen-SS as well several personal accounts concerning the end of the war and the fate of the volunteers of the Waffen-SS. Herr Kotlowski also provided several important photographs and biographical information.

Ekkehard Wangemann
Herr Wangemann supplied detailed notes about the formation and the battles of his Panzerjägerabteilung 27 which fought as part of Kampfgruppe "Schellong" during the battles in Pomerania in 1945. Herr Wangemann also supplied interesting facts concerning the political situation within the Flemish units and the Waffen-SS in general.

Paul-Albert Kausch
Paul-Albert Kausch was the commander of SS-Panzerabteilung 11 "Hermann von Salza" during the battles in Estonia. Herr Kausch provided important information concerning the battles that took place west of Narva and supplied some previously unpublished photographs as well as biographical information.

Lea Van De Wiele-Laperre
Mevrouw Van De Wiele-Laperre is the sister of Marcel Laperre, who was Schrijnen's platoon leader during the battles in the Blue Mountains of Estonia. She provided the only known photo of her brother Marcel and supplied important biographical details concerning her brother and the Laperre family.

Dries Anseeuw
Dries Anseeuw supplied an excellent report on his experiences as a loader in the PAK company during the battles in Narva. Heer Anseeuw also supplied photos and biographical information.

Alfons (Fons) Van Broeck
Fons Van Broeck was a motorcycle dispatch messenger with the anti-tank company and fought in almost every major battle of the war. Van Broeck assisted the author with information about the battles in Narva and supplied other important facts concerning the Flemish units.

Michael Van Ruymbeke
Michael Van Ruymbeke was a volunteer medic and served with Kampfgruppe Schellong during the final stages of the war. Heer Van Ruymbeke provided valuable biographical information concerning his experiences in the Waffen-SS.

René Bottu
Heer Bottu is the brother of Luc Bottu, who was a platoon leader in one of the infantry companies that fought in Narva. He graciously provided two photos of his older brother, Luc, as well as biographical information about his brother.

Luc De Bast
Luc De Bast relayed important information gathered from interviews with veterans of the Flemish units. He also supplied many excellent unpublished photos from his personal collection. Heer De Bast also arranged several interviews with veterans to help fill gaps concerning missing information.

Heinz Fleischer
Herr Heinz Fleischer provided a very rare photo of the view through the optics of a PAK gun from his private photo archive. Herr Fleischer is an active historian of his former unit, Heeres Sturmgeschützbrigade 276.

Mark C. Yerger
Last but not least I would like to thank Mark Yerger for his general support and encouragement concerning this book. Yerger is an accomplished author and historian of the Waffen-SS and is possibly best known for his series "Knights of Steel – the Development, Structure and Personalities of the 2. SS-Panzer Division." Mark graciously helped me get my start in researching the Waffen-SS and has tirelessly continued to help me during the past few years. Yerger also helped considerably by providing information on the movement of Battle Group "Das Reich" during the defensive battles in the Ukraine in early 1944, during which the Flemish Brigade was often subordinated to this unit.

Note on Source Material

A great portion of this book is comprised of "war stories" told repeatedly in the close quarters of the "Belgian Internment Camp" in Beverloo, Belgium, where the "German sympathizers" whiled away some of the best years of their young lives after the war. There the battered surviving veterans were stuffed into close quarters that lacked even the bare living essentials. It was at this camp where these stories were told again and again. It wasn't until 1950 that the last of the once proud Flemish veterans were released.

During Remy Schrijnen's prison term there, he made an effort to preserve the many stories about his comrades. He kept a notebook in which he carefully recorded many of the details concerning the men that surrounded him during the battles which he had fought in. In addition to general facts and dates, the voices of comrades that had been killed were also recorded. Much of this book is based on these stories. It should be noted that these stories are reprinted and marked by quotes and a footnote. These portions of the book are from third- and even fourth-hand sources.

During the search for new and additional material, many Flemish veterans supplemented the stories collected by Schrijnen with personal recollections. These statements and stories have been inserted into the framework of the story as well. Statements, opinions and stories that were taken from letters to the author are included in *italicized* text with a foot note.

Notes Kept in Captivity: Pictured here is Remy Schrijnen at his home in Hagen, Germany, in October 1996. He is reviewing one of the notebooks he kept while interned in the Beverloo POW camp in Belgium. After rehashing the war with his comrades, Schrijnen would write down what he had learned from them. He wrote in various colors of ink and in several different directions to make the notebook look like a scribble pad, hoping that the prison guards would not confiscate it. These stories are the basis for some of the first part and much of the second part of the book.

These recollections more often than not agreed with Schrijnen's outline of events that occurred within his sphere of the war. Sometimes certain facts and dates did not correspond at all, however. In each case, when questioned about the discrepancies, veterans responded that they had been asked to report on events that took place fifty years in the past and that their memories could only be trusted to a certain extent. An example is provided by a letter from Georg D'Haese:[1]

> *With all trust to my statements, you are not allowed to forget that Narva occurred over 50 years ago and that in the meantime, I, in contrast to Remy Schrijnen, only seldomly concerned myself with the past. It is therefore very well possible and hopefully understandable as well, that my memory can, on occasion, abandon me.*

---

[1] Letter to the author from Georg D'Haese dated Feb. 9, 1997.

Besides war stories, personal opinions and stories, the basic outline of the story was provided by general texts concerning the battles. A list of these texts is included in the bibliography.

• • •

In order to understand the motivations of the young Flemish soldiers who sided with the Germans in the Second World War, an understanding of the history of Belgium is required. Existing as an independent state since 1830, the young country of Belgium, now home to one of three locations of the European Union's European Parliament, has a very interesting history. Due to its relatively small size, Belgium has been forced to play the role of a pawn by greater European powers throughout its one thousand year history, while Belgium's cultural diversity has been the source of internal conflict which exists to this day.

This Book is Dedicated to all Flemish Soldiers
Killed or Missing in Action in the Second World War

1
Catalyst of Conflict:
A Brief History of Flanders and Belgium

Early Belgium History

Belgium is presently a country which contains three separate cultures, all with their own languages and customs. To the south, bordering France, Germany and Luxembourg, lies the region of Walloonia. The Walloons, who speak French, make up about 40% of the population. In the north, where Belgium borders the North Sea, the Netherlands and France, lies the region of Flanders. The Flemings, who speak Flemish, their own version of Dutch known as *Vlaams*, make up the majority of the population, some 60%. To the southeast live ethnic Germans, who have maintained their native German language and customs. This area was ceded by Germany to Belgium after the First World War. The ethnic Germans make up only a very small percentage of the population.

The area now known as Belgium was first inhabited by Celtic tribes known as the *Belgae*. After the Romans defeated the Belgae during the 50's B.C., they developed several cities, local industries and roads. Around 400 A.D. a Germanic people known as the Franks drove the Romans out of the northern region of what was then known as Gaul (ancient Western Europe which included primarily the regions of modern-day Belgium and France). This area became Flanders. The Frankish King, Clovis, established a kingdom that included, among other regions, Belgium. During the seventh century, descendants of Clovis gave control of the region to a family of Frankish rulers known as the Carolingians. Charlemagne, the

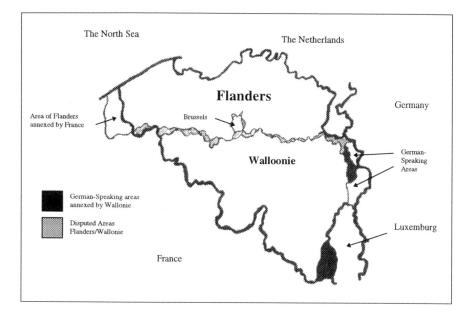

The North Sea

The Netherlands

Flanders

Germany

Area of Flanders
annexed by France

Brussels

German-
Speaking
Areas

Walloonie

German-Speaking areas
annexed by Wallonie

Disputed Areas
Flanders/Wallonie

Luxemburg

France

most famous of the Carolingian rulers, ruled the region from 768 to 814. In 843, Charlemagne's three grandsons divided the region into three kingdoms. During the following centuries, the Carolingians lost the greater portion of their power. During this time, Belgium became an important center of trade and industry and a feudal system developed. Under this system, merchant guilds sought charters from feudal lords, promoted the economic interests of the villages and granted special privileges to the merchants. This helped to form a rigid class system. It should be noted that a celebrated day in Flemish history is July 11, 1302, known as the "Day of the Golden Spurs." On this day a small Flemish army defeated the French in a large battle in Kortrijk.

Thereafter, during the 1300s and 1400s, the dukes of Burgundy ruled all of the Low Countries (Walloonia, Flanders, Luxembourg and the Netherlands). During this period, manufacturers and merchants alike prospered. The arts also flourished during this time. In 1477, the Austrian Hapsburg family obtained rule of the Low Countries. In 1516, however, the entire region came under Spanish rule. The Spanish, who were devout Catholics, persecuted the Protestants in the Low Countries. These actions led to a long Protestant revolt which began in 1566 and ended in 1581 when the Netherlands declared independence. The area of Belgium, however, remained under Spanish control. By separating the economy of the Low Countries, the economies in Flanders and Walloonia suffered greatly. Flanders and

Walloonia continued to suffer economically during the remainder of the 1600s until Spain gave the area to Austria as part of the settlement of the War of the Spanish Succession. During the time thereafter, Flanders and Walloonia regained their agricultural and commercial status. During this time the Austrians began to revise the administrative, economic, educational and legal systems which bound Flanders and Walloonia. While overhauling these systems, Austria did not take the cultures of the two regions into consideration. This lack of respect led to a united revolt against the Austrians which ended with the Belgians in control of their own country. The next year, however, the Austrians once again took control of the region. In 1794, the French arrived and drove out the Austrians. Walloonia and Flanders became officially a part of France in 1795. French rule ended after the defeat of Napoleon in the battle of Waterloo in 1815.

During the Spanish, Austrian and French occupations, French became the dominant language in Belgium, despite the fact that the majority of the population exclusively spoke Flemish. The dominance of the French language was especially reinforced during the French occupation, as the French replaced the existing legal and educational systems with their own. This was a great advantage for the Walloonian population, as French was their mother tongue. In order to be successful, upper-class Flemings were forced to maintain a fluent French. For the remaining Flemish population there was little opportunity for financial prosperity.

After Napoleon's defeat, political leaders from all over Europe gathered in Vienna to establish a new Europe. The results of this meeting, known as the Vienna Congress of 1815, united Flanders, Walloonia and the Netherlands into one country, known as the Kingdom of the Netherlands. The primary motivation for this unification was to form a strong barrier against possible renewed expansion attempts by the French. The economies in Flanders and Walloonia began to flourish with the union, but differences between the Dutch government and both the Walloons and residents of the French-speaking part of Flanders concerning education, language and politics led to discontent among the citizens of this new country. To make matters worse, the Flemings and Walloons were Roman Catholics and resented being ruled by Dutch Protestants, who treated them like second-class citizens.

Resentment toward the Dutch grew steadily until the French-speaking portion of the Belgian population, with the help of the French, decided to revolt against the Netherlands and secede from their control. The Flemings and Walloons formed an army to fight against the Dutch for independence. This army was not a united

Flemish/Walloonian army, though, as the officer corps was exclusively made up of Walloons. The French were said to have had a decisive influence on the formation of this new army.

Even though the Flemings helped to form this new army, they hardly did so for patriotic reasons. The majority of the Flemings that had joined had done so only for money. A "Flemish Army" was out of the question. The Flemings were primarily poor farmers who had no political power. The Walloons, on the other hand, were from the industrial part of Belgium and were rich in comparison to the Flemings.

The revolt began in August of 1830 and ended on October 4th with Belgium declaring its independence. In December, the major European powers of the time officially recognized the state of Belgium. Shortly thereafter, an agreement was signed which guaranteed Belgium's independence and neutrality.

Under its first King, Prince Leopold of Saxe-Coburg, Belgium was the first nation within the European mainland to industrialize. This industrialization mainly took place in Wallonia, with Flanders remaining primarily agricultural. Trade also rose sharply during the 1800s.

Despite Belgium's new found independence, industrialization and increasing economic trade, relations between the Flemish-speaking Flemings and the French-speaking Walloons grew increasingly tense. Up until this time, French was the only official language in Belgium, despite the fact that Flemish was spoken by the majority of the population. Despite the fact that the Flemings gained recognition of Flemish as an official language shortly after Belgian independence, the Walloons were very slow to accept this and maintained control of the government and society in general. Flemings, despite being citizens within the Belgian state, were at an extreme disadvantage due to this language barrier, and thus were unable to enjoy the same rights as their Walloonian counterparts. For example, the language of the judicial system remained French, which naturally caused many problems for the Flemings who were brought to court. Flemings accused of crimes could not understand the proceedings – and so it was that many Flemings were convicted of crimes without even fully understanding the charges brought against them and without ever being able to properly defend themselves.

The Flemings were primarily farmers and needed their children to help on the farm. Children began to work the farm at the age of twelve years (and sometimes younger) and because of this, school classes were only taught in the winter. Also, since French was the official language of higher education, the majority of the

Flemings were effectively eliminated from pursuing any career besides agriculture. The university courses taught throughout Belgium were conducted in French and the business language remained exclusively French. The language barrier remained the primary obstacle for Flemings to economically flourish within the Belgian state.

Belgium in the early Twentieth Century

In 1909, Albert, a nephew of Leopold II, became King of Belgium and consequently the leader of Belgium's military forces. On August 4, 1914, Germany invaded Belgium in the first part of a plan to overrun eastern and northern France. In order to fight the Germans, Albert needed to recruit soldiers from the entire population. To lure the Flemings, Albert promised them that upon their return from the front, they would be granted a "normal" Belgian citizenship. A "normal" citizenship implied that Flemings would receive the same rights as their Walloonian counterparts – that Flemings could take an active part in government and business and would get the opportunity to receive a university education. Many Flemings rushed to volunteer for the Belgian army and fight the Germans. Once again the Army was led exclusively by the French-speaking Walloons, despite the predominance of Flemish-speaking soldiers. The language of the officer corps was French and all orders were therefore given only in French. This created many problems during battle, as the Flemish-speaking soldiers could not understand their French-speaking leaders. Many Flemings were killed in battle unnecessarily as a result of this clearly avoidable confusion. It was the extreme bitterness and contempt felt by the Flemish soldiers about this tragic situation that formed the roots of Flemish nationalism, which would later grow into a united front.

It should also be noted that during the four years of fighting, several large battles took place between the Allies and the Germans on Belgian soil. The Germans advanced as far as the Ijzer river in western Belgium. During the course of the war, all of the towns in the vicinity of the front were destroyed. As a result, a great number of Belgians had bitter feelings toward the Germans.

During the German occupation, many of the population fled to France, Great Britain and the Netherlands. Organized resistance on the part of the civilian population did not really exist during the First World War as it did in the Second World War. The Allies did not officially recognize partisan warfare and did not support it. Still, in some places in Belgium, for example Leuven (Flemish)/Louvain (French)

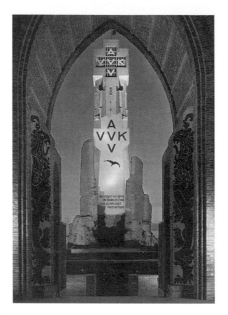

Memorial on the Ijzer River: This photo portrays the memorial to the Flemish soldiers killed in the First World War and is located in Diksmuide on the Ijzer River. The letters AVV – VVK stand for "Alles Vor Vlaanderen – Vlaanderen Vor Kristus" (Everything For Flanders – Flanders For Christ), which was the slogan of the embittered soldiers who returned from the front lines of the First World War to form the Flemish Front Party.

some people did resist the German occupation by carrying out acts of violence against the German authorities. In such cases the Germans took hostages who were executed because the guilty parties did not surrender themselves. In total several hundred people were executed.[1]

A portion of the Flemings saw a different side of the German occupation. Under German rule, the oppressive conditions enforced by the French-speaking population were partly relieved. For instance, the University of Ghent in Flanders was allowed to switch its language of instruction from French to Flemish. Also, during the war, an "independent Flanders" was called for by a part of the Flemish population and was supported by the occupying German forces. There was even a

---

[1] Later, in the Geneva and Hague conventions it was agreed by the allies (at that time primarily France, England, Italy and the U.S. – the Russians did not take part in these conventions) that partisan or civilian warfare was officially illegal. According to the new conventions, it was illegal to take part in war without wearing a recognized uniform. Within these rules it was clearly stated that occupying forces were permitted to execute civilians as punishment for the assassination of members of the their forces at a ratio of 3:1. The purpose of this rule was to avoid partisan warfare which was considered unfair. Ironically, the Allies did not adhere to this dictate of the treaty and actively supported underground resistance movements in all of the Western European nations.

"Council of Flanders," made up of some two hundred Flemish autonomists that were to be the nucleus of the new independent state. This idea received very little support from the rest of Belgium, however, and was never realized.

The newly established Flemish rights were quickly dissolved after the Germans were driven out of Belgium. It should also be noted that the Germans never actively recruited Flemish or Walloonian soldiers during the occupation. All Belgian prisoners of war remained in Germany for the duration of the war.

After the war concluded, King Albert refused to make good his promise to grant his "normal" citizenship to the Flemish soldiers who fought against the Germans and maintained his opinion that the "official" language of Belgium would remain French. This only served to intensify the bitterness felt by the Flemings towards their fellow countrymen, the Walloons as well as the Belgian state.

The Turbulent Inter-War Period

During the late 1800s and early 1900s, nationalism developed as an increasingly popular concept in Europe. The Versailles Treaty, which some view as an experiment in nationalistic theories, had carved several new borders after the Great War. Some countries found their borders generally corresponding to the different population concentrations and differences in culture and languages. The Austrian-Hungarian empire had been split in just this way, with the empire being forced to cede land to Italy and then split to form Hungary (Hungarian culture), Austria (Austrian/German culture) and Czechoslovakia (Czech and Slovak cultures under one government). This applied theory was not perfect, however, as the settlements were populated areas and not clear cut. Several German culture populations were still located within Czechoslovakia (primarily in Bohemia and Moravia)and governed by the new Czech government. Throughout Austria there were Hungarians and vice versa, so in that respect, the nationalist policies of the Versailles Treaty failed to unite all people of the same culture under one government.

The signing of the Versailles Treaty also affected Belgium as it abolished Belgium's neutral status. Just two years later, in 1920, the country signed a defense agreement with France. This obviously had a significant effect on the future role of Flemings and strengthened the bias in government to favor the Walloons. The Flemings now viewed Belgium not as an independent state, but as a French buffer-zone against possible future conflicts with the Germans.

Even though Flanders contained some sixty percent of the Belgian population, the official language of Belgium remained exclusively French and the government was dominated by French-speaking Walloons. The influence of the Flemish national party[2] grew stronger, however, and Belgian army officers were first allowed to speak Flemish with the men of the Flemish divisions serving in the Belgian Army in 1936. But as before, these new rules were difficult to enforce and were only slowly recognized by those in power.

In 1930, the Belgian Parliament officially recognized that the country consisted of two linguistic areas and began to install different administrations. This, like the other improvements, was only very slowly realized and was considered by the Flemish population to be a changes in name only.

In 1934, Leopold III became the Belgian King. He was the first Belgian King that could speak Flemish. As King, Leopold III tried to reassert Belgium's neutrality from France, but was unsuccessful. These ties to France were officially secret, but many Belgians knew of them, while others simply did not believe them. In any case, this contract was annulled. The Walloons did nothing more than accept the King. Only in Brussels was Leopold III well-liked. In Flanders the situation was different. The older generations liked the King while the Flemish youth did not.

After the Great War, the economic conditions throughout Europe were very poor. Due to the social and economic effects of the Great Depression, many European countries sought radical solutions for their suffering. Many countries throughout Europe were caught in an idealistic struggle for some new form of government that would save them. Democracy, then the current form of government, was viewed by many as too corrupt. Several new political parties formed, all with extremely different beliefs, but with one goal in mind: an end to the massive unemployment and staggering inflation that brought poverty and despair to much of Europe. Socialist, Bolshevist (as they were called before the term "communist" became popular) and nationalist parties sprung up everywhere. A large sector of the European population became involved in politics. In fact, the first political organization in Belgium to work together with a like-minded German party was communist in nature.

During the Great Depression, nationalistic parties surfaced in almost every European country and became dominant in several. The Italian Fascists under

---

[2] The Vlaams Nationale Partij was established in the early 1920s. Flemish nationalists were elected to the Belgian Parliament as early as 1919. By 1929 there were nine members of the Vlaams Nationale Partij in Parliament.

Mussolini, the Falangists under Franco in Spain, and the National Socialists in Germany under Hitler were the three dominant nationalistic parties. The Nazis were not only nationalists, they were a socialist worker's party as well and thus had to compete with the communists. The communists, who also claimed to be a party for the people, were dominant in Russia and had strong followings in Spain and France. The majority of the European population felt that in the end, European politics would be dominated by either German-led National Socialism or Soviet-led communism. A coexistence was out of the question.

• • •

Remy Schrijnen, who was born on December 24, 1921, in Kemptich, grew up during the post-war economic depression which greatly devastated the population in all of Europe. His father worked for the railway and had a family of eight children. Remy's childhood was a happy one, and he was close to all of his relatives. Schrijnen attended the American equivalent of grade school starting in 1927. Growing up in Kemptich, Remy received a nationalist-Flemish upbringing. His parents and the rest of his family viewed themselves as Germanic, friendly to Germany and other Germanic countries and anti-Belgian. Remy was brought up being taught these beliefs, and was strictly forbidden from enlisting in the Belgian army. He was constantly reminded to "never, ever wear a Belgian uniform and never fight against Germany!"

During his younger years, the rumors left over from the Great War were still circulating in much of Europe. The Prussians were constantly accused of war crimes and several incidents in which the Germans had supposedly cut-off children's hands and heads during their four years of occupation were circulating. Even though the Flemings joked about these rumors, the French-speaking population continued to keep them alive. The French press and the new film industry helped in this regard.

After the conclusion of the First World War, the Flemings formed several nationalistic parties and movements. The primary nationalistic parties and movements whose members served in the Waffen-SS were the *Vlaamsch Nationaal Verbond* or VNV (originally the *Vlaamsch Frontpartij*), *De Vlag* and *Verdinaso*.

The VNV was the most extreme nationalistic party and was devoutly Catholic in nature. The primary goal of the VNV was to form a Flemish state that would be completely independent from Belgium and Walloonia. The party was officially founded in the beginning of October 1933. The leader of the VNV, Staf (Gustave)

De Clercq, was elected on October 8, 1933. Remy's father himself was a member of this party from the beginning, when it was originally founded under the name *Vlaamsch Frontpartij* (Flemish Front Party). The original members of the Vlaamsch Frontpartij were veteran Flemish front-line soldiers. These nationalistic soldiers, embittered after the Great War had ended, had seen a re-establishment of Flemish rights within the Belgian state only to see them lost once again after the war ended and Walloonian dominance resurfaced.

The main beliefs of the VNV centered around the dissolving of the Belgian state and the formation of a union of Dutch-speaking regions under one government. Besides the Flemings, this included the Netherlands, Dutch and Flemings from the German Friesland and the Flemish regions of northern France. The symbol of the VNV was a triangle within a circle. The circle represented the union of the regions and the triangle represented the delta formed by the Rhine, Meuse and Scheldt rivers in the regions. Members of the VNV did not wear uniforms per se, but members of their militia did.

The party was considered by others to be a social-thinking front-party. The party grew during the thirties and with funding granted to the party by the National Socialist German Workers Party, or NSDAP, several members were elected to the Belgian parliament. Among those elected was Dr. Reimond Tollenaere, who was a lawyer and leader of the Black Brigade of the VNV (Dietse Militie – Zwarte Brigade), the paramilitary branch of the party's militia.

While this party was at first supported by the Germans, problems later developed during the war as differences of opinions surfaced concerning what exactly the Flemish volunteers were fighting for. The German leadership, both political and military, preferred to think that the Flemings were fighting for Germany and for Germany's favor, and not for their own nationalistic convictions. The members of the VNV, however, viewed their struggle as one that would free them from repression and control by *any* other state within Europe, not just from the Walloonian-dominated Belgium. It was a struggle for complete independence.

It should also be noted that many of the members also became embittered toward the Germans during the war, as they felt that on the front they were treated as mere cannon-fodder and that their lives and sacrifices somehow held less meaning compared to their German counterparts. Another sensitive issue was the fate of Flanders and the ideals of the VNV should the Germans win the war. Despite the differences of opinion between the members of the VNV and the Germans, the cadre of the Flemish units continued to be primarily made up of members of the VNV.

Dr. Reimond Tollenaere. Tollenaere was born in Oostakker, Flanders (Belgium) on June 29, 1909. He studied law in Ghent and was a political leader there. Later he became the Propaganda Leader for the VNV and Commander of the *Dietse Militie/ Zwarte Brigade* (Dutch Militia/Black Brigade) and held various posts within the VNV. On July 17, 1941 he volunteered for service in the Waffen-SS at Staf De Clercq's headquarters. In August 1941, he enrolled in leadership training for Germanic volunteers in Lauenberg, Germany and by the end of September he was promoted to Untersturm-führer (Second Lieutenant). He served with the 2nd Company of the Legion Flandern until his death in January of 1942.

De Vlag was neither a political party nor movement, but a cultural organization. The name "De Vlag" is an abbreviation for *Duits-VLaamse ArbeidsGemeenschap* (German-Flemish Workers Society) and also translates to "the Flag." This group held cultural exchanges with German organizations, such as "song evenings," plays, and held lectures on Germany in Flanders. Naturally, this organization was very pro-German. After the VNV turned down an offer by the Germans to be the nucleus for the Flemish Allgemeine-SS in 1940, the De Vlag movement expressed desire for Flanders to become a *Gau* (district) within the coming "Greater German Reich." This was not openly discussed by members of the movement, but was a known fact amongst the Flemish soldiers and termed the "Heim ins Reich" or "onward to our home in the Reich" concept. With this idea, Flanders was to become "a pearl in the crown of the Greater German Empire." Jef Van de Wiele was the leader of this organization. Members of De Vlag did not wear uniforms but their symbol was the black lion of Flanders on a yellow shield held in the claws of a black German eagle. This adequately symbolized De Vlag's philosophies and beliefs. Before the war, the De Vlag organization was relatively uninvolved in politics but later became a rival of the VNV.

Verdinaso was not a party, but a political movement. Verdinaso was short for *VERbond van DIets NAtionaal SOlidaristen* or Organization of Dutch[3] National

---

[3] Here the word "Dutch" encompasses all of the Low Countries or "Netherlands" whose inhabitants speak Dutch (Nederlands).

Socialists. The name Verdinaso was also seen in its abbreviated form, Dinaso. This organization was founded in 1932 by Joris Van Severen, a well-respected Fleming who had been one of the few Flemish officers who served in the Great War. This movement held beliefs both similar to and different from the VNV. Whereas the groups were united in their struggle to form the "Greater Netherlands," members of Verdinaso were anti-clerical in contrast to the devoutly Catholic members of the VNV.

While the VNV believed in a "united Netherlands," members of the Verdinaso movement sought to work with the Walloons (as of 1934), the Dutch and even the French. A reunion of the "17 Provinces," which included Holland and Luxembourg, was one of the movement's foreseen goals. In 1938, however, Verdinaso and Van Severen accepted the "Belgian Situation" and decided that it would be better to work only with the Flemings and the Walloons. This caused a break in the movement and a third of the members resigned.

Verdinaso was a small group but well known for their unyielding discipline and organizational skills. It should be stressed that while the VNV was an officially recognized political party in Belgium, Verdinaso was neither a party nor was it officially recognized by the Belgian government as an organization of any kind.

Members of the *Dinaso Militie* initially wore green-shirted storm trooper uniforms. In 1934, the militia was re-named the *Dinaso Militanten Orde* (D.M.O.) but a ban by the Belgian government prevented them from continuing to wear their green uniforms. The motto of Dinaso was *"Recht en Trouw"* (right and true). Their symbol was a combination of a plow, a sword and a gear within a circle. Their leader, Jef Françios, would later volunteer for the Legion "Flandern."

While Verdinaso was not politically connected to the VNV, after the Germans arrived in Belgium in 1940, all German-sympathizing splinter political parties and movements were forced to merge with the VNV.[4] This brought Verdinaso into the VNV party.

Other parties in Belgium during the 1920s and 1930s included the Catholic Party, the Socialist Party, the Liberal Party, the Rex Party and the Communist Party. The strongest political party in Flanders was the Catholic Party, while the Socialist Party was the strongest in Wallonia. The Liberal Party was very anti-Catholic and anti-Flemish and was known as a bourgeois party.

---

[4] Other small splinter parties/movements were the *Nationaal-Socialistische Beweging in Vlaanderen* (N.S.B. i V. or Dutch National-Socialist Movement in Flanders) and the *Volksverweering* (The People's Defense).

The Catholic, Socialist and Liberal Parties were the three strongest parties in Belgium. Trailing closely behind was the strongest of the three nationalist parties, the Flemish VNV. The Catholic party was a general Belgian political party and had both a Walloonian and Flemish wing. The VNV was very Catholic and maintained a "love-hate" relationship with the Flemish wing of the Catholic party. In the provinces of East Flanders and Antwerp, the Flemish wing of the Catholic party (KVV-Katoliek Vlaams Verbond) and VNV formed a coalition. With this coalition the requirement to be a ruling party was met.

The Rex Party and the Communist Party were other minor parties on the ballot. The Rex Party was a nationalistic party founded in Walloonia by Leon Degrelle. Despite its Walloonian roots, the party also existed in Flanders after 1936. The Communist Party was the biggest opponent of the nationalist organizations.

During the politically turbulent 1930s, Remy Schrijnen grew up in his hometown of Kemptich. He finished school in 1937 after which he found a job working in the coal mines. Schrijnen, then at the young age of 15, was very lucky to have found work, as unemployment was quite staggering during this period in Belgium. Schrijnen was also a bit young to be concerned about politics, but like his father, Schrijnen would eventually become a member of the VNV.

War Breaks out in Poland in the East – and then in the West

Early in the morning on September 1, 1939, the Germans abandoned the "flower wars" when they attacked Poland. These non-combat operations had annexed Austria, half of Czechoslovakia and returned the Memel District to the German Reich. The Memel District had been ceded to Lithuania by East Prussia in 1924. This time, however, the Germans unleashed their revamped armies in an unprecedented Blitzkrieg into Poland. After some three weeks of hostilities, the Germans occupied approximately half of the country while the other half would be left for the Russians to later invade and occupy.

The Germans would then go on to take Denmark and Norway. The attack on Denmark commenced on April 9, 1940, and the Danes capitulated shortly thereafter. Then it was on to Norway, where the Germans experienced difficulties. By the end of the hostilities in Norway, they had lost approximately half their Navy due to the intervention of the strong British Navy.

Following the German attack on Poland in September of 1939, the political climate in Belgium became very unstable. France and England had declared war on Germany. This was viewed in Belgium as a conflict between the Germanic and French peoples. The Walloons sided naturally with the French and the Flemings with the Germans. The uncertainty and panic that swept the country caused many conflicts.

On May 10, 1940, the Germans launched the war in the West, which would last less than a month and a half. Holland was taken in less than five days. The Germans had also launched their offensive, virtually unopposed, through the Ardennes Forest in southern Belgium. On May 14, the Germans crossed the Meuse and began the dash to the North Sea. After a few tactical difficulties, the Germans had driven the British Expeditionary force to Dunkirk. The Germans wasted their opportunity to destroy this force and the British were able to escape into the North Sea where they were picked up by their navy.

The Belgians fought well during these battles, but were unprepared for the more modern German army. Hitler had planned the attack of Belgium in a very detailed manner. To influence the success of the operation, he had planned the capture of the Belgian Army's most fortified strongpoint, Fort Eben Emael. This fort commanded the junction of the Meuse River and the Albert Canal. It was a modern, strategically located fortress and was regarded by both the Allies and the Germans as the most impregnable fortification in Europe, stronger than anything the French had built in the Maginot Line or the Germans in the West Wall. Constructed in a series of steel and concrete galleries deep underground, its gun turrets were protected by heavy armor and manned by twelve hundred men. It was expected to hold out indefinitely against the pounding of the heaviest bombs and artillery shells. It fell in thirty hours to eighty German soldiers, who, under the command of a sergeant, had landed in nine gliders on its roof and whose total casualties amounted to six killed and nineteen wounded.

As easy as the Germans made the capture of the "impregnable" fort appear, they had been well prepared for the engagement. During the winter of 1939-40 they had erected a replica of the fort and of the bridges across the Albert Canal and had trained some four hundred glider troops on how to take them. This careful preparation insured the fate of the surprised and dazed Belgian soldiers.

Jan De Wilde, later a member of the Legion "Flandern" and the "Langemarck" Brigade and Division related his experience as a member of the Belgian army fighting against the Germans:[5]

---

[5] Letter to the author from J. De Wilde dated Aug. 29, 1996.

In May 1939, I began my mandatory service in the Belgian Army, and indeed in a Walloonian regiment. When the Germans attacked Belgium on the 10th of May, my Regiment was in position on the German border. I took part in the retreat of the Belgian Army until reaching the Leie (Golden River) in the vicinity of the city of Kortrijk where I would later live for twenty years. That was about 200 km in the direction of the North Sea. On the Leie we fought. It was there that my company retreated under strong pressure from the Germans. My Walloonian group leader was wounded and had been left behind. I then decided to go back and retrieve my group leader with another soldier from my unit who was a volunteer. Unfortunately, on the way the volunteer was killed. I managed to find my group leader, but on our way back we were captured by the Germans.

After two attempts to escape the column of POWs on its way to Germany, I finally managed to get away. As I arrived home, I found that my house had been partly destroyed by a German artillery round. Luckily my parents were still at home.

After a few weeks the message came that Flemish soldiers serving in the Belgian army were to be released and that those that had escaped could pick up release documentation from the German authorities in Ghent. Somewhat later, I found out that my wounded group leader was being taken care of in a hospital in Ghent. I visited him often since his family lived in Lüttich which was some 200 km from Ghent.

After the Germans commenced their western offensive on May 10, 1940, the Belgian government began to collect itself to flee to France. Several officials also began to take prisoners considered to be "enemies of the state" and intern them in Brugge. These prisoners consisted of, among others, communists, Flemish-nationalists, Rexists and Jews. They were subsequently transported to France, where they were put into a prison in Le Vernet. Among the prisoners taken by the Belgian government for transport to France were Joris Van Severen and the leaders of Verdinaso. Even though Van Severen had chosen the "Belgian direction," which had all but broken his Verdinaso movement, he was still considered to be an enemy of the Belgian state. On May 20, 1940, after arriving in Abbeville, France, Van Severen was amongst 22 Belgians that were murdered by French soldiers. The fate of their leader split the remains of Verdinaso. Approximately half of the group remained under the leadership of Jef François, while the other half resigned. François would later serve with the Legion "Flandern."

On the morning of May 28th, King Leopold the IIIrd surrendered Belgium to the Germans, but only after strong urgings from the Belgian Cabinet's Prime Minister and Foreign Minister not to. Both officials wanted Belgium to remain opposed to Germany. They advised the king to maintain his powers in exile in Great Britain, just as the Queen of Holland and the King of Norway had done previously. Leopold, however, believed that the war would be won by the Germans and decided to stay in Belgium. This decision caused Leopold many problems after the war, but his defenders cite that he made the honorable decision to stick by his soldiers and the Belgian people. The Flemish people were generally pleased by the King's display of loyalty. The rest of the Belgian government fled to France.

After the war in Western Europe came to an end, many of the Flemings viewed their new German occupiers with mixed emotions. Some members of the older generations were receptive of the Germans, as they could easily remember the first occupation. But the First World War was already twenty-two years in the past, and by this time, new generations had arrived in Flanders. Others were too young during the First World War to remember what the occupation was really like. They still had memories of the rumors of children with cut-off hands and heads, and were not quite sure what to think of the Germans. There certainly were those who immediately greeted the German occupiers with open arms and those who deeply resented them.

But by the months of September, October and November 1940, the reputation of the Germans had changed. The German leadership viewed the Flemish POWs as Germanic and released them.[6] In Belgium this meant that the Belgian Army's Walloonian soldiers would remain in prison. All officers, Flemish or Walloonian, were to remain in prison. The Flemish officers held prisoner were given the opportunity to volunteer for the German *Arbeitsdienst* (work service) or as *Hilfsdienst* (help service) for the German Police.

More importantly, many Flemings had come to admire the discipline of the German soldiers and had found them to be polite and respectful of the Flemish culture. Indeed, as during any occupation, there were several incidents of civil crimes committed by German soldiers against the population. But these acts were illegal and the German occupation authorities dealt with them harshly. German soldiers convicted of such crimes were, depending on the incident, publicly executed. This only served to strengthen German support. By the end of November,

---

[6] Dutch and Norwegian prisoners of war were also released.

some 80% of the Flemish population considered themselves friendly to the Germans. It should also be stressed that 90% of the entire Belgian population believed in a final German victory. At this time, the Stalin-Hitler Pact was still in effect. This placed the Flemish communists on the side of the Germans as well. Further, food was plentiful. The war was at a stand-still and no great hardships were placed on the Belgian population.

In contrast with the First World War, the Germans did not waste this opportunity to bolster their manpower and began to set up various recruiting posts early in the fall of 1940. Many Flemings subsequently enlisted for service in the German Wehrmacht and other German organizations. Flemings would eventually be called to enlist in the Luftwaffe, Kriegsmarine, German Red Cross, the N.S.K.K. (National Socialist Vehicle Corps) as well as the Waffen-SS. Those that enlisted in the German Wehrmacht or other German organizations did so for a variety reasons:

- Pressure from the nationalistic Flemish political parties to volunteer.
- The corruption in Belgium – the government was viewed by the Flemings as a ruling democracy which was more similar to a dictatorship.
- The success of National Socialism in Germany. The Germans were well-known for their performance in the 1936 Olympics which were held in Berlin. There was also the attractive social conditions in Germany, most notably lengthy vacations and free health care for all citizens. The attractive sport and youth organizations were also highly visible.
- The singing German soldiers portrayed on billboards throughout the country: young, sporty, and well-disciplined.
- The desire to take part and the adventurous spirit of the Flemish youth.

Historians and the veterans alike agree, however, that the overwhelming motivation for enlisting was Flemish nationalism or better said, the resistance against the Belgian State. Although the official languages of Belgium were French and Flemish, the Flemish language was greatly repressed. This language difference was used by the French-speaking Walloons to maintain the effective rule of the entire country of Belgium, despite the fact that they were in the minority within the overall population. It should also be noted that the Belgian State itself was viewed as nothing more than an official French "buffer zone" between the French and the Germans by many.

Foreign Volunteers. Flemings enlisted in all branches of the German Wehrmacht (Army, Luftwaffe, Kriegsmarine and Waffen-SS) as well as the N.S.K.K. (National Socialist Vehicle Corps), the German Red Cross and other organizations.

Flemish Youth Step Up! Jules Geurts, the first Fleming to be awarded the Iron Cross 1st Class for bravery, poses in this recruiting poster with a Flemish German Red Cross nurse.

The Flemings also viewed the Belgian constitutional monarchy as very corrupt. This caused many to become apolitical. With the German re-occupation of Flanders, the Flemings once again hoped for a re-establishment of Flanders as an independent Belgian state.

After the Germans attacked the Soviet Union during the summer of 1941, the Catholic Church immediately expressed (although unofficially) its support for the Germans. This only served to add another reason to the list of motivations for the primarily Catholic Flemish youth to enlist. The danger of the communists, who were against religion of all kinds, was a popular discussion topic in Church and had often been spoken about. The Catholics had also launched a massive anti-communist campaign after some six thousand priests had been murdered by the communists during the revolutionary war in Spain.

The following excerpts from letters written by various Flemish veterans have been reprinted to help explain the motivations of the young Flemish soldiers who volunteered to fight with the Germans.

Georg D'Haese, who would later serve as commander of one of Langemarck's battle groups, volunteered because of his nationalistic convictions. D'Haese, like Schrijnen, also had Flemish nationalist parents and recalls:[7]

> *...as 15-16 years old sons of Flemish-nationalist parents, we were often on the prowl at night with paint, paintbrushes and hammers to paint over French street signs or other signs written in French or to smash them.*
>
> *...had we been able to love our country, we would have defended it and not fought against it. Under the conditions at that time we would have established a pact with the devil himself to attain an independent administration or to dissolve the Belgian State...*

And so it was that D'Haese, as many other of Flemish youths, began to consider enlisting in the German Wehrmacht

> *...so that Flandern, after many decades of repression, could finally achieve an independent administration as a state within the greater Belgian state. We wanted to achieve this required reformation, not as a "charity case" and were ready to fight on the side of the German troops.*

---

[7] Letter to the author from G. D'Haese dated May 11, 1996.

SS-Mann Georg D'Haese. Here D'Haese poses as a new volunteer of the 6. SS-Freiwilligen-Standarte "Nordwest." D'Haese was among the first Flemings to volunteer to fight with the Waffen-SS, doing so shortly after his 18th birthday.

The Young Worker: Remy had this picture taken in Kempten-Allgäu, Germany, during his stay there in 1940. Schrijnen first worked on the railroads and than in a factory. He was 18 years old at the time this picture was taken.

And so on May 23, 1941, at the age of 18, D'Haese enlisted in the Waffen-SS as well.

Herman Van Gyseghem, who served with "Langemarck's" Sturmgeschütz Abteilung (Assault Gun Battalion), had the following to say:[8]

> *...I was born in Ghent on May 6, 1923. My mother was an activist during the Great War. She was a teacher and it was completely normal that I also chose the general direction of Germany. Her maiden name was Hermann as her father was a German. If one wants to understand how it can come to be that someone would volunteer to fight for a foreign country, one should understand the history of that man's country. The Belgian state is an artificial state where the Flemings have the majority but have never been able to use*

---

[8] Letter to the author from H. Van Gyseghem dated Oct. 5, 1996.

this majority against the Francophiles. I will say one more thing to that: it was first in 1930, that is, 100 years after the Belgian State was established, that a Flemish University was founded. Until that time it was impossible to become an engineer or a doctor in any other language than French. That is one reason why some freely chose Germany.

A second reason: The wind that came from the East, the influence of the Olympic Games in 1936, the pictures and the stories about the beautiful youths, the happy workers, the chance to have one's own house and finally the possibility for a real vacation. I, as a student of Germanic languages, was completely open to these possibilities.

And then the third reason: Moscow or Rome. In the Catholic schools much was said about the danger of the "Reds." All of this together makes it understandable why I enlisted in the Waffen-SS and why my sister became a D.R.K. Schwester (German Red Cross Nurse).

Remy Schrijnen, then at the age of 17, was not immediately trusting of the Germans, however. In his opinion, the Germans had abandoned support of other countries, namely Finland, Estonia and Latvia,[9] so why not Belgium and Flanders too? While other children of nationalistic parents rushed to enlist in the armed forces, Remy had little desire to become a soldier and only sought work.

Remy, along with approximately two hundred and fifty thousand other Flemings and Walloons, volunteered to work in Germany. Schrijnen desired to work there so that he could learn more about the German people and their socialist system. Remy, a member of the working class, had worked with many Flemish former communists who had volunteered for work in the Soviet Union before the war. These acquaintances had told him many a tale of the hunger and suffering amongst Russian workers. Despite their hard labor, workers in Russia received no real freedom or benefits. The communists were seemingly a worker's party in name only.

Remy lived in Kempten-Allgäu (southwestern Bavaria) with the Eberle family, his sponsors. It was there that Schrijnen learned first hand about the socialist system which had been in place since the time of Bismarck. Under this system, everyone, regardless of social class, received free health insurance and many other

---

[9] These countries had been invaded by the Soviet Union after the signing of the Berlin-Moscow Pact.

[10] Letter to the author from R. Schrijnen dated Sept. 10, 1996.

benefits such as vacations, which in this time was atypical for a member of the working class. Remy Schrijnen recalls:[10]

> *...here a worker was more than just someone to be used, and employers had to think before they acted, as every worker was a respected member of society. Every citizen had duties and rights.*

Schrijnen felt more than at home in Germany and made many friends there. To this day he still corresponds with the Eberle family, his former sponsors, in Kempten-Allgäu.

The SS-Freiwilligen-Standarte "Nordwest"

On April 3, 1941 the formation of the 6. SS-Freiwilligen-Standarte "Nordwest" (SS-Volunteer-Regiment "Northwest") was ordered. It commenced the following week. This regiment was formed by placing volunteers from Flanders, Holland and Denmark under German leadership. Volunteers were mainly enlisted men and very few were officers. A total of six hundred men had enlisted by May 21st. The men were separated according to nationality, with the Flemish contingent of the regiment forming three separate companies. Unlike its sister regiments "Nordland" and "Westland," which were also based on a cadre of men from countries deemed Germanic, "Nordwest" was originally foreseen as a guard regiment, which would perform police and security operations. The manpower requirements of the war, however, would later change this status.

Basic Training for the Waffen-SS

Jan De Wilde, who volunteered for the Waffen-SS on April 14, 1941 and who was assigned to the Freiwilligen-Standarte "Nordwest," was kind enough to lend some insight into what it was like to be a new recruit during the Waffen-SS's basic training:[11]

> *We were trained by very disciplined and capable officers and NCOs in a modern military concern with every comfort. The physical training was very hard which strengthened our mental character. Everyday we would wake up at 0600 hours, then wash and immediately play sports four a half an hour (every day it was increasingly difficult). Then we would wash again, make our*

---

[11] Letter to the author from J. De Wilde dated Aug. 29, 1996.

New Recruits of the SS-Freiwilligen Standarte "Nordwest." Included here are Georg D'Haese and a few friends (sitting across from D'Haese is Ghijselijns) in a beer tent in St. Pauli in Hamburg, Germany, after enlisting in the Volunteer Regiment "Nordwest." This picture was taken in May 1941.

beds and clean our rooms, and then return to physical exercise or receive instruction. During the afternoon we would clean our part of the concern, then again sports, sports, sports, difficult and strenuous sports. Then we would perform exercises in tactics with live ammunition at the troop exercise grounds. Then we would perform shooting exercises with rifles, machine guns and live handgrenades. We were also instructed on how to take cover during artillery barrages.

We received exceptional instruction about battle tactics and the belief that one must prove himself in combat was impressed in our minds. After we performed our regular duties (during which we were never able to satisfy our superiors) the social relations between officers, NCOs and enlisted men were very friendly ("Duty is duty and schnapps is schnapps" was the slogan) although the respect for our superiors remained. We received little political instruction, but we did receive instruction about general politeness (how to act while on the street, in a train station or in a local pub). The Geneva and Hague Conventions for the conduct of war were impressed upon us and we were to fight and act in accordance with these rules. We were also given instruction on general hygiene (brushing our teeth and washing), which was a new concept for some of our rural countrymen.

War Breaks Out Between Germany and Russia

At 3:05 am on June 22, 1941, Remy Schrijnen, who was at this time a volunteer worker in southern Bavaria, heard a radio broadcast announcing that war had broken out between Germany and the Soviet Union. That same day, Schrijnen, then at the age of 19, volunteered for service at the local Waffen-SS recruiting post. The Waffen-SS recruiting policies were very strict, however, and in order to be deemed acceptable, an applicant had to conform to very strict qualifications: volunteers had to be at least 172 cm (approx. 5 feet 8 inches) tall, in good physical shape, have no police record and be racially acceptable. Despite submitting seven applications, the recruiters would not accept Schrijnen due to his relatively short stature of 164 cm (approx. 5 feet 4 inches).

While Schrijnen was busy trying to convince recruiting officers that he should be accepted, Regiment "Nordwest" was virtually split up. Only a few men remained, those who apparently did not meet the strict physical requirements of the Waffen-SS.[12] The unit would continue to exist as a training and replacement unit for "Flandern" and other Germanic units, however.

As a result, the original three Flemish companies of "Nordwest" became the basis of the "Bataillon 'Flandern,' " an exclusively Flemish unit (under German leadership) which was to fight at the front (and not perform security operations, as was planned for "Nordwest"). Apparently, the Germans needed all available manpower for the fight against the Soviet Union and decided to vastly expand the smaller foreign units. This was definitely a new possibility since the declaration of war against the Soviet Union had been responsible for a wave of new volunteers. In Flanders alone, some twelve hundred men and boys volunteered for service. The leaders of the four primary nationalist organizations, Reimond Tollenaere (Black Brigade/VNV), Jef François (Flemish Militant Order-Verdinaso), Suys (Rex-Flanders) and René Lagrou (Flemish Allgemeine-SS)[13] were among those who volunteered for the Waffen-SS. Their actions certainly inspired members of their organizations to do the same. All of these men would later serve in combat units on

---

[12] "Nordwest" was first set up as a guard unit for internal security and was not considered to be an SS-VT or Waffen-SS unit. When the unit was used to form the basis of a front-line combat unit higher qualifications were introduced.

[13] The Flemish Allgemeine-SS was formed in Antwerp in September 1940 by two pro-German Flemings, Ward Hermans and René Lagrou. Hermans was a former member of both the VNV and Verdinaso. The maximum enrollment was some 1,580 members. Due to the need for front-line soldiers, membership was greatly reduced during the war. This organization naturally had a lot in common with the De Vlag organization and openly advocated a much greater German control in Flanders. The leader of the De Vlag movement, Jef Van de Wiele, held honorary membership in this organization.

the Eastern Front. Surprisingly, though, the leader of the VNV, Staf De Clerq, did not initially endorse the Waffen-SS. De Clerq was apparently in favor of an independent Flemish unit for the fight against Soviet Russia. His reservations led to an agreement that a list of his demands for the unit be adhered to. The content of the agreement primarily concerned the welfare of the men, the structure of the unit and the nationalistic symbols (flags and uniform insignia) the unit was to bear. With this agreement, the formation of the "Freiwilligen Legion 'Flandern' " began. Although over twelve hundred men and boys had volunteered to serve in the Legion, they were subject to the same strict volunteer requirements as Schrijnen had encountered, which resulted in only some four hundred of these men were deemed acceptable.

• • •

A Flemish Legion of idealists, political activists and adventurers formed around the leadership of a German and Austrian officer corps. The young Flemings had mixed feelings about their new masters, who in many cases despised them and considered them unworthy of membership in any German army unit, especially the Waffen-SS.

Still, the Flemings followed the Germans into battle with a hardened pride. At first the men were pulled in and out of the front lines during the early stages of the mass confusion of the winter of 1941/42. Shortly thereafter, the Legion was put into action in Koptsy during the initial stages of the Russian winter counter-offensive – during some of the coldest weather the Germans would experience during the entire war. The Germans were not prepared for the treacherous conditions and the Flemings were flung into the front lines without proper winter equipment. The Flemings fought hard and proved themselves, even earning the recognition of the higher leaders of the Wehrmacht.

During the next stage of battles, the unit fought in the "Volkhov Pocket" and next around Leningrad. In the trenches surrounding the city there was static fighting which claimed many young lives. Thereafter, the unit fought around the Neva bend and finally in Krasny Bor. These final battles of the Legion forever forged the name Krasny Bor into the memories of the few soldiers that survived these harsh winter battles.

Despite the Germans' negative prejudices toward their young foreign volunteers, the Flemings continued to prove themselves to be not only loyal and formi-

dable soldiers, but more importantly a tightly-knit group bound in camaraderie. The continuous hardships of the brutal life on the front eased tensions between those with different beliefs united in their cause. By the end of the battles that took place in 1943, the Flemings had proven themselves to be reliable veterans of the Eastern Front in the eyes of their German superiors.

2

A Flemish Legion is Born

The Volunteer Legion "Flanders"

After the formation of the unit was complete, the order of battle for the Freiwilligen-Legion "Flandern" consisted of a leadership contingent and five infantry companies. Companies 1-3 were light infantry companies, each armed primarily with rifles and a few machine guns. The 4th company was deemed a heavy infantry company and consisted of three platoons, each armed with heavy machine guns and one platoon armed with heavy mortars. The 5th company was designated as the Legion's PAK (*Panzer-Abwehr-Kanone* or anti-tank gun) company and had two platoons with the small 3.7 cm PAK gun and one platoon with heavy mortars.[1] The Legion's manpower consisted of Flemings from Regiment "Nordwest," new Flemish volunteers and leadership corps. The combined total of the unit was some 1,112 men. Approximately half of the officers were Flemings, with Dr. Reimond Tollenaere, the leader of the Black Brigade of the VNV, serving in the 2nd Company as an Untersturmführer (2nd Lieutenant). Two other political leaders, Françios and Suys, also served as Untersturmführer in the 1st and 3rd Companies, respectively. The Legion's NCOs were almost exclusively German while more than ninety percent of the approximately one thousand enlisted ranks were Flemish. The structure of the unit was as follows:

---

[1] The Legion would later be supplemented with three 7.5cm PAK 97/38s, which utilized captured French barrels on German chassis.

SS-Freiwilligen-Legion "Flandern"

Stab mit Stabskompanie
(*Legion's staff with staff company*)
    Legion Kommandeur – SS-Sturmbannführer Michael Lippert [2] (G)[3]
    Adjutant - SS-Untersturmführer Günther Steffen (G)

1. Schützen-Kompanie: SS-Obersturmführer Peter Nußbaum[4] (G) (*rifle company – approximately 220 men*)

2. Schützen-Kompanie: SS-Untersturmführer Helmut Breymann[5] (A)[6] (*rifle company – approximately 218 men*)

3. Schützen-Kompanie: SS-Untersturmführer Hans Moyen[7] (G) (*rifle company – approximately 219 men*)

4. (schw.) Granatwerfer Kp.: SS-Untersturmführer Karl Neuhäuser (A) (*heavy mortar company – approximately 223 men*)

5. (Pz.Jäg.)-Kompanie: SS-Untersturmführer Karl Weingärtner[8] (A) (*anti-tank gun company, equipped with 3.7cm PAK guns – approximately 159 men*)

    Besides the Waffen-SS basic training, the Flemish officers – all former officers of the Belgian Army – had completed training at a Wehrmacht officer training school by the final phases of unit formation. Some volunteers had received NCO

---

[2] Lippert, according to several members of the Legion, despised the Flemings. He commanded the Flemings for less than one year, serving from July 12, 1941 to April 2, 1942. Active readers will recognize his name as the man who assassinated Ernst Röhm along with Theodor Eicke during the "Night of the Long Knives," the purge of the SA officer corps.

[3] G is for German - even though all of the company commanders were German, approximately 14 of the 25 officers of the Legion were Flemish.

[4] Nußbaum was killed in action on March 2, 1942 while serving as company commander for 1./ "Nederland."

[5] Breymann was killed in action in July 1944 while serving as battalion commander for II./SS-Panzer-Grenadier Regiment 48 "General Seyffard" (Niederländische Nr. 1).

[6] A is for Austrian.

[7] Moyen was promoted to Obersturmführer sometime in 1942 but later died of cancer in a field hospital. The spelling of the name "Moyen" has been disputed. Period source material contains the spelling "Mojen," but dependable sources cite that this is a common misspelling of the name.

[8] Weingärtner was killed on January 3, 1944 while serving as company commander for the 7.(Stg.)/ SS-Freiwilligen Sturmbrigade "Langemarck." He had been awarded the Iron Cross IInd Class on March 3, 1942.

training at a school in Braunschweig, Germany, while the *Pioniere* (combat engineers) and *Funker* (communications men) received specialty instruction at their designated schools. By October of 1941, the commander of the Legion "Nederland," Standartenführer Reich, ("Nederland" was training with "Flandern" in Arys, East Prussia) declared the unit "combat ready."

It is interesting to note that an official from the VNV and the Higher SS and Police Leader of Northern France and Belgium together paid the Legion a visit to investigate a number of complaints concerning poor treatment during training of the Flemish volunteers by their German leaders. During the visit the two officials learned that the complaints were indeed valid and the German official registered a formal complaint with the Reichsführer-SS, Heinrich Himmler. As a countermeasure, Himmler insured that all Germans serving with the Legion "Flandern" took a required course on Flemish culture. From that point on, any act of prejudice towards Flemings was strictly forbidden and was dealt with harshly.

The Legion was finally ready to depart to the Eastern Front in November 1941. At this time the fast-paced advances during the early stages of Operation "Barbarossa" (the invasion of the Soviet Union), were slowing down. The fatigue experienced by both the men and the wear and tear of their equipment from months of uninterrupted fighting, in addition to the increasingly cold temperatures and the vast expanse of the Russian wilderness, left the German lines incredibly thin. These factors contributed to the slow-down.

The Legion "Flandern" Arrives at the Front

As the Legion departed from the training grounds on November 10, 1941, the air was unusually cold – a prelude of what was to come. As the troops entered Russia on November 13th, the danger of partisans emerged as a reality. The 2nd SS Brigade's headquarters was located at Chudovo. The Legion was officially subordinated to the Brigade,[9] which consisted of a number of miscellaneous Waffen-SS companies and platoons, as well as the Reichsführer-SS's Escort Battalion. On November 23rd, several platoons from Legion were ordered to ready themselves for combat. The next day, these units were placed on the front but saw very little

---

[9] The 2. SS-Infanterie Brigade (mot) formed in May 1941 from SS-Infanterie Regimenter 4 and 14. The unit was later supplemented with the Begleit-Btl. Reichsführer-SS and the SS-Flak-Abteilung "Ost." The Brigade was intended to battle partisans in occupied territories. Due to the manpower demands required by the invasion of the Soviet Union, it was subordinated to Army Group "North" for action on the front lines. This 2. SS-Infanterie Brigade was the first German unit to command a foreign volunteer unit in battle, that being the Frw. Legion Flandern. The Frw. Legion Nederland and the Frw. Legion Norwegen would later fight under the command of the unit as well.

action. New Flemish legionnaires arrived at the front on December 3rd, having just completed training with the Standarte "Nordwest." Having seen practically no action, the Legion was relieved by a *Heer* (army) unit and sent back to Latvia on December 6th.

During what was to be a fairly short rest, the men of the Legion discussed their symbolic collar-tab insignia. There was a definite disagreement about this piece of insignia, as several members of the original "Nordwest" Regiment wanted the Flemish "Trifos" (a three-legged swastika) and the new members wanted the SS Runes. The primary argument favoring the use of the "Trifos" collar-tab was that it would be a symbol unique to the Flemish Legion, and thus an expression of their individuality and Flemish nationalism. Those in favor of the SS Runes preferred to wear the symbol of Germany's elite combat troops. It was finally decided upon, after much discussion, that the unit would wear the SS Runes. Despite this decision, this theme would continue to be a source of friendly disagreement amongst all members of the Legion, whether Flemish, German or Austrian.

As the German offensive was coming to a complete standstill in December, Stalin decided to inflict damage on the Germans in the same way the Germans had inflicted damage on his armies. The method was to cut off and encircle the Germans (which would leave them stranded) and then annihilate them. In order to execute this general plan in the north, General Vlasov and his army of some one hundred and thirty thousand men were given the order to come from Novogrod over the frozen Volkov river and frozen swamps to battle their way to the Baltic sea. This would serve to cut off the German's Army Group "North," led by General von Leeb. Stalin knew that the swamp areas were only weakly occupied by the Germans.

The general Russian winter offensive arrived in January 1942. By January 9th, the Flemings were once again called up to the front. They performed well in their first battle, re-taking the village of Koptsy in hand-to-hand combat against strong Russian forces. The temperatures were extremely cold, reaching 40 degrees F below zero. This had a devastating affect on the men as they didn't have any proper shelter and had to remain in the open.

Artillery barrages rained on the village and the men dug-in, while reinforcements from Standarte "Nordwest" arrived. On January 20th, the Russians launched a counterattack against Koptsy with the intention of re-taking it. The Flemings beat back the Russians, successfully inflicting major losses. Despite high Flemish casualties, Koptsy was still in German hands. On January 21st, tragedy struck.

No Winter Clothing: The large "great coats" the two Flemish soldiers here are wearing were never intended for severe cold conditions and had no insulation whatsoever. The unusually harsh winter conditions (with temperatures plummeting to as low as 50 degrees below zero), combined with a complete lack of warm clothing, resulted in numerous severe cases of frostbite and gangrene.

The Leader of the Black Brigade is Dead. SS-Untersturmführer Jack Delbaere, a Flemish officer serving in the Legion's 4th (heavy) Infantry Company, stands before the grave of SS-Untersturmführer Dr. Reimond Tollenaere in Podbyeryezhye, Russia. Tollenaere was 33 years old and had a wife and three children at the time of his death.

Untersturmführer Tollenaere (2nd Company) and Untersturmführer De Wilde (4th Company), also a Flemish officer, decided to inspect the Legion's forward lines. During the inspection, Tollenaere, located at a forward observation post, found himself in the middle of a Spanish (Spanish "Blue" Division) artillery barrage that was falling short of the Russians. Tollenaere did not survive the barrage of "friendly fire" and was the first of many Flemish officers to be killed on the Eastern Front.

Funeral services were given for Tollenaere in Brussels during the second week of February. Thousands of mourners attended. At the funeral it was announced that Tollenaere's younger brother Leo would volunteer for the Legion to replace his older brother.

Despite the conditions at the front, the German Army high command still took the time to praise the brave units in the east. In January 1942, the Legion was on of many units named in a Wehrmacht report:

> During the heated battles in the northern sector of the front, the Legion "Flandern" inflicted the heaviest casualties on the storming Russian troops.

Back at the front, the Legion was pulled out of Koptsy on February 4th for rest and refit. The Flemings were again praised for their efforts by a Wehrmacht bulletin on February 10th. They had registered two hundred casualties, but the 2nd and 4th Companies had counted seven hundred Russian dead. By February 14th, the Legion was back on the front lines, this time in Zyemptitsy, a village located just north of Koptsy. On February 23rd, the Russians launched a major attack, but were driven off after heavy battles which claimed many casualties. The Legion was beginning to feel the effects of their losses and several officers felt that the Legion was being unjustly bled, as if they were less valuable than their German counterparts. None of these complaints produced an ounce of sympathy from higher officials. The Legion's condition was not unique in this stage of the fighting at the Eastern Front. All units were suffering badly from the extreme cold, lack of food, shelter and adequate equipment, not to mention the mounting casualties. Jan De Wilde, then an SS-Mann (private) in the *1. Kompanie* recalls:[10]

> *...when the ground along the Volkhov front had frozen two meters deep, we needed explosives and grenades to dig graves for our fallen comrades.*

---

[10] Letter to the author from J. De Wilde dated March 10, 1997.

Also, in certain positions along the lines we would pile the dead bodies of Russian soldiers on top of each other and cover them with snow so that we could lay in some kind of protection since we couldn't dig trenches.

On March 2, 1942, the Legion received new battle orders. They were to conduct a counterattack that would force the Russians behind an important road which ran between Zyemptitsy and Vyeshki. The attack began with a platoon from 1st Company getting bogged down in a field by accurately placed Russian fire. The problem was quickly remedied by calls from an encouraging officer to continue moving forward. The men moved on and the attack was registered as a success on its first day. The Legion also received some support from the Spanish "Blue" Division, which covered one of the Legion's flanks during the advance.

The next day, the German attack continued. The Flemings advanced in unison with the Spanish "Blue" Division, which was fighting at its side. The weather remained extremely cold, with day-time temperatures reaching a high of only -25° F. On March 4th, the majority of the men remained in their positions while others unsuccessfully attempted to push a small Russian defensive position out and away

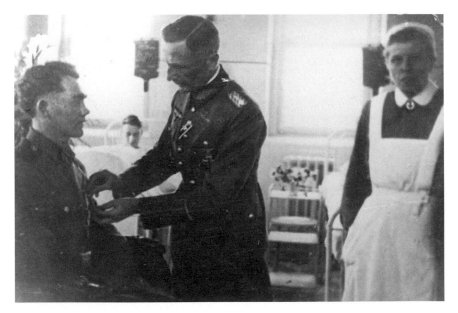

A High Price to Pay: Pictured is Flemish Legionnaire Josef De Becker who is being awarded the Iron Cross IInd Class by an Army General after loosing both of his lower legs and his entire right arm in battle during the winter of 1941/1942.

from the Flemish lines. The next day, "Flandern" was ordered to change positions. The day was calm in comparison to the previous few days fighting. Only artillery fights took place. On March 6th, the Legion was again prepared for offensive operations. The battles began at 0820 hours and ended at 1700 hours later that evening. This day was very successful for the Legion since they had managed to penetrate the Russian positions around Zyemptitsy and finally throw them out of the village. "Flandern" spent the next day trying to pry out small localized pockets of concentrated Russian resistance. The next day, the attack was declared both complete and successful by the commanding army corps. Of the original 388 legionnaires registered on March 2nd, only 101 remained on March 9th. Luckily the number of dead was relatively low and many of the casualties were cases of severe frostbite as the extremely cold temperatures continued to take its toll on the *Oostfronter*. Their excellent performance earned the Flemings the official praise of the Wehrmacht's high command. Their commander, Obersturmbannführer Lippert, was promoted to Standartenführer.

The fighting continued for a few more icy months. In March 1942, just before the rage of the battles was about to end, "Flandern" was praised once again:

> The Legion "Flandern" successfully threw the enemy from their positions and among other things managed to overtake 25 enemy pill boxes in heavy close combat.

By March 16th, the Legion, having been replenished with soldiers who had recovered from their wounds, was again ready for battle. The Russians shelled Flandern's positions between March 18th and April 2nd. At this time the Legion was positioned on the front between two Army units. On April 2nd, several Russian tanks appeared in the Flemish sector and their PAKs were helpless against them. The Spanish "Jagdkommando 12," a group of tank hunting specialists, managed to take care of them, though. Later that day another attack came, this time with Russian infantrymen riding atop several T-34s. This second battle lasted four hours. On April 4th came yet another attack, but this time the famous German 8.8 cm FLAK guns (*Fliegerabwehrkanone* or anti-aircraft guns) were put to good use against the Russian tanks, which were no match against the firepower of this big gun. The following days were calm and on April 11th, "Flandern" was pulled out of the front lines to Chichulino. The Legion had now been reduced to a battle group and was put together with other fragments of the 2. SS-Infanterie-Brigade to

Stuck in the Mud: Three Flemish Legionnaires from the 4th Company pose in front of a truck stuck in the Volkhov swamp area. Notice the gas mask on the headlight.

form a larger battle group. The battle group engaged in artillery duels with the Russians until April 18th. On April 20, 1942, the Legion was assigned a new commander, Obersturmbannführer Vitzhum.[11] The Legion spent the next month as part of a battle group. This battle group was positioned next to the swamps and marshes running along the Volkhov river. At the end of May, approximately one hundred new volunteers arrived after completing training in Graz, Austria.

By June 1st, the Flemings became part of a wall of what was termed as the "Volkhov Pocket." The masses of Russian troops that had attacked with General Vlasov were now stuck in the swamps that ran along the Volkhov river. The Legion was positioned along the edge of the swamp with the task to contain the Russian forces trapped there.

A general offensive against the encircled Russian positions began on June 16th. The Legion fought in conjunction with the *58. Infanterie-Division* and the *4. SS-Polizei-Division*. In the Pocket were remainders of six Russian infantry divisions and two tank brigades. At first the Legion wasn't directly engaged in the battles, but rather served as support. On June 20th, the remaining members of the Legion were combined with a Spanish battalion and a convalescence company to form a new battle group. This battle group advanced on June 21st in spite of the

---

[11] Vitzhum was commander for less than one month, serving from June 20th through July 15, 1942.

fact that their vehicles were bogged down by the extremely poor swampy conditions.

The first battles claimed several casualties as the Russians were using illegal exploding "dum-dum" bullets which would rip open large holes in the bodies of their victims. By the end of the day, though, the Flemings had completed their objectives and had managed to capture a few Russian bunkers. They had advanced approximately one hundred and fifty meters into the pocket. June 22nd began with a German artillery barrage and later the men of Flandern advanced and eliminated some more Russian bunkers. During the battles, two of the Legion's officers were wounded, but decided to stay with their troops. Fighting continued on June 23rd and 24th. On June 25th, the Russians attempted a break-out, but this attempt was concealed by well-placed German artillery fire. By June 25th, the Legion's troops were reduced by a further fifty men. On June 26th, the Legion was positioned in the south and east with a battalion from the 2. SS-Brigade and a battalion from a Spanish regiment. Meanwhile, Legion "Nederland" was in the north. The battles lasted for three days and the German forces made good ground.

During the fighting the Legion's commander, Obersturmbannführer Vitzhum, was called away. Hauptsturmführer Gerhard Hallman, the first staff officer from the 2. SS-Infanterie Brigade, served as his acting replacement. During the battles the Flemings had relied on help from volunteer Russian deserters now serving in the Legion as *HIWIs* (*Hilfswillige* or volunteer helpers). Some of these HIWIs would remain volunteers until the end of the war.

The Legion was relieved in early July. The battle against the Volkhov Pocket was now over and deemed a complete success by the German high command. The Russians had lost some one hundred thousand soldiers killed and another thirty thousand were taken prisoner. One of those thirty thousand was the Russian General Vlasov. Before the end of the war Vlasov would lead a volunteer Russian army – in the strength of approximately two divisions (some fifteen thousand men) – under German command against Stalin's communist forces.

The Legion's performance was praised in a Wehrmacht Bulletin in late June. During an inspection during the first week of July, General Lindemann awarded Jules Geurts with the Iron Cross 1st Class. Geurts had served as a foot messenger (runner) for Untersturmführer Tollenaere before Tollenaere was killed. On July 14th, the Legion's new commander, Hauptsturmführer Conrad Schellong, arrived from having just served with "Nederland."

Conrad Schellong: Pictured above is Hauptsturmführer Conrad Schellong shortly before his transfer to the staff of the SS-Freiwilligen-Legion "Nederland." Schellong was born on February 7, 1910 in Dresden, Saxony. He completed middle school and later took training in business. After completing his studies in 1927, he remained in Dresden to work full-time at a firm where he had served as an intern. He was employed as a salesman until 1931, at which time he was laid off. He remained unemployed until 1933 when he took a job working the land on a farm in East Prussia. In June 1932, he joined the SA and was shortly thereafter transferred to the SS. After Hitler's rise to power, he served in the Hilfspolizei. In February 1934, he submitted a request to transfer to the SS-Oberkommando "Sachsen" which later became the SS-Wachtruppe "Sachsen." Schellong served in SS-Totenkopf-Regiment 1 "Oberbayern," which originated as a "Wachregiment" (guard regiment) but was transformed into a combat regiment and incorporated into the SS-Totenkopf-Division. Schellong served with "Oberbayern" from 1937 until 1942, where he held various leadership positions (including company commander and battalion adjutant). While with "Oberbayern," Schellong won the Iron Cross Second Class. He was then transferred to the SS-Freiwilligen-Legion "Nederland," and served first as a staff officer and then as a battalion commander, during which he was awarded the Iron Cross 1st Class. Schellong was given command of the Legion "Flandern" on July 16, 1942 and remained with the Flemings until the end of the war. Many Flemish veterans reported that Schellong was "not used to foreigners" and "very disciplined." Due to these two personality traits Schellong, "maintained a certain distance from his soldiers."

What is now St. Petersburg, Russia was then known as Leningrad. Leningrad was an icon on the Russian Front, as the Germans laid siege to this city throughout almost the entire war, but were never able to conquer it. Just a few miles from the city's borders were a series of trenches that ran around about 3/4 of the city, south from the Finnish Gulf and then east into Russia. The Germans were not only unable to take the city, but they were also unable to completely encircle it. The Russian city was supplied from food and other vital stuffs from the east, most of which was primarily reserved for the soldiers defending its periphery.

Beginning on July 24th, the Legion "Flandern" began to take positions in the trench system partially surrounding the city. By this time "Flandern" was in no condition to return to combat, but the Leningrad front needed every available man. As the boys arrived at the front they found conditions to be a bit different than what they were used to and it took a few days to get acclimated. The first week of August saw the arrival of a contingent of one hundred and fifty new volunteers and veterans who had just recovered from their wounds.

While "Flandern" was taking positions, they experienced heavy enemy artillery fire. The companies were spread out along the line, with the heavy weapon sections being overlapped so that no section would be too weak. It wasn't long before the Russians drove their tanks into the Flemish lines. During the beginning

More Iron Crosses: Commander Schellong awards more men of the Legion with the Iron Cross, 2nd Class. This picture was taken in late summer/early fall of 1942 in Alexandrovka, a village bordering Leningrad, where the Legion's 5.(Pz.Jäg.)Kompanie was positioned. The NCO assisting Schellong is Oberscharführer Viertelmann.

Trench Warfare: Pictured above is an artist's modern rendition of a press photo which was printed in an issue of the "Völkischer Beobachter," a popular German newspaper of the time period. Sitting in the trench is Georg D'Haese who reported: *Here I sit in a "water position" before Leningrad. The trenches were very close to the city and we could easily see the city's large buildings. The floor of the trenches consisted of 30-40 cm of water and muck. We would dig holes in the walls of the trenches so that we could sit somewhat dry and sometimes even sleep for a few minutes. Ten to twenty meters away sat the Russians in the very same trenches. The Russians would repeatedly try to take our positions, but during later counter attacks, we were able to "clean-out" the enemy positions.* A special thanks to Erik Neitzke for his artwork.

of the second week of August, several T-34s attacked Flemish and Latvian positions. Artillery guns from the Legion "Nederland" sent the tanks on the run, however, and the danger quickly disappeared. By mid-August, the Legion was fully deployed and ready for combat. The Flemings now lived in a series of waterlogged murky trenches, similar to those on the Western Front in the First World

Artist's Rendition of Leningrad through the Eyes as the Legion. This is the view of the city of Leningrad as seen by the soldiers who occupied the trenches surrounding the city.

War. The water was more than a foot deep and cases of "trench foot" were common.

In the middle of August the Russians made use of loudspeakers to greet the newly arrived Legion and harass the men with propaganda. This was a prelude to a four-hour artillery barrage which lasted into the early hours of the morning. After the barrage concluded, Russian patrols raided the Legion's lines but were easily driven back. The Luftwaffe arrived with several Stukas the next day to further aggravate the Russian patrols. After a few attacks from the air, things again became calm along the trenches. A week later, a platoon-sized Russian patrol attacked the lines. Several Legion groups were involved in night fighting which lasted until the early hours of the morning. September began with artillery barrages and the Russians continued to use their loudspeakers to harass the Flemings. Despite the many broadcasts about the excellent conditions on the other side, a few Russian soldiers defected to the Legion. The fighting which took place in the next months involved local patrol troop skirmishes. No real battles took place and there was no give or take concerning the position of the front lines. Casualties were also low.

Flemish Soldiers in the Trenches: Pictured above on the right is Wim Daelman (who was later killed in action) and another unknown legionnaire (on the left). Here they sit in a makeshift trench before Leningrad in July 1942. Notice the handy heavy machine gun and the Flemish coat of arms in the background.

Schrijnen Enlists in the German Military

While the Legion was busy fighting in Russia, Schrijnen remained in Kempten-Allgäu where he continued to work and apply for admittance to the Waffen-SS. Finally, after submitting his seventh application, he gave up and applied for service with the German *Gebirgsjäger* (Mountain Troops) which had its main office located in Kempten-Allgäu. At first Remy was not aware that Flemings could serve in branches of the German Wehrmacht other than the foreign legions of the Waffen-SS. When he found out, he immediately volunteered. Nonetheless, Schrijnen would have preferred to join the Legion "Flandern" and fight alongside his countrymen.

Somewhat disappointed, he departed for basic training in July 1942. To Schrijnen's surprise, he received a transfer to the Waffen-SS on August 1, 1942, shortly after arriving at the mountain trooper training grounds. Schrijnen was sent to Klagenfurt, where all Germanic legionnaires, Flemings, Danes, the Dutch, Finns and Swedes were sent. Volunteers from Wallonie and France were sent to the Wehrmacht; only Germanic volunteers were sent to the Waffen-SS.[12] Needless to

[12] This would later change. Eventually almost all foreign volunteers found themselves fighting within the ranks of the Waffen-SS.

say, Remy was more than satisfied with his transfer and was proud to be together with volunteers from across northern Europe. Schrijnen reported that the training was very hard, and that the recruits also visited several political lectures, the topics of which centered on anti-communism. He was later sent to Graz (Austria) and then Hilvorsum (Holland), where he continued his training at the *Panzerjägerschule* (tank hunter school). In Hilvorsum Remy had an advantage over some of the other Flemish comrades since he had learned German during his time working in Kempten-Allgäu. He served as a runner for August Knorr, a German, who would later become his *Kompanie-Chef* (company commander). Unterscharführer Kirmse, also a German, recommended Schrijnen for *Panzerjäger* training. There he also met Alfons Gradmayer, another German, who would later be an Unterscharführer and Schrijnen's PAK gun commander.[13] August Knorr later recalled his time with Schrijnen in Hilvorsum:[14]

> "...in Hilvorsum we trained our recruits so that they were capable of serving in every position and Schrijnen never knew that we noticed him. Since he could speak a good 80% Bavarian, we all became friends. Gradmayer and I used to jokingly make fun of him, but he never seemed to care or notice."

Little is known of Schrijnen's training, but several of his comrades have commented on Schrijnen's personality at this time. Marcel Laperre, later Remy's platoon leader, reported that Schrijnen was:[15]

> "...very hard on himself during training. He also demanded the same of his comrades. I thought that Schrijnen must be a natural-born soldier, with a sense of adventure, a go-getter with little regard for himself."

With the Legion "Flandern" as a Foot Messenger

At the end of 1942, Schrijnen and his fellow trainees from Hilvorsum departed for the northern sector of the Russian front. They traveled through East Prussia, Lithuania, Latvia and Estonia, stopping along the way. During these stops they were greeted by friendly people until crossing over into the area west of Leningrad. Finally in Russia, Remy Schrijnen and his comrades got their first glimpse of the Russian countryside:[16]

---

[13] It should be noted here that Knorr, Kirmse and Gradmayer were all members of the staff at the Panzerjägerschule in Hilvorsum. It was not until late 1943 that they were transferred to the Flemish unit, which at that time would be rechristened the *Sturmbrigade "Langemarck."*

[14] Schrijnen notebook.

[15] Schrijnen notebook.

[16] Letter to the author from R. Schrijnen dated May 13, 1996.

Schrijnen in Hilvorsum: This photo was taken at the *Panzerjägerschule* (anti-tank gun school) in Hilvorsum in 1942. Remy is the fourth soldier from the left in the top row.

...we were all astonished by the poverty of the Russians, I mean, in the name of all non-German volunteers, I must admit that it convinced us that we stood on the right side. It was sad to see this worker's and farmer's land, this so-called worker's paradise. There was poverty and suffering everywhere, even the Russians themselves admitted it.

Schrijnen said that as an admirer of Adolf Hitler, he volunteered to start his military career as a *Fußmelder* (foot messenger). Hitler had won the Iron Cross 1st Class serving as a runner during the First World War. Due to his *Panzerjäger* (anti-tank gun) training, Remy was assigned to the *5.(Pz.Jäg)Kompanie*. His company commander was Hauptsturmführer Willi Dethier and his platoon leader was Untersturmführer Johannes Gläser. Marcel De Jaeger was responsible for training Schrijnen. Being a foot messenger entailed delivering messages alone from his unit to neighboring units and back again. It required many long hikes through swamps, hilly areas as well as through many combat zones. A foot messenger was a soldier who mostly only fought for himself. He was often alone, day and night, and frequently found himself running, ducking and generally just trying to out-smart enemy sharp-shooters. The foot messenger also had to know how to make his way through an artillery barrage or to find his way through or around combat

Schrijnen in the Trenches: A rare photo of Remy in 1943 when he was one of the Legion's foot messengers in the mucky trenches before Leningrad. This photo was taken in the Zappe, as described by Jan De Wilde.

zones. All this, not to mention the bitter cold and wicked snowstorms of northern Russia, made for a difficult job. During his time as a foot messenger, Schrijnen got to know several of his comrades fairly well, comrades he would be acquainted with throughout the war. Among them were Paul Rubens, Juul Fieremans and Fons Van Broeck. Fieremans and Van Broeck were *Kradmelder* (motorcycle dispatch riders) and Rubens was a foot messenger like Remy. Remy recalls his life as a foot messenger:[17]

> *...I wanted to be a brave soldier, but I knew that as a foot messenger I would mostly be alone. Life was bitter cold and there were a lot of snowstorms, but we had very good winter clothing. I often listened when the 'alte Hasen' told their many stories about what good fighters the Russians were.*

Back in Russia on the Leningrad Front

In October, the Legion received over two hundred men who arrived along with Untersturmführer Jack Delbaere who had been recovering from his wounds. The Legion was again at full strength, which allowed groups of men to be rotated out of the lines to take a rest.

---

[17] Letter to the author from R. Schrijnen dated May 16, 1997.

Alfons (Fons) Van Broeck: Fons Van Broeck was born on June 11, 1914 in Beveren-Waas He completed the American equivalent of high school but then had to find a job due to the financial status of his family (which was a common occurrence in this time). In May 1941, he volunteered for service in the Waffen-SS. Van Broeck, who was twenty-six years old at this time, reported that he volunteered for nationalistic reasons. Shortly after signing up he was transferred to the Freiwilligen Standarte "Nordwest." Van Broeck took part in the battles on the Volkhov river, on the Leningrad front and in Narva. For a motorcycle messenger, Van Broeck was highly decorated and by the end of the war he had been wounded three times and was awarded the Kriegsverdienstkreuz (War Service Cross), the Ostmedaille 41/42 (Eastern Front Medal), the Wound Badge in Black and was also presented with the Iron Cross IInd Class for the battles in Narva in the summer of 1944.

Juul Fieremans: Pictured above is Juul Fieremans who was a Kradmelder and close comrade of Remy Schrijnen. Remy fought together with Fieremans for much of the war.

During his first few weeks on the front, Schrijnen got the opportunity to get to know his platoon leader Unterscharführer Heinz Gödecke and his company commander Willi Dethier personally. As a foot messenger he would often have to run messages back and forth between the two. During one notable instance, Gödecke was positioned quite far away, and in order to get to him as Dethier had prescribed, Remy would have to take a longer route which led through numerous swamps.

The swamps could be avoided, in reality, but this was forbidden, since a short cut would require that he pass through several villages which were occupied by Russian snipers. Messengers almost always carried secret orders, orders which could not be transmitted by wire or radio. Therefore all "short-cuts" were strictly forbidden. Snipers had already claimed the lives of many runners. But Remy, trusting his instincts, decided to take the short-cut and save himself the misery of going through the swamps. As he arrived, Gödecke had just received a phone call from Dethier. As Remy stood before Gödecke with message in hand, Dethier informed Gödecke that Schrijnen would be arriving in a while with a message from him and that he should call him the minute that he arrived. Gödecke, somewhat confused, answered that Remy was already there. Dethier, realizing that Remy had not followed his orders became irate and told Gödecke to have Remy return immediately. Gödecke, with a smile on his face, took the message and told Remy to return immediately and report to his commander. Remy, knowing what he could expect from his commander when he got back, took the short-cut again. And there he was, at the end of the street that went through the village, waiting for him. As Remy approached him, Dethier pointed to the sign that read: "ENTERING THIS STREET IS FORBIDDEN, IT IS SURROUNDED BY THE ENEMY AND IS UNDER FIRE FROM SNIPERS." Remy then answered:[18]

> ...a foot messenger must bring his messages in the shortest possible time and therefore must always use the shortest path to his destination, and besides, that sign doesn't say anything about messengers.

Dethier responded, *"Recklessness isn't the same thing as courage"* and ordered him to do two hours of calisthenics. Schrijnen, an enthusiastic soldier, recalls his first combat:[19]

> *My first combat experience: Yes, I arrived with my message in the midst of an infantry attack. The infantry men were fighting hand-to-hand with the Russians and, forgetting that I was a foot messenger, I grabbed a shovel and jumped right into the middle of the fight. We blew bunkers, took prisoners and won the battle. As soon as the fight was over, I ran back to the rear lines and reported to the commander. I saluted him, but by this time I just didn't care*

---

[18] Letter to the author from R. Schrijnen dated Nov. 10, 1995.
[19] Letter to the author from R. Schrijnen dated May 17, 1996.

Detour: Careful – it is forbidden to go any further – take detour.

anymore, commander here, commander there, it was then that I finally knew that I could stand by my comrades in battle. Commander Dethier stood there with the commander of the infantry and they looked me over and were laughing. Dethier said, "You goof, you're pretty lucky." I thought to myself "Yeah, whatever." But the other commander praised me, "As a foot messenger, you're good in combat." I didn't really care, for me what happened only seemed natural.

New equipment began to arrive in October and the Flemings received real winter clothing for the coming frigid months. The new winter gear was quickly put to good use, since the temperatures had once again fallen below zero by November. At the end of November, the Russians made an attempt to disrupt the Legion's lines with strong forces. The battle began with several penetrations, but the many barbed-wire obstacles the Legion had put up effectively slowed down the attack. The slow-down enabled the Legion's machine gunners to inflict heavy casualties on the Russians. Things looked grim in several positions along the line, but arriving patrol troop reinforcements managed to put an end to the danger.

Patrol troop skirmishes continued well into December. The appearance of the trenches had changed, however, and the winter clothing was now more than a

Hauptsturmführer Willy Dethier: Shown above is Willi Dethier, on the left as a Hauptsturmführer of the Allgemeine-SS and on the right as a Hauptsturmführer of the Waffen-SS. The picture on the left was taken in early 1940 when Dethier was on assignment with the SD (German security service). The photo on the right was taken sometime after his promotion to Hauptsturmführer of the Waffen-SS on November 9, 1942. Dethier was born on May 17, 1910 in Düsseldorf, Germany. At the age of 21, Dethier enlisted in the Allgemeine-SS. By April 1933 he had been commissioned as an officer and continued to serve with the Allgemeine-SS in several leadership and clerical positions. During his time with the Allgemeine-SS, Dethier was twice promoted (his final rank was Hauptsturmführer) until transferring in February 1940 to the Waffen-SS (then known as the "SS-Verfügungstruppe"), where he was assigned the rank of a senior NCO. After completing his basic training (which included training to be a leader in a PAK unit), he received his commission as an Untersturmführer of the Waffen-SS and transferred to the staff of the II. Bataillon of the 2. (mot.)SS-Infanterie-Brigade. On March 20, 1942, Dethier was transferred to the SS-Frw.-Legion "Flandern" where he served as Kompanie Führer for the 5th (heavy weapons) company. After the Legion was expanded into the 6. SS-Frw. Sturmbrigade "Langemarck," Dethier served as Kompanie Chef of the 9th (heavy) anti-aircraft gun company. During this time he was recommended for the German Cross in Gold by the leader of his I. Batterie, Obersturmführer Karl-Heinz Gustavson. The recommendation was primarily based on his exemplary performance during the Brigade's battles in Ukraine in early 1944. The recommendation was not approved. Dethier was a very capable officer and was chosen to serve as the Brigade's temporary commander for the wounded commander Schellong from March 8 to May 3, 1944. In June 1944, Dethier was reportedly assigned to oversee the formation of SS-Flakabteilung 27 for the forming 27. SS-Division "Langemarck," but this unit was never formed (the SS-Panzerjägeratbeilung 27 contained Langemarck's FLAK units). Dethier was considered to be a "fine man" by the men of the Brigade. He survived the war and remained in contact with his Flemish comrades until his death sometime in the 1960s.

necessity. During the third week of December the Legion was assigned to take out a series of Russian bunkers which lay behind a minefield, but the attack failed. Before the Flemings got a chance to make another attempt at the bunkers, extremely harsh winter conditions forced a pause in the fighting.

Tragedy struck during the second week of January, as Jules Geurts, the first Fleming to win the Iron Cross 1st Class, was killed by a sniper. The Legion's anti-tank company was removed from the unit and subordinated to the 4. SS-Polizei-Division, which was also fighting along the Leningrad front. The remaining portions would have to make do without them and received several new heavy mortars, anti-tank guns and the necessary personnel from Germany to form an anti-tank platoon. In February, the 4. SS-Polizei-Division was replaced by Latvian units. The 5. Kompanie spent a portion of its time instructing the Latvians on the use of their heavy weapons. By mid-February, the 1st, 2nd and 3rd companies were placed in reserve and positioned behind the lines of the Spanish "Blue" Division in the vicinity of Krasny Bor.

On February 12, 1943, the Russians initiated an offensive aimed at blowing open the area of the front further south of Leningrad. The Spanish "Blue" Division was attacked by three Russian divisions. The Spaniards were hard hit and lost over a third of their combat strength in the first hour of the battle and a further third by the end of the day. At this time the Legion was still in reserve but was quickly grouped with several Latvian units and sent to a section held by the (*Heeres*) 254. Infanterie Division. This division had performed well during the Russian attack and had the situation well in hand. The Legion was transferred shortly thereafter to positions behind the Spanish "Blue" Division.

During the difficult and violent fighting on the front, the young legionnaires received many encouraging letters from friends and family. These letters served to console the young men and boys and strengthen their inner convictions during this difficult time. Others took the time to write letters to the boys on the front as well, including political leaders, government officials and members of the Church. Each letter told them how much the people back home appreciated their deeds and how much they respected their courage. Georg D'Haese received a letter from a Flemish Catholic priest who, among other things, wrote to him:[20]

> *...I very much want to tell you that I very much appreciate and am very*

---

[20] Letter to the author from G. D'Haese dated Nov. 29, 1996.

Winter Trenches: As winter arrived the wet and murky trenches froze stiff. Jan De Wilde, who supplied the picture on the left, reported "...at a certain place along our trenches (we called it the "Zappe"), the Russian trenches were only eighty meters away. The Russians attacked our trenches continuously and in our trenches we sometimes fought man against man. The Russians were never successful in breaking through our position, they were always beaten back. Many Legionnaires were killed or wounded there. Our companies had to be relieved on a regular basis."

much amazed at your courage and your simple deed, a deed which has such hard consequences.

...I hope that your sacrifice and the sacrifice of your comrades will lead to the annihilation of this hellish Bolshevism, so that Christ will remain King in the hearts of all people, and so that our homeland of Flanders will remain Catholic and that our Catholics will be and continue to be Flemish! And that will be because our dear God will sympathize with your fight and your comrade's fight for him and for those things which remain dearest in our hearts.

By the end of February, Schrijnen had acquired quite an education from his messenger comrades Juul Fieremans and Fons Van Broeck which helped him to survive. Remy claimed to have learned quite a bit from these two and he credits his experience as a foot messenger as a major factor in his survival of the war. Schrijnen reported:[21]

---

[21] Letter to the author from R. Schrijnen dated Feb. 9, 1996.

By early 1943 I felt at home on the front and I had a reputation of being a fast messenger. It was at about that time that we heard about Rottenführer Gerardes Mooyman, who was the first non-German soldier to receive the Knight's Cross as a Panzerjäger in the Legion "Nederland." This was a great day for us all, we were proud of this Germanic volunteer.

Later in February, the Flemings changed positions and stayed in the trenches until March where they remained engaged in small patrol-troop operations. The spring weather began to melt the snow and Flemings soon found themselves wading through ice water. The Legion was placed under the subordination of the 254. Infanterie-Division. The Russian army once again went on the offensive beginning in the third week of March. The lines held by the 254. Infanterie Division were broken and the Russians began to raid their bunkers. The remnants of the Spanish "Blue" Division also experienced difficulties. The Legion was therefore transferred behind the Spaniards. After about a week the Spanish lines were so weak that "Flandern" was sent in to re-occupy their positions. The Flemings had earned respect among the leaders of the German high command and the task they were given was more suitable for a unit twice their size. The Flemings were to begin on March 22nd after the Luftwaffe's Stukas and several artillery barrages softened up the Russians. The attack began with the support of several Tiger tanks. With German artillery shells accurately in front of the advancing Flemings, the legionnaires were able to advance quickly. As the German Panzers reached their forward-most positions, the Flemings were on their own. They approached the Russian trenches with fixed bayonets and grenades ready at their sides. They fought with such fervor that the Russians began to abandon their positions. The Legion then occupied the entire series of lines, which were large enough for a unit twice their size.

During the following night, a Russian deserter stumbled into the Legion's lines. He informed them of a coming Russian tank attack. Sure enough, the next day the Russians appeared with their tanks, but the Legion was ready with their anti-tank weapons. These weapons were mostly just mines and bundled hand grenades, which would offer only light resistance against a larger tank attack. Luckily for the Flemings, an 88 mm FLAK/PAK gun battery appeared and began knocking out the T-34s, not to mention the Russian infantry that was following. This helped but did not turn the tide of the battle. As the situation began to look somewhat grim for the Flemings, Kommandeur Schellong rallied the entire unit, including the

Gerardes Mooyman: At right is a formal studio portrait of Gerardes Mooyman, while the picture below shows Mooyman standing before his 7.5 cm PAK 97/38 (notice the numerous "kill" rings). Born in the Netherlands on September 23, 1923, Gerardes Mooyman was 19 years old when he volunteered for service in the Waffen-SS. Before enlisting, he completed courses in a trade school for locksmiths, but later became an assistant to a pharmacist. Like many other Germanic volunteers, he started his career in SS-Freiwilligen-Standarte "Nordwest," a unit which, as discussed earlier, consisted of volunteers from Flanders, the Netherlands and other Germanic countries. After completing training for Panzerjäger in Hilvorsum in the Netherlands, Mooyman transferred to the SS-Freiwilligen-Legion "Nederland." During the Russian offensive in the northern sector of the Eastern Front which began in January 1943, Mooyman, a Sturmmann and R*ichtschütze* (no. 1 gunner) of a 7.5 cm PAK crew, knocked out four T-34s and blocked a local Russian advance. Shortly thereafter Mooyman was promoted to Rottenführer. Another Russian offensive came one morning in February, during which Mooyman annihilated another seven T-34s. During this en-

gagement his Geschützführer was killed, requiring Mooyman to perform his duties as well. That very afternoon came another attack during which Mooyman's skill continued, allowing him to score another six Russian tanks. This brought his score to seventeen knocked-out enemy tanks. For his contribution to halting the Russian offensive, Gerardes Mooyman was awarded the Knight's Cross on February 20, 1943.

70

non-combatants (drivers, cooks, etc.). The Russians sought to exploit one point in the lines and hand-to-hand combat was raging in the trenches. The tide of the battle turned, however, after two of the lead tanks ran into trouble. The first one hit a mine which broke its tread and the second fell victim to a magnetic mine that was well-placed on its chassis by a Flemish legionnaire. This served to stall the advance as the two tanks blocked the forward progress of the others. The remaining Tigers and 88s now had easy pickings. The Russians, recognizing this, retreated. The Russian losses, as well as those of the Legion, were staggering. The Russians attacked once more (March 28th), but the attack was weak and quickly faltered. On March 30th, the unit was removed from the front lines. Of the 450 Flemings only fifty remained. Jan De Wilde reported:[22]

> *...by April '43 the Legion had fought its last but worst battles in Krasny Bor on the Neva river. The Legion received its 'coup de grâce' and pulled out and was sent to Debica (Poland). The Legion had been on the front for an uninterrupted 15 months, much of that time in snow (in winter a continuous - 35 C, with a worst temperature of -52 C). During the entire time we never received any potatoes, vegetables or fruit.*

The Army Corps was impressed with the Legion's performance and word got way to the Reichsführer-SS. Himmler was also greatly impressed with the Legion's performance and started drafting plans for an expansion of the unit into a Brigade.

For a short period of time in April, several members of the Legion spent their time building barbed-wire obstacles to be placed along the lines and serve to slow down advancing Russians. By May, the entire Legion was in Debica training for their next assignment.

• • •

By the end of the spring of 1943, despite the initial uncertainty of the German command, the Flemings had proven themselves to be dogged and reliable soldiers. The German and Austrian leaders were impressed with their accomplishments and steadfastness in heated and uncertain situations.

Despite their excellent military reputation, the political convictions of many of the Flemish cadre remained uncertain in the eyes of officers within certain circles

---

[22] Letter to the author from J. De Wilde dated Aug. 6, 1996.

of the German leadership. Politics remained a primary topic of conversation amongst the ranks and many of the Flemings were not quiet about their devotion to their homeland and not to the German Reich. Numerous German and Austrians sympathized with these nationalist Flemings, while some did not. Still others forced themselves to remain politically aloof.

Other Flemings, those who were members of the De Vlag movement and the Flemish Allgemeine-SS, did not voice the same concerns as their VNV compatriots. The Germans were more than aware of these factions as well as their separate and different beliefs.

Before the conclusion of the Krasny Bor battles, plans for an enlarged Flemish brigade were being carried out. By this time the favor of the war was increasingly on the side of the Russians. The fact that Himmler enlarged the Flemish unit with more manpower and better equipment is a testament to the favorable opinion the Germans had for the fighting ability of the Flemings. On the other hand, inconsiderate administrative moves made by Himmler damaged the reputation of the Germans in the eyes of many Flemings.

Despite political complications and differences, the Flemings remained loyal and obedient soldiers who continued to fight bravely and make the sacrifices that the Eastern Front required.

3

The Freiwilligen Legion "Flandern" Becomes the Sturmbrigade "Langemarck"

A New Unit Designation

As the Volunteer Legion "Flandern" began to regroup and recover in Debica from the battles in Ukraine, they learned that the name of their legion would be changed. Instead of being a foreign legion serving alongside the Germans within the Waffen-SS as opposed to having a separate army of their own, the new unit designation would serve to distance the unit from its Flemish-nationalist roots even further. Many of the men of the Legion were insulted upon hearing about the name change. Ekkehard Wangemann, the former German commander of SS-Panzerjägerabteilung 27 reported:[1]

> *To explain the strange name "Langemarck" another word. During the First World War in the Flemish village of Langemarck,[2] a company of volunteer German students initiated an attack against a stronger French unit while singing the German national anthem. The German volunteer unit was completely annihilated. Therefore the name "Langemarck" became a patriotic symbol for the Germans. By the way, the Flemings as well as the Germans in the Division were not in agreement that the name should be changed. It would have been correct to maintain a name such as "Flemish Volunteer Division."*

---

[1] Letter to the author from E. Wangemann dated April 8, 1997.
[2] Langemarck is spelled "Langemark" in Flemish.

Unfortunately, there were other volunteer units which had these unnecessary changes which only served to insult the nationalistic feelings of the unit's members.

The name Langemarck was perhaps a weak attempt at best to somehow associate Flanders with Germany using some kind of a patriotic namesake, but in reality the new unit designation bore a name that had little or no meaning to the Flemings or even the Germans serving in the unit. It is unknown why exactly the name was changed, but several of the Legion's members speculated that the Germans ultimately planned to integrate Flanders (along with other Germanic countries) into a "Greater German Reich." Besides the change in the unit's designation, the oath taken by the Legionnaires was also to be changed with the addition of an oath to Adolf Hitler as the leader of the Greater German Reich. This enraged many of the soldiers and rumors of a flat-out refusal to take the new oath circulated. After all, the majority of the unit, some 50-60% of the men, was made up of members of the VNV, the Flemish nationalist party. The members of this party sought a completely independent Flemish state and wanted little or nothing to do with the Germans. They were fighting alongside Germany to achieve this new status – not be incorporated into another country only to remain an oppressed secondary power, as the situation in Belgium clearly reflected.

But it should be noted that there was indeed a considerable portion of members of the unit that *did* foresee a free Flemish state within a Greater German Reich. These were primarily the members of De Vlag and the Flemish Allgemeine-SS, which made up some 30-40% of the Flemish unit. These men welcomed the change of name. These political topics were the sources of lively debate while the men were situated in the barracks.

The relationships between the Flemings and their German counterparts remained mixed. There were some Germans that outright despised the Flemings while others were much more friendly towards them. The Austrian officers in the unit also had mixed relations with the Flemings, but in general their reputation was better than that of the Germans. Many of the Flemings were defiantly nationalistic and the German leadership knew it. How the Germans felt about Flemish Nationalism can only be speculated upon as no documentation concerning this topic is known to exist. There are reports that the higher German leadership issued an order for the unit to remove their "Legion Flandern" cuff-titles and Flemish lion sleeve shields from their uniform in late 1943. This caused an uproar among the members of the unit and it appears as if this order was never realized. The men later received "Langemarck" cuff-titles and were allowed to retain their national sleeve shield. Even the German officers wore them, along with the "Trifos" (three legged sun-wheel) collartab. As before, the collartab also remained a heated discussion topic. Remy Schrijnen reported:[3]

> *At one time we were ordered never to wear the SS runes again and that the collartab was to be replaced by the sun-wheel collartab. We cut off our runes and sewed on the new patch. Then came another order that we could decide for ourselves which collartab we chose to wear. I had been insulted at the order to remove the SS runes and decided then never to wear them again. For the rest of the war I only wore the sun-wheel collartab.*

Still another insult was dealt to the Flemish Legionnaires in early 1943. The Wallonisches-Infanterie Bataillon 373 of the German Army would be incorporated into the Waffen-SS as the SS-Sturmbrigade "Wallonien."[4] Despite the fact that the Walloons were not a Germanic people, their unit was to be incorporated into the Waffen-SS, until then considered to be purely Germanic. The Flemings had been proud of the fact that they were recognized as a "Germanic" people by the Germans and had been given preferential treatment over the Walloons. This new order nullified these feelings. Still worse was the fact that the Walloons were able to retain the name of their homeland, "Wallonie," in their unit designation. Also, no unit collar patch was ever ordered for this unit and the Walloons only wore the SS runes throughout their existence within the Waffen-SS.

On to the Training Grounds in Milovitz

Late in May, the Flemings were transferred from Debica, Poland to Milovitz, a village in the vicinity of Prague, Czechoslovakia. The official formation of the SS-Freiwilligen-Sturmbrigade "Langemarck" began there. The primary cadre of the unit consisted of the remaining elements of the Legion "Flandern," and included those who had been recovering from their wounds up to this time. The foreseen strength of the Brigade was a combined total of seventeen hundred offic-

---

[3] Letter to the author from R. Schrijnen dated June 16, 1997.
[4] In October 1943, this unit was redesignated as the 5. SS-Freiwilligen-Sturmbrigade "Wallonien." This unit was lead by the leader of the Walloonian Rexist party, Leon Degrelle.

ers, NCOs and men – far more than were available. In order to try and make up for this deficiency, a campaign to recruit new members was initiated in Flanders. Members of many different Flemish political parties and Catholic church groups were hit up the hardest and the results were satisfactory. On July 27, 1943, the last three hundred men arrived from Ghent, which insured the training could proceed as planned.

Toon Pauli, who would later serve as a Richtschütze in Unterscharführer Freese's PAK crew, reported:[5]

> *My father owned a candy shop in Antwerp and I was supposed to become a candy maker! During my time in school I was in the KSA (Catholic Youth) and at the beginning of the war I switched over to the NSJV (Nationaal Socialist Jeugd Verbond), the Flemish National Socialist Youth Organization. Then, after the beginning of 1941, I joined the Allgemeine or Germanic SS. At the end of December 1941, I received a teaching position in Germany and was with the Germanic SS in Düsseldorf. I volunteered for the Waffen-SS at the end of April 1943. On May 19, 1943, there was a catastrophe as a dam in the vicinity of my job was annihilated by English planes. The bakery was destroyed by the water and I received vacation leave. I then returned to Antwerp where I volunteered for the Waffen-SS once again. At the beginning of July 1943, I was called up and first went to Sennheim, then Breslau and then Milovitz to the 6. Kompanie.*

All training courses were conducted at Milovitz with the exception of NCO (most of the NCOs came from the SS-Unteroffizierschule "Lauenberg"), officer training (most of the officers had received their training at the SS-Junkerschule "Bad Tölz") and Pionier (combat engineer) training (which took place in Pikovitz). For all practical purposes it can be assumed that the officer corps consisted approximately of half Flemings and half German nationals.[6] The German officers had either served with the "Legion Flandern" or had been transferred to "Langemarck" from other units. Sturmbannführer Conrad Schellong continued as commander.

With a promotion in status from legion to brigade, the Flemings received more and better equipment than they were supplied in the past. The intended structure of

---

[5] Letter to the author from T. Pauli dated Oct. 14, 1996.
[6] Based on an officer list for the Brigade provided by Mark Yerger and completed and corrected by Georg D'Haese.

the Brigade reflected this fact and consisted of a brigade staff and two battalions. The first battalion was to consist of three infantry companies (companies 1-3) and a fourth heavy infantry company equipped with heavy machine guns and heavy mortars. The second battalion, a heavy battalion, was to consist of four companies (companies 5-8) possessing infantry cannons, anti-tank guns (PAKs), assault guns (Sturmgeschütze) and anti-aircraft guns (light and heavy FLAK), respectively. But, due to lack of equipment and personnel typical of this time in the war, the Brigade was forced to organize with what it could. The actual organization of "Langemarck" was not much different than planned and was as follows:

SS-Freiwilligen-Sturmbrigade "Langemarck"

Brigade Stab (*brigade's staff*)
    Kommandeur – SS-Sturmbannführer Conrad Schellong (G)
        Adjutant – SS Untersturmführer Wilhelm Teichert (G)

Stab Kompanie – Untersturmführer Rudolf Six[7] (G)
    (*staff company*)
        I. Zug – Kradschützen - SS-Oberscharführer Taktasch (G)
        (*motorcycle dispatch rider platoon*)
        II. Zug – Pioniere - SS-Untersturmführer Karl Prade[8] (G)
        (*combat engineer platoon*)
        III. Zug – Funker - SS-Untersturmführer Hendrik Van
        (*signals platoon*)   der Abeele (F)
        IV. Zug – Kriegsberichter - SS-Oberscharführer Van Hulse (F)
        (*war reporter platoon*)

1. Kompanie – leichte Infanterie - SS-Obersturmführer Kurt Mahrenholz (G)
    (*light infantry company equipped with rifles and light grenade launchers*)
    I. Zug   -   SS-Untersturmführer Karl-August Jenssen[9] (G)
    II. Zug   -   SS-Untersturmführer De Backer[10] (F)
    III. Zug   -   SS-Hauptsturmführer Andreas Cambie[11] (F)
    IV. Zug   -   SS-Oberscharführer Peters (G)

---

[7] Killed in Action in May 1945.
[8] Killed in Action in February 1944 in Ukraine.
[9] Killed in Action on January 3, 1944 in Ukraine.
[10] Killed in Action on January 1, 1944 in Ukraine.
[11] Killed in Action on March 8, 1944.

2. Kompanie – leichte Infanterie – Untersturmführer Sven Martenson[12] (G)

I. Zug	-	SS-Hauptscharführer Steiniger (G)
II. Zug	-	SS-Untersturmführer Johann Güldentope (F)
III. Zug	-	SS-Obersturmführer Delft (F)
IV. Zug	-	SS-Untersturmführer Andreas Stevens (F)

3. Kompanie – leichte Infanterie – Untersturmführer Vogel (G)

I. Zug	-	SS-Untersturmführer Herbert Kahrl[13] (G)
II. Zug	-	SS-Untersturmführer Georg Bruyninckx (F)
III. Zug	-	SS-Untersturmführer Demeester (F)
IV. Zug	-	SS-Hauptscharführer Laublicher (G)

4. (schw.) Kompanie – Untersturmführer Leo Van der Weeën[14] (F)
(*heavy infantry company, equipped with heavy machine guns and heavy mortars*)

I. Zug	-	SS-Hauptscharführer Ollendorp (G)
II. Zug	-	SS-Oberscharführer Blum (G)
III. Zug	-	SS-Oberscharführer Huber (G)
IV. Zug	-	SS-Oberscharführer Goemans (F)

5. (I.G.) Kompanie – Untersturmführer Willi Köhn (G)
(*heavy infantry gun company, equipped with infantry cannons and heavy machine guns*)

I. Batterie	-	SS-Untersturmführer Remi Bogaert (F)[15]
II. Batterie	-	SS-Hauptscharführer Wagner (G)
III. (schw.) Batterie	-	SS-Hauptscharführer Blohm (G)

6. (Pz.Jäg.) Kompanie – SS-Hauptsturmführer August Knorr[16] (G)
(*anti-tank gun company, equipped with 7.5 cm PAK guns*)

I. Zug	-	SS-Untersturmführer Anton Kotlowski (A)
II. Zug	-	SS-Untersturmführer Hugo Mortier (F)
III. Zug	-	SS-Oberscharführer Alfons Gradmeyer (G)

---

[12] Killed in Action, date unknown.
[13] Killed in Action on February 24, 1944 in Ukraine.
[14] Killed in Action on February 15, 1944 in Ukraine.
[15] Killed in Action on March 4, 1944 in the Ukraine.
[16] Missing in Action on March 5, 1944 in Ukraine.

7. (Stg.) Kompanie – SS-Hauptsturmführer Karl Weingärtner[17] (A)
(assault gun battery with staff and transport column platoon)

I. Batterie - SS-Untersturmführer Friedrich Ritzau (G)

II. Batterie - SS-Untersturmführer Johannes Glaser (G)

III. Batterie - SS-Untersturmführer August Heyerick (F)

8. (lcht. FLAK) Kompanie – Untersturmführer Otto Uytersprot (F)
(light anti-aircraft company equipped with 2 cm FLAK guns. The formation of this unit was never completed due to lack of equipment and actually consisted of only one battery)

I. Batterie - SS-Untersturmführer Issel (G)

II. Batterie - SS-Oberscharführer Tinke (G)

III. Batterie - SS-Oberscharführer Johannes Weber (G)

9. (schw. FLAK) Kompanie – SS-Hauptsturmführer Willi Dethier[18] (G)
(heavy anti-aircraft company equipped with 8.8 cm FLAK guns. The formation of this unit was also never completed due to lack of equipment and actually consisted of only one battery)

I. Batterie - SS-Obersturmführer Karl-Heinz Gustavson (G)

II. Batterie - SS-Untersturmführer Cesar Geerts (F)

III. Batterie - SS-Untersturmführer Meelmann (G)

10. (Marsch) Kompanie – SS-Untersturmführer Wilhelm Schaumann (G)
(served as a reserve company and was not with the Brigade for its first engagement)

Langemarck's total strength: 42 officers, 162 NCOs and 1,864 enlisted men. 137 Russian volunteer helpers (HIWIs). Total: 2,205 men.

The Structure of the 6th Company

The Wehrmacht's specified strength of a divisional anti-tank unit consisted of a staff, three companies and a replacement company. Twenty-two officers, three officials, 132 non-commissioned officers and 551 enlisted men were required to

---

[17] Killed in Action on January 3, 1944 in Ukraine.
[18] Killed in Action in February 1945.

bring such a unit to full strength. A full-strength anti-tank gun unit was equipped with 45 personnel vehicles, 91 trucks and 78 motorcycles – 46 of which had side cars. Each company had four platoons, three with heavier guns and the last with lighter guns.

The strength of the Brigade's 6. Kompanie was much weaker than that which the Wehrmacht had specified. It consisted of a single company with only three platoons. Assuming a staff and personnel size equal to that of a platoon, it can be estimated that the strength of Langemarck's PAK unit was only a combined total of approximately 150 officers, NCOs and men – a mere 27% of that specified by the Wehrmacht.

The following outlines the structure of the company and includes its designated leaders. This list of names serves as a quick reference for the reader, as many of these men are mentioned throughout the continued text of this book.[19]

6. (Pz.Jäg.) Kompanie/6. SS-Freiwilligen-Sturmbrigade "Langemarck"

Kompanie Führer: SS-Obersturmführer August Knorr[20]
I. Zug – SS-Untersturmführer Anton Kotlowski (A)[21]
    1. Geschütz – SS-Unterscharführer Gustav Freese[22] (G)[23]
    2. Geschütz – ?
    3. Geschütz – SS-Unterscharführer Eduard Reeb (G)
II. Zug – SS-Untersturmführer Hugo Mortier[24] (F)
    4. Geschütz – SS-Unterscharführer Lincke (G)
    5. Geschütz – SS-Unterscharführer Blaha (G)
    6. Geschütz – SS-Unterscharführer Heinz Gödecke (G)
III. Zug – SS-Oberscharführer Alfons Gradmayer[25] (G)
    7. Geschütz – SS-Unterscharführer Kirmse (G)
    8. Geschütz – SS-Unterscharführer Kleinmann (G)
    9. Geschütz – SS-Unterscharführer Dahlhoff (G)

---

[19] The following structural composition of the PAK Kompanie is at best an approximation. It was constructed based on statements made by surviving members. These statements did not agree at all times. It should also be noted that the structure of this unit changed almost on a daily basis while in combat. Leaders were killed or wounded and several members of the unit became sick and had to be taken out of action.

[20] At the time of formation, August Knorr was designated as "Kompanie Führer." This position is considered temporary or that of a trial basis. After being promoted to Hauptsturmführer, Knorr became a full-fledged Kompanie Chef.

[21] (A) for Austrian. Kotlowski had been wounded in mid-November 1941 during large-scale tank attack. At that time he held the rank of Unterscharführer. After recovering from his wounds he attended the Junkerschule Braunschweig where he was training in close combat with tanks. Kotlowski was

August Knorr: Pictured above is August Knorr, on the left as an Oberscharführer serving with SS-VT Regiment "Deutschland" and the right as the new company commander of the 6.(Pz.Jäg.)Kompanie in Knovitz. He was born on May 18, 1909 in Redwitz an der Rodach (Bavaria). As a youth he attended a trade school. He served in the German Police from October 1927 to November 1934 and then joined the SS-VT on December 1, 1934. He was given the rank of Scharführer and was assigned to 15./SS-VT Regiment "Deutschland." On September 1, 1935 he was promoted to Oberscharführer and on April 15, 1937 he was transferred to SS-Regiment "N" (Nürnberg). Later, on August 1, 1938 he was transferred to 14./SS-Regiment "Der Führer." Knorr fought in the Western Campaign as platoon leader from November 1939 to May 1940 during which time he was promoted to Hauptscharführer. In June of that same year, he was promoted to Sturmscharführer. In April 1941, he took part in the Balkan Campaign, after which he was commissioned as an Untersturmführer. He served in Operation "Barbarossa" as a Kompanie Truppführer and a Zugführer (platoon leader). In early March 1942, he suffered a complicated fracture on a finger caused by grenade shrapnel. After his recovery he was placed with the SS-Panzer-Jäger Ersatz Abteilung (tank hunter replacement detachment) in Hilvorsum (where Remy served as his runner). He was promoted to Obersturmführer on June 21, 1942 and from mid-January until the end of February 1943 took a course at SS-Panzertruppenschule "Wünsdorf." From there he was transferred to the Sturmbrigade "Langemarck" where he served as Kompanie Führer (company commander or "Chef" on a trial basis) for 6.(Pz.Jäg.)/"Langemarck." Knorr was promoted to Hauptsturmführer January 30, 1944 during the defensive battles which brought the Brigade to Jambol and his position as "Kompanie Chef" was confirmed. On March 5, 1944, shortly after Remy was wounded, Knorr was officially reported missing in action. Knorr was a highly decorated soldier. He had been awarded the Iron Cross First (1941) and Second Class (1940) very early in the war. He had also earned the Infantry Assault Badge in Bronze and the Wound Badge in Black. He was married and had one child.

---

transferred to "Langemarck" after receiving his commission as an Untersturmführer and was thus a new face amongst the Flemings.

[22] Stan Verlackt was Richtschütze (Schütze I), Toon (Anton) Pauli was Ladeschütze (Schütze II) and Jan Withaigels was the driver for Freese's crew.

[23] (G) for German.

[24] According to Anton Kotlowski, Untersturmführer Alois Herzog (G) was platoon leader of this platoon before being transferred after approximately 3 months.

[25] Killed in Action on or around January 6, 1944. Alfons Gradmayer or Brahmeyer, the true spelling of Gradmayer's name has not been determined. One source states that Gradmayer was actually a Hauptscharführer.

Anton Kotlowski: Pictured above is Anton Kotlowski, the new platoon leader of the first platoon. On the left he is shown as a new recruit in the SS-VT Standarte "Deutschland" and on the right as an Unterscharführer while at the Panzerjägerschule in Hilvorsum, Holland. Kotlowski was born on April 24, 1920 in Braunau am Inn, Austria. He enlisted in the SA in February 1938 and two months later transferred to the SS-Verfügungstruppe. By November 1940 he was an Unterscharführer. While taking courses at the SS-Junkerschule (officer candidate school) Braunschweig beginning in February 1943, he was promoted to Standartenjunker in April 1943 and then to Standartenoberjunker prior to leaving the school at the end of May 1943. He received his commission as an Untersturmführer three months later on September 1. While serving with the Brigade, he was platoon leader for the I. Zug of the 6. (Pz.Jäg.) Kompanie. After the spring battles he assumed the duties of company commander August Knorr who was killed in action in March 1944. When the Brigade regrouped in the summer of 1944 he was again given the command of 6. (Pz.Jäg.) Kompanie. During the war, Kotlowski earned the General Assault badge, the Eastern Front medal, the Wound Badge in Black and the Iron Cross First and Second Class. He reportedly was also awarded the German Cross in Gold. Kotlowski ended the war as an Obersturmführer and now lives in Vienna with his family.

Each *Geschütz* (cannon) had its own crew which, at full strength, consisted of a gun commander and seven crew members. Each crew member was assigned to perform a specific task. As specific as their tasks were, the men were to have a good working knowledge of the functions of the other members of the crew, since in combat there would certainly be casualties requiring men to substitute for their killed or wounded comrades. Six of the positions were given numerical designations and the soldiers referred to the positions by both their numerical designation

Hugo Mortier: Pictured above is Hugo Mortier shortly after receiving his commission as an Untersturmführer. In the fall of 1943, Mortier was the new platoon leader for the second platoon. Born on September 1, 1921 in Ghent, Mortier spoke Dutch, French and German. Prior to enlisting in the Waffen-SS on April 29, 1941, he had passed his college entrance exams and was a member of the Flemish-German Worker's Society. After training at Sennheim, he was transferred to Klagenfurt where Regiment "Westland's" ("Wiking" Division) training and replacement battalion was located. While holding the rank of Unterscharführer, he later served with the "Wiking" Division – first with 12./ "Nordland" and then later with 6./ "Nordland." On February 1, 1943 he entered the officer candidate school Bad Tölz. Mortier was admitted at the rank of Junker but was later promoted to Standartenjunker. After successfully completing his final exams, he was promoted to Standartenoberjunker on July 31, 1943. Later, after returning to regular service, he received his commission as an Untersturmführer on September 1, 1943. Mortier was severely wounded during the second week of January 1944 while serving as platoon leader for the 2nd Platoon of "Langemarck's" anti-tank company. After his recovery he was transferred to several training and replacement battalions. On April 23, 1944, he was transferred to the "Defense Staff Scheveningen" from the home unit, the SS-Pz. Jäg. Ausb. u. Ers. Abt. 1 "Nordwest" (Anti-Tank Training and Replacement Battalion 1), where he served as a temporary company commander. On June 20, 1944 he returned to "Langemarck" and later served with the 27. SS-Division. Mortier survived the war after earning the Iron Cross IInd Class, the Eastern Front Medal, the Infantry Assault Badge and the Wound Badge in Black.

and their function. For instance, the no. 1 gunner could be referred to as either *Schütze I* or *Richtschütze*. A *Schütze* was also a Waffen-SS rank equivalent to a private, but crew members could have the rank from *SS-Schütze* (private) up to *SS-Rottenführer* (corporal). That is not to say that men with higher ranks did not serve as crew members, but this was most usually not the case. The following is a list of the crew's positions and their duties. It will serve as a reference for the continuation of the text:

Outline and Description of a Typical German PAK Crew

Position: Duties

Geschützführer: The *Geschützführer* (gun commander) commanded the PAK crew. He held the rank of a non-commissioned officer in most every case, usually that of *Unterscharführer* (senior corporal). The Geschützführer often chose his own crew, picking the best available men to serve his gun. Typical commands issued by the Geschützführer were:

LADEN!	(load the cannon)
FEUER FREI!	(fire at will)
PANZER VOM LINKS!	(tank coming from the left)
PANZER VOM RECHTS!	(tank coming from the right)

Schütze I: The *Richtschütze* (no. 1 gunner), was the senior crew member and was next in line to take the place of the Geschützführer should he become wounded or killed in action. He also took the Geschützführer's place if he had to attend to his duties elsewhere, but his primary responsibility was to aim and fire the gun. If the Richtschütze was an experienced and proven gunner, the Geschützführer usually gave him the freedom to aim and fire at will. This was quite common as the noise during a battle made it almost impossible for the Richtschütze or other crew members to hear the commands.

Schütze II: The *Ladeschütze* (loader) had the primary responsibility of loading the gun.

Schütze III: As a *Munischütze, Schütze III* handed the shells to the loader, *Schütze II*.

Schütze IV: Also a *Munischütze, Schütze IV* was responsible for handing the shells to Schütze III as well as for organizing and keeping munitions supplies ready for the gun's crew.

Schütze V: The *MG-Schütze* (machine gunner) was positioned in front of the PAK to protect it from attacking infantry.

Schütze VI: The *Munitionschlepper* (ammunition runner) was responsible for retrieving munitions supplies for the gun crew. The Munitionschlepper was also responsible for retrieving other supplies, food, etc. for the men.

No numerical designation: The *Fahrer* (driver) drove the half-tracked vehicle which towed the gun. The Fahrer, when not driving, was on hand during combat to help the other crew members. He was also responsible for entrenching his vehicle before a battle so that it would not be damaged by shrapnel, etc.

New Position for the Foot Messenger

After having returned from battle with the Legion "Flandern," Remy had had enough of his messenger job and was ready to try something new. Having completed training in 1942 at the Hilvorsum *Panzerjägerschule* (tank-hunting school) where he served as Company Commander August Knorr's runner, he was qualified to serve in one of the armored companies. Knorr and Gradmayer, who were both new to the Flemish PAK unit, had taken a liking to Remy during their time together at the Hilvorsum training grounds. Both wanted Remy to be their driver. Schrijnen refused, however, stating that he wanted to prove his worth on the front lines as a member of a PAK crew.

Remy's wish was granted and he was assigned to the *III. Zug* (3rd platoon) as Richtschütze for the 9. Geschütz under Unterscharführer Dahlhoff. Dahlhoff's crew at the beginning of the Brigade's combats was as follows:

9. Geschütz – SS-Unterscharführer Dahlhoff (G)

Schütze I:	Remy Schrijnen (F)
Schütze II:	Albert Desremeau[26] (F)
Schütze III:	Anton Dersmenscheck[27] (F)
Schütze IV:	Hektor Gijse[28] (F)
Schütze V:	Gaston Troch[29] (F)
Schütze VI:	Doorisen[30] (F)
Fahrer:	Paul Rubens (F)

[26] Desremeau was a Rottenführer and survived the war.
[27] Killed in action in the "Jambol Pocket," March 1944.
[28] Gijse survived the war and passed away sometime in the 1960's.
[29] Killed in action in the "Jambol Pocket," March 1944.
[30] Reportedly missing in action in the "Jambol Pocket," March 1944. Doorisen was supposedly not in Remy's crew at the end of February. Little is known about him.

While both Dahlhoff's and Kirmse's crew were made up of men with front-line experience, Kleinmann's crew was made up of inexperienced men. Remy knew a good number of the men in his company well. Many had served with him in the Legion, including (besides Knorr): Blaha, Gradmayer, Mühlbauer and Kirmse. Dahlhoff, Kleinmann and Freese were new to the Flemish unit. They were all Germans and had known each other previously while serving in the German police in Hamburg. From there they were transferred to the *Waffen-SS Unterführerschule* (Waffen-SS NCO school) at Lauenberg where they completed a leadership course just prior to arriving at the Milovitz training grounds. It should be noted that Remy was still good friends with his old messenger comrades from the Legion Flandern, many of whom continued with the Brigade. Among others, Juul Fieremans and Fons Van Broeck were still Kradmelder (motorcycle reconnaissance) messengers for Knorr's Platoon.

The 7.5 cm PAK Gun

Whereas the Legion Flandern had been primarily using the 3.7 cm PAK gun, the Brigade was to be equipped with the relatively new long-barreled 7.5 cm PAK 40. The 3.7 cm PAK had proven to be a weak gun as early as 1940 during the western campaign. As Operation "Barbarossa" began in 1941, the 3.7 cm gun was proven to be a complete failure against armor. It was only effectively utilized against infantry and light vehicles. Engagements against the Russian T-34, KW I and KW II earned it the nickname "gun for knocking on tanks." The slightly larger 5 cm PAK (which was developed beginning in 1938) also proved to be a failure in the presence of T-34s. In search of a solution, the Germans began to mount captured French 7.5 cm barrels from artillery cannons to their 5 cm PAK chassis. The also modified the gun by welding on a make-shift muzzle brake to the end of the barrel. The purpose of the muzzle brake was to reduce the recoil of the gun. This gun was known as the 7.5 cm PAK 97/38 (97 being the model year for the French barrel and 38 being the model year of the German chassis). This gun was completely manual.

Development of a new model, the 7.5 cm PAK 40, began in 1939. Due to the fast pace of the western campaign and little need for a heavier weapon, the production of this gun did not commence until sometime in the spring of 1941. Due to a lead time of approximately six months, the gun did not see action until May of the following year.

The design of the 7.5 cm PAK 40 (which the Brigade received) was based on the 5 cm gun and many of the features from this lighter gun were maintained. By changing the material of the spars from aluminum to steel, the gun performance could be increased due to the stability offered by the increased weight in the back of the gun. Like its predecessor, the gun utilized a muzzle brake as well as a double shield to protect the gun operators. As stated previously, the muzzle brake decreased the recoil of the gun after being fired. This allowed the use of lighter-weight materials. The double shield was constructed of two 4 mm shields set 25 mm apart from one another.

The gun used three types of ammunition, depending on how the gun was to be utilized. For direct targets or regular tanks, there were *Panzergranaten* (anti-tank shells). For heavy tanks, there were *Hohlraumgranaten* (hard core shells). The hard core shells, weighing in at 3.5 pounds, weighed approximately half of what the anti-tank shells weighed, the benefit of which was increased muzzle velocity. These lighter weight shells traveled at up to 2080 miles per hour, which was approximately a 17.5% increase in speed. This increase in speed corresponded to a 16.5% increase in armor penetration, reaching just over six inches. A third type of ammunition was the *Sprenggranate* (anti-personnel shells), which exploded like a shotgun, spraying shrapnel over a wide area. This type of ammunition was used against infantry and lightly armored vehicles, and, according to Remy Schrijnen, was by far the most frequently used form of ammunition.

Training and then – Off to the Front

The Brigade's training in Milovitz was typical, that is, difficult and necessary for what the men were about to experience. It was during this training that Remy's reputation began to take root. Schrijnen, having previously served in the PAK company as a runner, was very excited about his new assignment. As discussed previously, Remy received his PAK training in 1942 at the training grounds in Hilvorsum. He was finally assigned to a PAK crew during the training which took place at Milovitz. As many of his former comrades reported, he was very attentive during instruction and asked many questions. It is safe to say that Schrijnen took his PAK training very seriously.

At the beginning of December 1943, Sturmbannführer Conrad Schellong reported that the Brigade, now re-designated as the 6. SS-Freiwilligen-Sturmbrigade "Langemarck," was ready for action. A parade in Prague on December 6th marked

A PAK Gun at Milovitz: Shown here is a 7.5 cm PAK gun used by the Brigade for training at the Milovitz training grounds. (The Legion had used a limited number of these guns in combat as well). An attentive eye will notice that the muzzle brake on this gun is different than the normal German design. Due to a shortage of guns at the front, the Germans used French 7.5 cm barrels which had been designed in 1897 and utilized by the French artillery in the First World War. The Germans mounted the barrels from this gun (which had been captured after the French campaign) to their 5 cm PAK chassis, producing a new gun deemed the "7.5 cm PAK 97/38." The odd looking muzzle brake was designed and added by the Germans to reduce the recoil of the gun. The difference in performance between the PAK 97/38 and the completely new German 7.5 cm PAK 40 was very noticeable, as the French version was fully manual and the German version half-automatic. The half-automatic guns could be fired at a much faster rate. Schrijnen also notes that the German version was also a more powerful gun, as it had a longer barrel and utilized longer shells. For the battles that were about to take place, the Brigade would be fully equipped with the 7.5 cm PAK 40.

the conclusion of the formation. It was a very festive occasion for the men. The strength of the Brigade, intended to be at least seventeen hundred men, ended up being over 2000, as several contingents of recruits trickled in during the training period. The excess in strength lay primarily in the enlisted ranks, with the non-commissioned ranks lacking three hundred men and the officer ranks lacking twenty.

While "Langemarck" was still in Prague, the *2. SS-Panzergrenadier-Division "Das Reich"* was busy forming *Kampfgruppe "Das Reich"* in southern Russia. The Division, which was still almost at full strength, was to be withdrawn from the front lines for a transfer to France where it was to reform as a full-fledged Panzer division. The members of "Das Reich" had many months of tense offensive and defensive fighting behind them. In early November the Division had retaken the city of Shitomir. During the following two months the Division had had to withstand numerous counterattacks in the area between the villages of Korosten, Boroditschev and Radomyschl. After the German Army leaders were informed of the planned withdrawal of the unit, they demanded that a battle group be formed to remain on the lines as all men were needed. The complete absence of "Das Reich" would put have put an extreme burden on the German front. The formation of the Kampfgruppe concluded on December 19, 1943. Oberführer Heinz Lammerding would lead the battle group which had a strength of approximately five thousand men.

After successfully taking part in a small operation to retake a lost village, "Das Reich" was ready to take a short break for the holidays. The men knew that letters and gifts from home were on the way to the front and were looking forward to a somewhat festive occasion. The Russians, however, had different plans and at 0600 hours on Christmas Eve they launched a major offensive which completely surprised the Germans.

Back in Prague the men of "Langemarck" had just finished up the Christmas celebration when they were put on alarm due to the grim situation at the front. Schrijnen himself had just finished celebrating his twenty-second birthday. On December 26th, the Brigade departed by train heading east to the front lines which now lay somewhere between Kiev and Shitomir. They arrived there on December 30th and spent New Year's Eve preparing for the coming battle. The pressure was on and the *"alte Hasen"* were aware of what was to come, while the new recruits were awaiting their baptism of fire. Their task: hold open the front lines to let through retreating elements of battle group "Das Reich."

While the men were digging in and preparing their positions, the call came: RUSSIAN TANKS APPROACHING! Most of the troops ran by Gradmayer's Panzerjäger in fear of the Russian tanks while they prepared their positions in the vicinity of a supply road. Gradmayer ordered Dahlhoff's crew to set up sixty meters to the right of the road while Kirmse's crew was positioned seven hundred meters to the right of Dahlhoff and Kleinmann's crew seven hundred meters to the left. As seven T-34's poked their barrels over a small hill at a distance of approximately five hundred meters, the PAKs were ready. Geschütz Kirmse could not attack for unknown reasons. Geschütz Kleinmann was also in position but did not attack either. Dahlhoff's PAK had better luck and Remy scored three direct hits in a row, knocking out three of the T-34s. The other four, recognizing Remy's good aim, fled back to their lines. Schrijnen and his men knew that the crews of the first two

Geschütz Dahlhoff, January 1944: Shown here is an artist's depiction of Unterscharführer Dahlhoff's crew in position in Ukraine after the conclusion of a battle in during the first weeks of 1944. From the left is the MG-Schütze, Gaston Troch, Geschützführer Dahlhoff, Richtschütze Remy Schrijnen, Ladeschütze Albert Desremeau and finally Schütze III, Anton Dersmenscheck. The three rings around the gun's barrel mark the crew's first three T-34s.

tanks had been killed and watched as three men in the last tank burned to their death. A fourth crew member from the final T-34 managed to escape the fire and was taken prisoner. Langemarck's infantry, noticing the success of the PAKs, rushed back to their positions. So it was that during their first action on the front, Dahlhoff's crew earned its first three "kill" rings. The day was not a total success, however, as Dahlhoff's crew reported that Kleinmann and his crew had faltered due to coward-ice in the face of the enemy. They also later found out that battle group "Das Reich" broke out somewhere else.

Later that night the men got into a small fight with some Russians who had strayed from their units. After the small skirmish they managed to capture some American rations, which were noted as a welcome change. After the men had finished eating, Remy decided to depart on his own personal reconnaissance mission. He took off to check out a village which lay a short distance behind his unit's positions. As he approached the village, he heard several Russian soldiers singing. He immediately ran back to Dahlhoff to report his discovery. Dahlhoff and his men then decided to greet the New Year 1944 by spending the day running through the village occupied by the Russians, tossing grenades in open windows and torching buildings with gasoline. They also took the opportunity to destroy several of the Russian's vehicles.

Elsewhere in the Langemarck sector, Dries Anseeuw, the Richtschütze in Unterscharführer Lincke's crew, had knocked out his first tank early that morning. Toon Pauli, the Richtschütze in Unterscharführer Freese's crew, knocked out the second. Unfortunately it turned out that the tanks they hit were "Das Reich" Panzers retreating from the Shitomir pocket.

From January 2nd though the January 5th, Gradmayer's platoon was ordered to head south to support Kampfgruppe "Das Reich," which was having difficulties blocking the Russian offensive. During these battles, Dahlhoff's PAK crew found themselves mainly fighting against Russian infantry, switching over to their Sprenggranate ammunition. Up to this point, Gradmayer's platoon and Knorr's company had performed with mixed results – but what luck they had was not to continue. For January 5th and 6th, Gradmayer's PAKs were to be positioned in Tschudinov to stop a Russian advance where Geschütz Kirmse and Geschütz Dahlhoff performed well. Gradmayer lost his first PAK, however, as Geschütz Kleinmann was placed in reserve for security reasons. It was obvious to the men and their leader that Kleinmann and his crew could simply not perform in the face of the enemy. To continue to send them into action would not only endanger their lives, but the lives of their comrades as well.

While arriving in Tschudinov on the 5th, they also found out that the others had mistakenly knocked out two Das Reich Panzers. The men took position in Tschudinov and were now supported by the 2 cm FLAK platoon and were once again assigned to Langemarck. The next few days of fighting would cost Langemarck many men. On January 6th the Brigade found itself engaged in heated battles which teetered back and forth between offense and defense in Olszanka. The bad luck the men of the PAKs had experienced continued. Just as the Russians began their first attack, the 2 cm FLAK platoon was called off to support another unit elsewhere. At this time Gradmayer was with Dahlhoff's crew, but unable to observe the situation properly. Frustrated, he took off to Kirmse's PAK, positioned six hundred meters to the right, to observe from there. The fight erupted and from then on Dahlhoff and his men heard nothing from neither their platoon leader nor Kirmse's PAK. Later, a messenger arrived to report that the platoon lost both its leader and the second of its PAKs. Geschütz Kirmse suffered a direct hit which killed Gradmayer, Kirmse and the crew's Schütze I and II. Just over a week after being brought to the front, Knorr's IIIrd Platoon was almost completely wiped out, and the bad luck would continue. At 3 a.m. on January 7th, an order arrived that Knorr and his men were to retreat to an area near Burkovzy. After traveling a few kilometers, Kleinmann and his group caught up with the retreating men and reported to Knorr that their PAK had suffered a direct hit. Knorr was somewhat skeptical of the report and ordered Remy to take a few men and find out if Kleinmann was telling the truth. Upon arriving at the PAK, Remy and his men found that it was a building that had suffered a direct hit and not Kleinmann's PAK. The gun, which was positioned next to the building with the tow truck, was covered with beams and other rubble. By now the Russians were crawling in this area and it would be impossible for the men to tow the gun back without making themselves noticed. They decided instead to place mines under the wheels of the gun and cover them with dirt. They then uncoupled the gun from the truck and pulled the truck away. Next, they set the truck on fire to alert the Russians, so that they would hopefully come and investigate and then try to recover the PAK, setting off the mines that the men had hidden under the wheels. Remy then returned to Knorr to make his report. It was then that Schrijnen and his men learned that Kleinmann would be sentenced to seven continuous years at the front. Schrijnen notes that this case was not an infrequent occurrence on the front and that there were many who failed and later punished because of it. The men felt, however, that Kleinmann's punishment was light. They thought that had he not been German, he would have been shot for this act of cowardice.

Remy Schrijnen later commented about this incident:[31]

> ...we thought he would get either a bullet or a court-marshal. Even if he got the latter we definitely thought he would get a death sentence which would be surely carried out. Kleinmann's punishment was not a good example for us because if it was one of us it would have surely been a death sentence. We then asked Dahlhoff why this didn't happen with the German Unterscharführer.

Dahlhoff, Schrijnen's *Geschützführer*, responded:[32]

> "...I don't know either. I knew Kleinmann and Freese for a long time while with the Police in Hamburg. All three of us were transferred to the

---

[31] Letter to the author from R. Schrijnen dated May 17, 1996.
[32] Schrijnen notebook.

Mortier and Kassberger: Above are Kassberger (who was a reserve platoon leader) on the far left and Hugo Mortier on the far right. The officer in the center is an infantry officer. It was long rumored that Kassberger had committed suicide during the breakout from Jambol as the fighting got thick and the men were suffering from extreme exhaustion. In 1997, however, the veterans of the Brigade learned that Anton Kotlowski had been in contact with Kassberger since the end of the war and that he had been living in Austria.

Waffen-SS in the summer of 1942. We went to NCO school and Kleinmann was a good student, but a miserable failure at the front. I think that it was only normal that the men found his sentence unjust, as a coward remains a coward and Kleinmann's men seemed to have lost trust in themselves as well."

Knorr's IInd Platoon leader, Hugo Mortier, was severely wounded in the face the next day. Knorr assigned SS-Hauptscharführer Mühlbauer to take over as platoon leader while forming a new IInd Platoon, reducing the strength of the company from three to two platoons:

II. Zug – SS-Hauptscharführer Mühlbauer
    5. Geschütz – SS-Unterscharführer Blaha
    6. Geschütz – SS-Unterscharführer Heinz Gödecke
    9. Geschütz – SS-Unterscharführer Dahlhoff

As the Brigade reached Burkovzy they were afforded a few days rest. It wasn't until January 10th that the fighting started again. The Russians had pressed on and were now only fifteen kilometers from Sseverinovka, where the majority of the Brigade was located. Brigade units in Burkovzy pressed on and reached the others in Sseverinovka on January 12th.

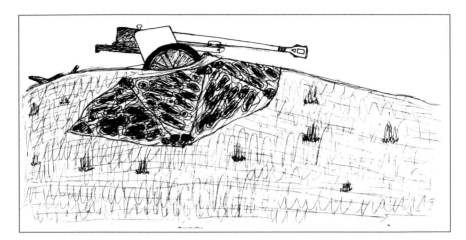

The "Kopfstellung": It was during the battles in Ukraine that Remy Schrijnen developed his "Kopfstellung," which, roughly translated into English, means "head position." While the accepted position of a PAK gun was a dug in position, low to the ground on a flat section of terrain, Remy developed a positional strategy which appeared to be quite different and was even considered dangerous. In contrast to a normal PAK position, Remy sought a small hill or a flat of terrain that was slightly elevated. This position, in Remy's opinion, offered several advantages. First, the opponent could not see behind the gun's position. Since the gun was at a position which was higher than the surrounding terrain, there was no background which would help enemy tanks to more easily judge the distance at which Schrijnen's gun stood. This made Schrijnen's gun a more difficult shot. Secondly, a gun firing down on a tank from a position above it was more likely to hit armor head-on. The armor of a Russian tank was designed to deflect rounds and was sloped. Firing at the sloped armor from a position below the tank increased this deflection effect, while firing from a position above it served to negate it. Schrijnen also had his own ideas about camouflaging the gun. While viewing old press clips from the German newsreels, one notices the massive dust clouds formed when an anti-tank gun is fired. In order to better conceal his position, Schrijnen's crew would lay Zeltbähne (shelter quarters) in front and to the sides of the gun to hinder any of these dust clouds from forming. This served to make the gun's position even less noticeable. Schrijnen first utilized this method on January 5, 1944 in Tschudinov and found it to be "good and secure." Both Gradmeyer and Knorr were of the opinion that the position was too dangerous, as they thought it would be easy for enemy artillery observers to spot the position. After a while, though, they reluctantly allowed Remy to continue to use this method. Remy continued to position his gun in this manner for the rest of the war and claims that it greatly contributed to his success as a Panzerjäger.

The Russians would often shoot at the German supply wagons in hope that they were full of ammunition. It was in Sseverinovka that one of the PAK munitions trucks was hit. Remy noticed the fire and ran and jumped into the truck to save the valuable ammunition. Dahlhoff called for him to get out but Remy ignored him. He threw out the ammunition crates from the wagon and then found the source of the flame. After moving several boxes out of the way, he saw a shelterquarter and used it to extinguish the fire. Right in the vicinity of the fire was the gas tank. A lucky save.

A Richtschütze's View: The picture above shows a view through the optics of a PAK gun. The small triangles lined up from left to right allow the Richtschütze to time the movement of his target, while the large triangle in the center is the focal point of the shot. A Richtschütze would also have to adjust the height of the gun properly depending on the distance of his target.

The defensive battles continued, the men fought during the day and retreated at night. Every day, day in and day out, night in and night out, the men were constantly on the move. There was no time for sleep. Sometimes the fighting was mild, other times it was heavy. Luck can hold out only so long, though, and a while later, Remy received his fourth wound, this time shrapnel in the buttocks. In the same battle, Mühlbauer was also wounded, having taken some shrapnel in his legs. This gave the men a chance to compare each other's wounds. Remy exclaimed: *Man, you belong in a field hospital! Have you seen the puss coming out of your leg?* The two then just laughed it off. Despite being wounded and having received orders from the medics to evacuate to the field hospital, both men remained with their crews. It was at about this time that Knorr was promoted to Hauptsturmführer (January 30, 1944). Schrijnen was awarded the Wound Badge in Black on February 10.

During the month of February the Brigade retreated slowly in the direction of Jambol. On approximately February 17th, the Brigade was ordered to make its way to Tschepetovka, where they were to take part in a battle against partisans. As it would turn out, however, the partisans were really Russian patrols which were penetrating the German lines. The intent of the enemy was to break through the lines in the north near Kiev and in the south near Tscherkassy and head west.

Chantraine's PAK Crew: This picture was taken on January 15, 1944 in Sseverinovka. From left to right Anton Pauli (Ladeschütze), Stan Verlackt (Richtschütze), Jan Withaegels (Fahrer), Unterscharführer Chantraine (reserve Geschützführer) and Frans Mapans. Chantraine had replaced Unterscharführer Freese, who became ill and was evacuated.

Digging In: Here, two soldiers of the PAK company dig in before another battle. The soldier on the left is a "Munischlepper" as evidenced by the pack strung around his neck for dragging munitions.

More Supplies for the Brigade: Here the men of the Brigade unload more supplies and ammunition during the winter/spring of 1944.

These two penetrations were to turn to the south and north respectively, and surround the German troops in a large pocket.

It was about this time that Remy was recommended for the Iron Cross 2nd Class by his company commander, August Knorr. Knorr, a German officer who had known Remy since his assignment at Hilvorsum, had watched over him during his time as a no. 1 gunner. One time during a heated battle, as the situation became dangerous and the Russians continually turned up the pressure, Remy sent his crew back behind the main lines and remained at his gun alone, loading, aiming and firing the PAK all by himself, an act that would later become his trademark. As the others arrived behind the lines near the command post, Knorr appeared and wanted to know what was going on. After the group explained the situation, Knorr ran out with his field glasses to see what was going on. There he saw Remy operating the gun on his own, loading, aiming, firing. Without any regard for his life whatsoever, the company commander ran out into the middle of the battlefield and, after stumbling through several craters, made it to the gun. Remy was somewhat shocked to see his commander and without a word, Knorr immediately took the place of the loader. They continued to act as a two-man team, firing and loading, firing and loading, as incoming Russian anti-tank fire

Sturmmann Gaston Ide and Unterscharführer Cyriel Sardeur: Gaston Ide was a member of the PAK Kompanie's staff and Cyriel Sardeur was a reserve Geschützführer. Notice the Russian tommy gun on the truck, this was the weapon of preference for the German "Landser."

became concentrated on them. They remained there until the last Russian anti-tank gun was destroyed. A token of camaraderie. Schrijnen held his company commander in high regard:[33]

> ...Knorr remains for me one of the best, or better said, the man that every man could depend on to carry out any assignment.

Conrad Schellong approved Knorr's recommendation for Remy's Iron Cross 2nd Class and Schrijnen was given the award in February.[34] Remy was the first member of the PAK Company to receive the Iron Cross Second Class. Congratulating their comrade on his new award, Gödecke and Blaha,[35] both veterans who had known Remy since his time with the "Legion Flandern" proclaimed:[36]

> "...Yes, it's the former runner from the Legion Flandern, now a no. 1 gunner, proven in battle, with a crew that has yet to suffer a single casualty!"

Knorr added to this stating:[37]

---

[33] Letter to the author from R. Schrijnen dated Dec. 13, 1996.
[34] Schrijnen was officially awarded the Iron Cross 2nd Class on May 26, 1944.
[35] Blaha, then an Unterscharfuhrer, was promoted to Oberscharfuhrer sometime on April 20, 1944, but was badly hurt in a motorcycle accident a few weeks later and never returned to "Langemarck."
[36] Schrijnen notebook.
[37] Schrijnen notebook.

"...In Remy sit a dozen devils. He has no idea what fear is. He's a go-getter, not like any other, not dumb, but able, and that damned Kopfstellung! Where other PAKs immediately flee, Geschütz Dahlhoff remains."

There would be no time for a formal award ceremony, and Schrijnen would have to wait some time before receiving the award. At about this time, the gun's crew lost their gun commander as Dahlhoff was promoted to SS-Oberscharführer and subsequently transferred to a new position as Kompanietruppführer.[38]

During his time as a Geschützführer, Dahlhoff had been satisfied with the performance of his crew:[39]

...Yeah, my men, the heart of my crew was the trio. They never asked what they should do. They were always the first to get to work and immediately started building our positions and digging trenches whenever we would arrive somewhere new. The stories I could tell about their scout patrols... I was grateful to my crew, since as I arrived on the front for the first time, Desremeau, Rubens and Schrijnen helped me, even though I was to be their superior.

On February 22nd, Remy's new gun commander, Alfons Van Kerkhoven, himself a Fleming, arrived at the front to take over the crew with several other men fresh from *Unterführerschule Lauenberg* (NCO school located in Lauenberg, Germany). Van Kerkhoven's crew was as follows:

9. Geschütz – SS-Unterscharführer Alfons Van Kerkhoven (F)

Schütze I:	Remy Schrijnen (F)
Schütze II:	Albert Desremeau (F)
Schütze III:	Anton Dersmenscheck (F)
Schütze IV:	Hektor Gijse (F)
Schütze V:	Gaston Troch (F)
Schütze VI:	Kamiel Horre (F)
Fahrer:	Paul Rubens (F)

---

[38] The Kompanietruppführer was responsible for the company's messengers. Dahlhoff usually had three to four under his group. Dahlhoff went on to serve as platoon leader for the I./SS-Panzerjäger Abteilung 27 (27. SS-Division) and was badly wounded on April 22, 1944, during the defensive battles in Schöningen an der Oder (Germany).

[39] Schrijnen notebook.

There were no worries when Van Kerkhoven arrived, as he was already an experienced front-line soldier, having previously fought as a Munischütze in the former Legion's 5. Kompanie. The defensive battles began that day and Langemarck found itself positioned first in the vicinity of Zaslav and later continued fighting while making its way through Vaskovszy, Klembovka, Krzyvoluka and Bjelgorodka. After those villages came Michnoff, Dvorez and Sinjutki which lay north and north-west of Bjelgorodka.

During these battles it was always the same PAK that was deployed in the hot spots of the battle, whether in defense, to destroy the famous Russian PAK Riegel or to support Langemarck's infantry companies. During this time Remy and other members of the PAK company were afforded the opportunity to conduct several makeshift reconnaissance operations, as one of their crew members, SS-Mann Dersmenscheck was somewhat fluent in Russian. Dersmenscheck was a Fleming of Ukrainian heritage. His parents had immigrated from Ukraine to Flanders after the conclusion of the First World War and he had learned to speak Ukrainian (a language very similar to Russian) from his parents while growing up. Juul Fieremans recalls: [40]

> "...Gaston Troch, Schrijnen and Dersmenscheck used to go behind the lines to conduct their own reconnaissance patrols. Dersmenscheck, a Ukrainian-speaking Fleming who came to Limburg with his parents after 1918,[41] played "listening post" in a Russian uniform near the Russians. When the three returned they reported to Knorr, who immediately brought Dersmenscheck to Teichert – Schellong's adjutant. Later Knorr told me what Dersmenscheck had found out."

Knorr: [42]

> "...what Dersmenscheck and the other two turned up is unbelievable. These three fellows are as valuable as an entire company. I won't be splitting them up any time soon as Dersmenscheck and Troch both told me, 'Without Remy you can forget it. He is our man and the soul of our company. He gives the best advice and always finds his way out of bad situations in battle. He leads us without even knowing it.'"

---

[40] Schrijnen notebook.
[41] His family fled the Bolshevik Revolution in Russia.
[42] Schrijnen notebook.

On February 28th, the first men reached Jambol. To the new replacements, the village appeared to be a relatively calm place, but the more experienced noticed something disturbing lurking in the background. To the west of their positions they saw horse mounted soldiers riding to the south and knew that they were Russians. On February 29th, as the rest of the Brigade arrived in Jambol, they found the units there already bogged down in heavy defensive battles. These battles were some of the bloodiest battles that the Flemings would ever see. There was no recognizable HKL (main fighting line). Groups of men were splintered and spread about with no means of communication. The intensity and confusion of the battles has been attributed to the massive retreat of the Wehrmacht units at this time. It wasn't until Langemarck was subordinated to Kampfgruppe "Das Reich" that any stability could be realized. Lammerding, still the commander of the "Das Reich" battle group, gave the Brigade freedom of movement. During the next days the Russians succeeded several times in breaking through the Brigade's main lines around Jambol, but these breakthroughs were always repulsed.

It was during these battles that Van Kerkhoven was badly wounded. The remaining men in Schrijnen's crew were ordered to be evacuated some two hundred meters to the rear for security reasons. Remy was left to operate the PAK by himself, firing, reloading, aiming, again all by himself. It was on March 2nd, during the beginning of the climax of the battles, that Schrijnen's PAK suffered a direct hit. Schrijnen survived the hit but was badly wounded. Schrijnen reported:[43]

> *...I was deployed to battle against Russian Panzerjäger, trying to take out the Russian PAK Riegel and it was then that I met my match – it was a better Russian Panzerjäger that took me out.*

On March 3rd, Commander Schellong issued the order to evacuate the village. The mixed *Sturmgeschützbatterie* (assault gun battery) from battle group "Das Reich"[44] came to help with the evacuation. The majority of the Brigade's vehicles were able to safely retreat, with the exception of the 6. Kompanie. The anti-tank company were to be the last to evacuate the village (the PAKs were often deployed to cover the retreat of the infantry units), found itself once again under

---

[43] Letter to the author from R. Schrijnen dated Aug. 28, 1997.

[44] The mixed Sturmgeschützbatterie contained all kinds of vehicles including Panzers from the Panzer regiment. The commander of this unit was German Cross in Gold winner SS-Obersturmführer Hermann Bolte. See Yerger, "Knights of Steel - The Structure, Development and Personalities of the 2. SS-Panzer-Division," p. 144 for a detailed report on the little-known battle group.

Edmond Van Winckel: SS-Mann Edmond Van Winckel was Hauptsturmführer Knorr's driver. He was killed along with Knorr after receiving artillery fire while driving Knorr during the retreat on March 5, 1944. The artillery fire reportedly knocked the two men from their vehicle and thereafter they were run over by Russian tanks.

fire from enemy infantry. It was on March 5, 1944 that Hauptsturmführer Knorr, along with his driver, Edmond Van Winckel, were hit by an artillery shell while retreating in their staff car. Several men witnessed the incident and reported that the round knocked both of the men from their vehicle. Reportedly still alive, they were subsequently run over by Russian tanks. Both were assumed to have been killed. Due to the ongoing retreat, their bodies could not be recovered. They were officially reported as missing in action. According to Jan De Wilde, the Flemings had good relations with the Russian population and they helped the Brigade to flee from the encircling Russian forces.

On March 8th, Sturmbannführer Schellong was wounded on the hand and was evacuated. It was then that Schrijnen's former Kompanie Chef, Hauptsturmführer Willi Dethier, took over as temporary commander. Due to the confusion, many troops were still located in and around Jambol. On March 18th, the Russian offensive reached the Dnjestr and Jambol was completely surrounded. The Flemings were still located in the village along with 6-8 Sturmgeschütze from Kampfgruppe "Das Reich." The crews of the Sturmgeschütze were the victims of a concentrated attack and were completely annihilated. The men had been fighting for days and were completely cut off from supply lines and therefore had no rations or ammunition. Survivors of the "Das Reich" battle group who escaped the inferno in the city report that the surviving Flemish and German soldiers were

rounded up in an open field. They were then forced to completely strip out of their boots, pants, tunics and underwear there in the snow. Bare naked they were rounded up like a herd of cattle by Russian tanks and then slaughtered by their machine guns.[45]

The bitter defensive fighting continued. On March 19th, the survivors of the Brigade reached Staro-Konstantinov. More than seventy-five percent of the original 2,200 plus men of Brigade were registered as casualties, but the men were forced to reorganize and take position before Proskuroff.

The defensive battles and the constant retreating and fighting continued through mid-April. It was then that the Brigade, reduced to a mere fragment of its former strength, could take a few days to rest. The rest wouldn't last for long however, as the surviving remnants loaded a train in Jaslo (Poland) and headed to Debica where they were to rest and refit. At this time, Remy was still in the hospital recovering from his wounds. On March 17th, Schrijnen was awarded the Wound Badge in Silver, having been wounded a total of seven times.[46]

---

[45] See "Division Das Reich," Band V, by Otto Weidinger.

[46] The wound badge was awarded in three grades: Grade I (black) for up to two wounds, Grade II (silver) for three to four wounds and Grade III (gold) for five or more wounds. Even though Schrijnen had been wounded seven times, he had not received seven wound "points" at this point in time, as a soldier only received a point if he was forced to evacuate to a field hospital. Therefore, in the case where a soldier refused to evacuate for care in a field hospital - as Schrijnen often did - no wound badge point was recorded.

The New 6. SS-Freiwilligen Sturmbrigade

Starting in May 1944, the Brigade began its rest and refit. The Brigade was also to undergo a relative expansion and the new structure of Langemarck was planned as follows:

Brigadestab   *(Brigade Staff)*
 Brigade Kommandeur - SS-Obersturmbannführer Conrad Schellong (G)
      Adjutant -   SS-Obersturmführer Wilhelm Teichert (G)
I. Bataillon
 Bataillon Kommandeur - SS-Hauptsturmführer Wilhelm Rehmann (G)
      Adjutant -   SS-Untersturmführer Walther van Leemputten (F)
  1. Kompanie -   SS-Untersturmführer Frans Swinnen (F)
  2. Kompanie -   SS-Untersturmführer Henri Von Mol (F)
  3. Kompanie -   SS-Untersturmführer Georg D'Haese (F)
  4. Kompanie -   SS-Untersturmführer Van Ossel (F)
  5. (Pz.Jäg.) Kompanie - SS-Untersturmführer Marcel Laperre[47] (F)
II. Bataillon
 Bataillon Kommandeur - SS-Hauptsturmführer Johannes Oehms (G)
      Adjutant -   SS-Obersturmführer Ludwig Plabst[48] (G)
  6. Kompanie -   SS-Untersturmführer Wilhelm Schaumann (G)
  7. Kompanie -   SS-Untersturmführer Tops (F)
  8. Kompanie -   SS-Untersturmführer Demeester (F)
  9. Kompanie -   SS-Untersturmführer Jack Delblaere (F)
  10. (Pz.Jäg.) Kompanie - SS-Untersturmführer Anton Kotlowski (A)

Brigade schwere Kompanien: *(Brigade's heavy companies)*
  11. (Art.) Kompanie -   SS-Obersturmführer Horst Hinrichs (G)
  12. (Stg.) Kompanie -   SS-Hauptsturmführer Willi Sprenger (G)
  13. (lt. FLAK) Kompanie - SS-Untersturmführer Otto Uytersprot (F)
  14. (schw. FLAK) Kompanie - SS-Untersturmführer Karl-Heinz Gustavson (G)

It should be noted that the above structure was only the planned structure of the Brigade. It was never realized. As the men arrived in Knovitz, there was no-where near enough personnel to fill two battalions. Many of the men had been

---

[47] For a biography and photo of Marcel Laperre, turn to page ?.
[48] First name not confirmed.

Rehmann and D'Haese: This picture was taken at Knovitz in the summer of 1944. Third from the left is the foreseen commander of the I. Bataillon, Hauptsturmführer Wilhelm Rehmann. On his right is Untersturmführer Georg D'Haese, who had just returned to "Langemarck" after successfully completing course work at the Waffen-SS officer candidate school in Bad Tölz, Germany. D'Haese, who shortly before this picture was taken had received his commission, was assigned to command the 3. Kompanie.

either killed or lay wounded in a field hospital. Therefore, the 6. (PAK) Kompanie would remain, as before, the 6. (PAK) Kompanie. Schrijnen's old Kompanie Chef, Hauptsturmführer August Knorr, was officially reported missing in action during March and was assumed to have been killed. Untersturmführer Anton Kotlowski took over for Knorr and was now designated as Kompanie Führer. Marcel Laperre, who had just arrived from the Junkerschule Bad Tölz (officer candidate school), was the foreseen Kompanie Führer of the 5. Kompanie, but was for the time being a platoon leader under Kotlowski. Laperre's platoon consisted of the most experienced tank hunters. Upon his return, Remy would be assigned to Laperre's platoon. It is unknown what the status was concerning Platoon Leader Hugo Mortier's recovery at this point in time, although he would eventually recover and return to battle in the last chapter of the war. Alfons Gradmayer, platoon leader for the III. Zug, had been killed in action very early in the fighting in Ukraine. It is unknown who the other two platoon leaders under Kotlowski were.

Back with the Brigade

After recovering from his wounds to the point where he was mobile enough to stand and walk on his own, Schrijnen was given a recovery pass and released from the hospital. After several weeks of recovery, he was to report for a physical, where doctors would judge if he was healthy enough to return to the front. Schrijnen decided to skip the physical and set out to catch up with his comrades in Knovitz during the first week in July. As he greeted his comrades, the first thing that he did was ask where his men were. It was then that he learned that while he was in the hospital many of his comrades had been killed. From the leadership ranks, Company Commander August Knorr was missing in action and Platoon Leader Mühlbauer and Obersturmführer Müller[49] were no longer alive. The majority of Schrijnen's PAK gun crew had survived. Of his old PAK crew, Albert Desremeaux, Hektor Gijse, Kamiel Horre, Paul Rubens and Gaston Troch were still alive. Anton Dersmenscheck was reported killed.

Remy's new platoon leader, Marcel Laperre, was fresh from the famous SS-Junkerschule (officer candidate school) Bad Tölz and did not have any front-line combat experience. The first day back with the troops, Remy met his new platoon leader, who reported: [50]

"...Yeah, Dahlhoff, Fieremans, Fons Van Broeck, Tollenaere and even Spieß Wallow[51] had told me so many stories about this 'boy wonder,' who appeared to me to be pretty small. I saw him for the first time in July 1944, as he returned from the hospital. The first thing he did was ask about his men. And then that crack about the silver and bronze close combat clasp for the men of the heavy weapons companies. So many men were not awarded them, but Schrijnen was awarded the silver because he had been with our men since the time of the Legion, around Leningrad. Schrijnen turned down the badge, however, and for the rest of the war he never wore it. After turning it down he said out loud so that the whole company could hear him, 'I had five or six close combat days and not thirty. Us PAK, FLAK and infantry cannon men, why should we be talking about all of these close combat days?' This com-

---

[49] Obersturmführer Müller (a German) was a leader in 6. Kompanie and was responsible for social affairs (for example, when one of the soldiers wished to get married, he would make the arrangements, etc.)

[50] Schrijnen notebook.

[51] The Spieß was a staff position. The Spieß was termed the "mother of the company" by the soldiers. He was responsible for all sorts of administration task and looked after the welfare of the soldiers. Hans Wallow held the rank of Oberscharführer.

Awards for the Veterans of the Ukraine: Shown here is a well-known photo of Conrad Schellong handing out Iron Crosses to the members of the Brigade who distinguished themselves during the battles in Ukraine during the first months of 1944. It is possible that this picture could have been taken on May 26, 1944, the date that Schrijnen was officially awarded the Iron Cross IInd Class. At this time Schrijnen was still in a field hospital recovering from his wounds. Schellong is pictured here with the German Cross in Gold, which he received for his performance during the battles in and around Jambol. The recommendation for the award was written by Heinz Lammerding, who was the commander of the "Das Reich" battle group. The Brigade had fought along side "Das Reich" during the Jambol battles and at other times it was subordinated to this unit. It is very interesting to note that Schellong was recommended for the Knight's Cross by Lammerding in January 1945 for the very same battles that had taken place in Jambol in March 1944. One can speculate that the latter award could have had some sort of political significance since the 27. SS-Division had no Knight's Cross winners other than Schrijnen. Schrijnen, a Fleming,, was, up until that time, the only recipient of that award in the entire unit. The picture above also clearly shows Schellong's missing finger which he lost during the battles in Jambol.

ment made the NCOs look on with envy. Even Kotlowski was shocked by Schrijnen's hard words. 'Yeah,' said some NCOs, 'that's easy for him to say, he already has a few medals.' "[52]

If it is not clear in the paraphrase above, it can be assumed that Schrijnen did not accept the award because he did not feel that he deserved it.

On July 11th, the men took the time to celebrate a Flemish holiday, the "Day of the Golden Spurs." On this day in 1302, a small Flemish army had defeated the French army near Kortrijk, Flanders. During the next few weeks following this fest, Remy spent his time trying to get back in shape. Once again he took his training very seriously. Laperre continued: [53]

"...this man came to my platoon and the first thing I thought was that he must have a troubled heart, but he posed no problem for me since he trained like a recruit during the exercises. He only wanted to do combat training and he did so with Grootaers[54] as Geschützführer. Yeah, Schrijnen had combat experience and Kotlowski had warned me: 'Let him do what he wants. On the front he has the best nose, success after success, all without any casualties – at the front he acts as if he is on his own.' Normally it is the Geschützführer who is the one to pick his crew, and I was surprised to learn that Kotlowski let Schrijnen pick his own Geschützführer and men instead. Schrijnen tried not to draw any attention to himself, but even though I gave Grootaers permission to run the training, I could tell that it was really Schrijnen that was training the gun's crew. I watched how he made Gaston Troch and Van den Beamten into good MG-Schütze. Schrijnen demonstrated and explained, '...from the hip out, release the safety catch, with lightly bent knees and feet spread apart, firmly standing on the ground, don't hold the weapon too high. Hit your opponent between the knees and the stomach continuously so that his body sinks together, no shot should pass him by.' That is what was most important for

---

[52] The close-combat clasp was a highly respected award which was awarded based on "points" received for hand-to-hand combats unsupported by armor. A point was awarded for each engagement and was recorded in the recipient's Soldbuch. The award came in three grades: Grade I (bronze) was awarded for 15 points, Grade II (silver) for 30 points and Grade III (gold) was awarded for 50 points. The clasp was primarily intended for infantry soldiers, but was awarded to members of other units as well. See Angolia, *"Military Awards of the Third Reich"* for more details about this interesting award.
[53] Schrijnen notebook.
[54] Grootaers had arrived at Langemarck's position on the front in early 1944 as an Unterscharführer-Anwärter (NCO candidate - since he had no front-line combat experience) along with Unterscharführer Van Kerckhoven, who replaced Unterscharführer Dahlhoff.

Remy, whether in defense or close combat. He was not the kind of person that wanted to draw attention to himself, but he knew what he was talking about. Always wide-awake, it was as if he slept day and night. Always in a good mood and ready to help, regardless of any benefit to himself. Kotlowski said to me later, 'You won't believe it when you go to the front and have Schrijnen in your platoon.' As for me, I observed this man when he talked about his comrades and never about himself, that was his character, his modesty. He must not have known what kind of a reputation he had. A few of his men, those that were still alive, said that he was a fixated man, be it in attack or fighting infantry, tanks or anti-tank gun lines. He fought for days along the highway to Jambol. Gödecke and Blaha told me many stories about Schrijnen, all without a trace of jealousy, that he sneezed at every action and risked everything. I remember the hard look in his dark eyes as someone mentioned the German generals who had been captured by the Russians and now spent their days at the front using loud speakers to call out to the German soldiers to desert. 'Pigs!,' he said, but I couldn't say that because they were our pigs, 'Such cowards, traitors, I am going to have to get them in my fingers!' What should I as a young junior officer have thought? Love of his fatherland, of being a soldier, heroism, or is he just plain tired of life in general?"

Laperre often asked Kompanietruppführer and Oberscharführer Dalhoff about his time with Schrijnen:[55]

"He was with us at Hilvorsum in 1942 as a recruit and trained as a Panzerjäger. Remy took his training very seriously. He learned everything and asked many questions. His training with camouflage definitely stayed with him. In close combat with a pistol or a shovel, only three places were important for him, 'when you stab do it either in the throat or the stomach or just below the belt, those are the soft parts, unprotected and deadly. If you stab too deep, twist and then pull out. If you have a bullet still in the chamber, shoot it, everything must happen quickly – only think about the three places.' Remy, his game with his shovel, in the face or the throat... As Panzerjäger we didn't see Remy do this that often. Remy was also a fast runner, put the cannon here, roll it there and then march! march! march! It didn't matter if Remy and the rest of the crew had to drag the gun themselves or if they used a truck

---

[55] Schrijnen notebook.

Albert Desremeau: Pictured here is Albert Desremeau. Desremeau was a Fleming who was born in northern France. He was an experienced PAK crew member and had previously served in the 5th company of the Legion "Flandern" as a Munischütze for Geschützführer Unterscharführer Behling, Sardeur (Cyriel), and Blaha. He survived all of the battles with the Legion and Desremeau served as Remy's loader for the battles in Ukraine from January to March 1944.

Grub: Shown here are members of the PAK company lining up for chow after a hard days work in Milovitz. From left to right, Bert Baele, Plattevoet, Mussche, Paul Rubens and ?. Rubens was the driver for Grootaer's crew.

to bring it into position. Remy used to say 'liever bloode Jan dan doode Jan' (a Flemish saying for 'better a dumb man than a dead man' – here he is referring to dragging the gun when he says 'better a dumb man'), and that one should never underestimate one's opponent. 'Sweat saves blood' Knorr and Gradmeyer had said to us quite often – and it was true. I learned more from Rottenführer Desremeau and Sturmmann Schrijnen than I had learned in a half year at the NCO school. It showed that the men had already been in action. Desremeau had been on the front since 1941 and it was strange, he got along with Schrijnen like no one else. I don't know if it was because Schrijnen would jump in and help any man, which he gladly did for anyone, or because he stood guard in the cold or under the worst conditions. When something was reported somewhere, Desremeau, Dersmenscheck, Troch and Horre didn't

Schrijnen's New Platoon Leader: Marcel Laperre was born on May 29, 1923 in Bissegem, Flanders. As one of the disillusioned Flemish veterans of the First World War who had fought against the Germans under the Belgian flag, Laperre's father was very active with the history of Flanders and also served as mayor of Bissegem. Marcel was one of seven children. He could speak French, Dutch and German. Laperre enlisted in the Belgian Army in September 1939. At the age of just 17 he attended the Belgian Officer Candidate School in Turhout. Laperre was a member of the strictly disciplined organization "Verdinaso" and the badge seen on his Flemish Allgemeine-SS uniform is a Verdinaso Loyalty Badge. During the brief hostilities with Belgium, the Germans had surrounded the Belgian officer candidate school that Marcel was attending and the faculty, staff and students were taken prisoner. Laperre was imprisoned as a POW from the end of August 1940 until mid-December 1940. After his release Laperre earned a living serving as a translator at the airport in Wevelgem. From there he found work with the Flemish Allgemeine-SS at their Jungklaus post in Brussels. Next he enlisted as a volunteer for the Waffen-SS in early July 1943. After basic training he was sent to the Waffen-SS Officer Candidate School Bad Tölz in October 1943. Laperre completed the course in mid-March 1944 and left the school as a senior NCO. From there he was transferred to the elements of "Langemarck" training in Knovitz. On June 21, 1944 he received his commission as an Untersturmführer and departed a month later with the men of Kampfgruppe "Rehmann" for the battles in Narva. He survived the battles and continued to serve with the 27th Division as platoon leader under Untersturmführer Anton Kotlowski in Panzerjägerabteilung 27. At the end of the war, Laperre was killed by the Russians shortly after being taken prisoner. Apparently, Laperre had shot a Russian soldier in the leg before surrendering. Frans Van Mol, who was with Laperre at the time, was not executed and survived to tell the story of his fate in prison after the war. According to his sister Lea, Marcel had enlisted in the Waffen-SS due to his nationalistic and Catholic (anti-communistic) beliefs. Marcel was considered to be an excellent leader by his former comrades and had been recommended for the German Cross in Gold by his Kompanie Führer, Untersturmführer Anton Kotlowski.

Schrijnen's New Company Commander: Walking to the right of Sturmmann Remy Schrijnen is Untersturmführer Anton Kotlowski.

wander a step away from their gun. They were always ready. In the bunker during free time Desremeau would come to tell us stories. The new ones listened attentively about the hard times the Legion Flandern had experienced in 1941-1942 in the Volkov Pocket, in the Neva-bend. 'You can ask the holes in my stomach,' Desremeau used to say."

Laperre continued: [56]

"...at times, if the situation required it, we would have to drag the heavy PAK gun to another position, sometimes for kilometers. Even the Geschützführer helped sometimes. During a field exercise Remy said to me, 'In action the Zugführer is allowed to and should take a grip as well.' I had no idea and was unaccustomed to this kind of work, but took part in it anyway. It was the summer of 1944 and carrying the gun everywhere in the field made me sweat heavily. Kotlowski laughed when I told him this story, about Schrijnen's bold comment and how I got suckered into pulling the PAK all over the field."

" 'Yes,' said Kotlowski, 'Remy was trained very hard by Hauptsturmführer Knorr and Oberscharführer Gradmayer at Hilvorsum, but he was the best trainee

[56] Schrijnen notebook.

in the entire Panzerjäger school. Maybe you would like to be transferred to another Zug?'

" 'No, no, I have no idea what will happen to us at the front,' I replied.

" 'With men like D'Hollander, Fieremans, Van Broeck, Blaha, Grootaers, Tollenaere, Chantraine and the other fighters and with Spieß Wallow you have the best of the company. Whether you are in their vicinity, or serving as Geschützführer, the men are more than good and you also have the most successful Richtschütze. We'll never understand him, he makes his own decisions without asking very many questions. He recognizes every bad situation better and quicker than the rest of us,' answered Kotlowski."

Kotlowski seemed also to be somewhat wary of Schrijnen. He often told Laperre: [57]

"...in Schrijnen you have one of the best and most experienced Richtschütze, but don't try to influence him or change his ways, because he has a seventh sense, a certain instinct, he can smell danger and bring it on."

Kotlowski and Schrijnen had some differences and it wasn't in either of their characters to conceal them. Despite this, they did not let their disagreements carry on, as if they held a distant respect for each other. During exercises Schrijnen would remind Kotlowski: [58]

"You have a lot to learn, Untersturmführer, if you ever want to become a Knorr..."

• • •

In 1944, the northern sector of the Eastern Front became known simply as "Narva" to those who fought there. There, in the northern-most sector of the front, bordering the Gulf of Finland, lay the III. (germanisches) SS-Panzerkorps. This was the Germanic Corps – comprised not only of Germanic soldiers, but also of pan-Europeans. They fought in one of the last great struggles against the communist Russian forces. Shoulder to shoulder, the Europeans fought mostly to their death. As the blood flowed from the Danish, Dutch, Estonian, Flemish, Norwegian, Swedish, Swiss, Walloonian and German soldiers, all of whom comprised

---

[57] Schrijnen notebook.
[58] Schrijnen notebook.

PAK Crew in Training: Here the young volunteers exercise dragging the gun, which they often had to do, sometimes in combat if it became necessary. This picture was taken at Knovitz during the summer of 1944.

Firing Practice: Here members of the Brigade take target practice in Knovitz.

this pan-European corps during the continuous Soviet onslaught, Narva became a symbol of steadfastness for the young men who fought there.

Because of Langemarck's relatively small size, it was often utilized by the higher German command as a plug to fill gaps in the front. Since the Russians were clever enough to always search for the weakest point in the line and exploit it with all their masses, the Flemings often viewed themselves as the Wehrmacht's sacrificial lamb.

This time it was the gap where Waffen-SS Regiment 48 "General Seyffardt" of the 23. SS-Freiwilligen-Grenadier Division "Nederland" would have been. During the rapid retreat to the west, this Regiment and parts of the Division's reconnaissance battalion lost communication with other units and became completely surrounded and decimated by the Russians. Despite desperate attempts to save them, very few survivors ever made it back to the German lines. Those who survived relayed the story of the Regiment's total destruction.

The battle to the west of the Estonian city of Narva was certainly one of the bloodiest battles the Flemings would ever experience. Some, such as motorcycle messenger Fons Van Broeck, said that it was the most difficult. Others, such as company commander Georg D'Haese, cite Krasny Bor as a more difficult episode in the Fleming's battle history. One thing is certain, the battle was indeed bloody and the majority of the soldiers of the Langemarck battle group would find their final resting place on the battlefields there.

During these battles, which inflicted a casualty rate of better than 90% in only four days, the daring Richtschütze would again prove his worth in battle.

4

Narva 1944

On to the Blue Mountains of Estonia

Some two months after the Brigade arrived in Knovitz to regroup, commander Schellong received an order to send a strengthened battalion to Narva. The Flemings were once again called up to plug a gap in the front, this time in support of the III. SS-Panzerkorps under the command of Obergruppenführer Felix Steiner. Schellong, who was still recovering from wounds he suffered during the battles in Ukraine earlier that year, needed to remain in Knovitz to continue overseeing the training of his re-forming brigade. Therefore he could not take part in this significant chapter of the Fleming's battle history. Due to the slow progress concerning the re-forming brigade, Schellong chose what existed of the foreseen I. Bataillon,[1] commanded by Hauptsturmführer Wilhelm Rehmann, to be sent to the front, since it was the most complete. On July 19th, the strengthened battalion, designated as Kampfgruppe "Rehmann," marched past its commander and loaded onto a transport train which ran non-stop from Beneschau (near Knovitz) in Czechoslovakia to Toila, Estonia, where Obergruppenführer Steiner's command post was located.

As the men were gathering their equipment to load the train to the front, there was a certain excitement in the air. They were all aware of the task that stood before them. They knew that what they were actually about to partake in was a suicide operation and that hardly any of them would return. Despite this, their

[1] "Foreseen" indicates that this battalion existed on paper only. There never was enough men, material or sufficient equipment to fully equip this battalion.

mood seemed to be somewhat relaxed and the men took the time to joke carelessly as they loaded the train. Kotlowski, noticing this, stopped by to poke one last jab at Schrijnen:[2]

"There you go again, laughing like a honey horse cake..."

"Jawohl, Untersturmführer, too bad for you, since you can't come along with us!" Schrijnen retorted smartly.

As the battle group departed for Estonia, it consisted of four infantry companies and a platoon from the Panzerjäger company. After passing several army units who waved to them as they went by, they arrived in Toila, Estonia, on July 24, 1944. It was in Toila that Untersturmführer Ossel was relieved of his command of the 4. Kompanie and assigned to an Estonian unit company which had lost all of its officers to casualties. Ossel's platoons were divided up amongst the remaining three companies.

Schrijnen's Kompanie Führer, Anton Kotlowski, had chosen Marcel Laperre's platoon as the only heavy weapon unit to accompany the infantry companies. Laperre's platoon consisted of the best and most experienced gun crews, while Laperre, himself a newly commissioned officer, had no previous front-line experience whatsoever. Kotlowski was the only remaining PAK leader with any front-line combat experience, but, like Schellong, would stay with the rest of the PAK men training with the remaining elements of the Brigade in Knovitz. The final pre-engagement structure of the battle group was as follows:[3]

Kommandeur:	SS-Hauptsturmführer Wilhelm Rehmann (G)
Adjutant -	SS-Untersturmführer Walter Van Leemputten[4] (F)
Arzt (Doctor):	Leutnant Dr. Hertgens (G – from the Luftwaffe)
1. Kompanie:	SS-Untersturmführer Frans Swinnen[5] (F)
2. Kompanie:	SS-Untersturmführer Henri Van Mol[6] (F)
3. Kompanie:	SS-Untersturmführer Georg D'Haese (F)
PAK Zug:	SS-Untersturmführer Marcel Laperre (F)

---

[2] Schrijnen notebook.

[3] Other officers and battle group leaders included Hauptsturmführer Hutten, Untersturmführer Van Bockel (Platoon Leader, 2. Kp.), Oberjunker Lucien Bottu (Platoon Leader, 2. Kp.) and Oberjunker Roger Groenvinck (Platoon Leader, 1. Kp.). Hutten was an officer from the former Belgian army and did not enjoy the formal German Junkerschule officer training. He was in charge of organizing the building of the bunkers before the battle. According to D'Haese, he was wounded during the fighting, left shortly and then returned. It is unknown if Hutten survived the war.

[4] Van Leemputten was badly wounded on July 28, 1944 and later died of his wounds on August 15, 1944. He was awarded the Iron Cross IInd Class for bravery in battle on August 1, 1944.

[5] Killed in action on July 26, 1944.

[6] Killed in action on July 26, 1944.

Remy Schrijnen was in the Kampfgruppe's PAK Zug. The platoon was structured as follows:

Zugführer: SS-Untersturmführer Marcel Laperre (F)
   1. Geschütz: SS-Unterscharführer Bert D'Hollander[7] (F)
   2. Geschütz: SS-Unterscharführer Eduard Reeb (G)
   3. Geschütz: SS-Unterscharführer Jef Grootaers[8] (F)

Laperre was lucky, for he would be surrounded by veterans during his first trip to the front. Bert D'Hollander, a Fleming, and Eduard Reeb, a German, had been veterans since serving with the Legion Flandern. Jef Grootaers, a Fleming, had been at the front with Langemarck from sometime in February 1944 until the unit was relieved for rest and refit. Before arriving at the training grounds in Knovitz, he had completed a leadership course at an NCO school. Remy held the rank of Sturmmann and served again as Richtschütze, this time for Grootaers. Grootaers' crew included men of various enlisted man ranks:

Schütze I: Remy Schrijnen (F)
Schütze II: Emil (Miel) Sobry[9] (F)
Schütze III: Kamiel Horre[10] (F)
Schütze IV: *unknown*
Schütze V: Van Dem Beamten (F)
Schütze VI: Adrian Heusdens[11] (F)
Fahrer: Paul Rubens (F)

While the Flemings were on their way to the front, the Russians had occupied Hungerberg and Riigi. The Russian's 3rd Baltic Army, twenty divisions strong, now stood across from the "Narva Army." The entire front was in flames. The Russians were to attempt a pincer movement which was to encircle the III. (germ.) SS-Panzerkorps and destroy them. All along the "Tannenberg Line," the Germans were preparing for the coming battle.

---

[7] Killed in action on July 26, 1944.
[8] Killed in action on July 28, 1944.
[9] SS-Sturmmann Emil Sobry survived the battles in the Blue Mountains and was officially awarded the Iron Cross IInd Class for the battles on August 17, 1944.
[10] Schrijnen reported that Kamiel Horre was killed during the battles in the Blue Mountains.
[11] SS-Oberschütze Adrian Heusdens survived the battles in the Blue Mountains and was officially awarded the Iron Cross IInd Class for the battles on August 1, 1944.

Staff Members: Shown here from right to left are: Leutnant Dr. Hertgens, Hauptscharführer and Spieß Hans Wallow and Untersturmführer Willi Köhn. Dr. Hertgens had been serving in the Brigade for some time, despite his membership in the Luftwaffe. He was the doctor on hand during the battles in Narva. Hans Wallow served as the "Spieß" (technical sergeant) for the anti-tank gun platoon in Narva. His position as "Spieß" is indicated by the double rings of NCO tresse around his sleeves. Wallow was a German who was well-liked by his Flemish comrades. Willi Köhn first served as an officer in the Legion's 3. Kompanie and went on to command the Brigade's 5. Kompanie. He did not attend the battles in the Blue Mountains. This picture was probably taken in Knovitz during the summer of 1944.

PAK Leaders: Pictured here kneeling left to right are: Sus Nauwelaerts and Jef De Kesel. Standing left to right are· Eduard Reeb, Bert D'Hollander, Unterscharführer Behling and Alfons Van Kerkhoven. This picture was taken in Slusk in 1942. Both Reeb (pictured here as a Sturmmann), and D'Hollander (also pictured here as a Sturmmann) attended the NCO school in Lauenberg and returned to "Langemarck" as Unterscharführer to became Geschützführer in Laperre's PAK platoon. Unterscharführer Behling was a long-time PAK veteran since the formation of the Legion. Van Kerkhoven had returned from Lauenberg in time to see the end of the battles in the Ukraine. Van Kerkhoven was Schrijnen's second Geschützführer during the Ukraine battles in early 1944 until becoming wounded at the end of February.

Here were the young Flemings – in the Blue Mountains of Estonia – where they were to plug the gap in the front. [12] To their left was the Gulf of Finland, to their right marshes and in front lay a forest, from where the enemy would come. It was here that the battle group of four hundred men would rule the Blue Mountains for just four days – four eternities.

The Eve of the Battle: July 25, 1944

The men arrived at night and immediately began preparing their positions. The first order issued to the battle group was to build up their positions on Orphanage Hill. The city of Narva and the positions around the bend of the Narva river

---

[12] Ironically, Sturmbannführer Helmut Breymann, an Austrian who had once commanded 3. Kompanie "Flandern" and had previously been transferred from the Legion to command the II. Bataillon of Regiment "General Seyffardt," was one of the few who made it back to the German lines. However, Breymann was killed during the subsequent fighting along the Tannenberg Line.

Men of the 3. Kompanie: Shown here are leaders from the 3. Kompanie in Knovitz. From left to right: Unterscharführer Frans Werrebroek, Unterscharführer Valeer Janssens (the double tresse loops at the base of his shoulderboard indicate an SS-Junker or "potential officer"), Standartenoberjunker Georg D'Haese, Unterscharführer Albert Rits, Unterscharführer Kamiel Smekens, an unknown and Unterscharführer Willi Selders. Frans Werrebroek was a Gruppenführer who did not take part in the battles in Narva. According to D'Haese, Werrebroek was "one of the most loyal, brave and dependable soldiers during the heavy fighting in the Volkhov pocket and before Leningrad, where he fought as a Sturmmann." Werrebroek, who was the only soldier in this group to be awarded the Iron Cross Ist Class, went on to serve as a Gruppenführer (same as Geschützführer, only for the infantry) for the 5. Kompanie of Battle Group "Schellong" for the battles in Pommerania. He survived the war. D'Haese was the commander of the 3. Kompanie and Valeer Janssens was his Schirrmeister. As Schirrmeister, Janssens was responsible for the company's vehicles. Janssens survived the battles in the Blue Mountains and also the war. He passed away in 1991. Albert Rits was a platoon leader and took part in and survived the battles in Narva. After the war he was a leading manager for a hotel in Argentina where he died a mysterious death. Kamiel Smekens was a Gruppenführer but did not take part in the Narva battles. He was later killed in Belgium by a British fighter plane. Willi Smelders was a Gruppenführer and was awarded the Iron Cross IInd Class for the battles in Narva. He survived the war as well. Among the men in the wagon are Boterberg (fought in Narva), Van de Putte (did not fight in Narva) and Coen (did not fight in Narva).

had previously been evacuated. The German's new defensive line, the "Tannenberg" line, was subsequently occupied. To the right (south) of Kampfgruppe "Rehmann" was the Division "Nordland." To the left (north) was the Brigade "Nederland."

The companies of battle group "Rehmann" were facing east and positioned on a six hundred meter long stretch of land between Orphanage Hill and the edge of the forest (which was directly across from them). It was from this forest that the Russians would come.

The battalion bunker was positioned on the eastern foot of Orphanage Hill. It overlooked the battle group's companies. The battle group's leaders were only in the bunker before the battle. The bunker was manned primarily with numerous foot messengers and medics. The medic's bunker, where Dr. Hertgens was set up, was located on the north-east side of Love's Hill. The 1. Kompanie under

Oberjunker Luc Bottu: Luc Bottu was born on August 6, 1923 in Zolder (Limburg), Flanders. Bottu had one sister and one brother and had attended a military school in Sint-Truiden (Limburg). He was a member of the VNV and is pictured above in the traditional VNV/Black Brigade uniform. Bottu joined the Waffen-SS and took his basic training in April 1943. Thereafter he attended the 3rd Germanic Class at the Junkerschule Bad Tölz and had not yet been commissioned an officer at the time of the battles in Narva. The battles in Narva were this young soldier's first.

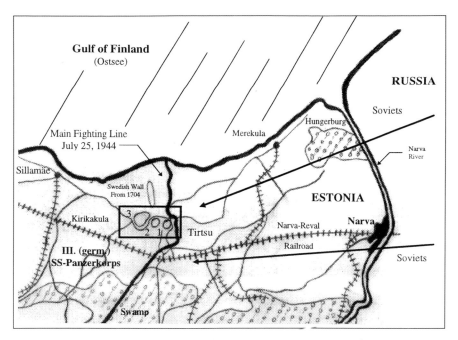

The Tannenberg Line: Above is the situational map describing the situation at the front shortly before the fighting began in the Langemarck section on July 26, 1944. The Flemish Brigade was situated on the three hills which are denoted by the boxed-in area. To the north was the "Nederland" unit and to the south was "Nordland."

Untersturmführer Frans Swinnen was on the right (south), the 3. Kompanie under Untersturmführer Georg D'Haese was on the left (north), while the 2. Kompanie, under Untersturmführer Henri van Mol, was in the middle.

The guns of the anti-tank platoon were spread out in support of the infantry companies. Hauptsturmführer Rehmann ordered Geschütz D'Hollander (no. 1) to a position on Orphanage Hill, a position that the veterans in the PAK company did not agree with. In their opinion, the gun would be too close to battlefield, from where the Russians would be attacking. Geschütz Reeb (no. 2) was positioned along the road coming from the forest and where it ran past the northeast edge of Grenadier Hill. Geschütz Grootaers (no. 3) was positioned to the right of Reeb.

First Day of Battle: July 26, 1944

This was the first day of battle. Narva was burning. Russians were everywhere. During the first Russian attack, the first officer was killed. Untersturmführer

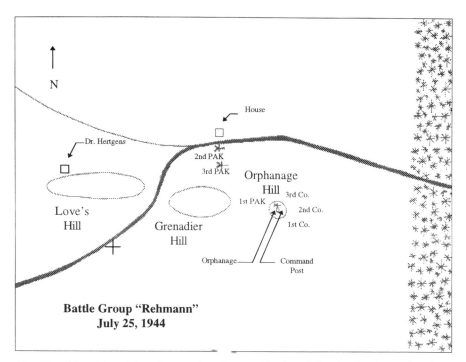

The Blue Mountains: Above is a rough scale magnification of the situational map that show Langemarck's initial positions on July 25, 1944. The map was constructed with the help of Remy Schrijnen, Georg D'Haese and Dries Anseeuw. To the right (east) was the forest from which the Russians attacked. Between the forest and Orphanage Hill was approximately six hundred meters of flat land. The first hill was called the Kinderheimhöhe (Orphanage Hill) and was so named since an orphanage sat on the top of the hill. It was approximately seventy-five meters wide, seventy-five meters long and about eighty-five meters high. D'Hollander's PAK Gun was located on this hill and looked out over the terrain of the field in front of the hill. Hauptsturmführer Rehmann's command post was located on the front slope of the hill. The infantry companies were spread out as shown in front of the hill in the field. The second hill was called the Grenadierhöhe (Grenadier Hill) and was about one hundred and fifty meters wide, three hundred meters long and eighty-five meters high. It was located approximately two hundred meters behind Orphanage Hill. To the north of this hill, close to the road, were the two remaining PAKs. The second gun, which was commanded by Eduard Reeb, was located to the south of the road. Grootaer's gun was located further south. The third hill was called the Liebeshöhe (Love's Hill) and was approximately one hundred meters wide, four to five hundred meters long and had a height of approximately seventy meters. It was located approximately one hundred meters behind Grenadier Hill. Dr. Hertgens and his medics were located on the northwest side of the hill.

Swinnen, Kompanie Führer of the 1. Kompanie, died in battle while fighting on the field between Orphanage Hill and the edge of the forest.

Marcel Laperre reported on the first day of the battle:[13]

---

[13] Schrijnen notebook.

"Yes, the gents, Norwegians, Danes, Dutch and Estonians, Teutonic fighters, all there for the most difficult of battles, Germania's greatest sons were there for the strongest bleeding of their Nordic-Germanic people. What luck, at Narva it showed that there was still a part of the Teutons that had not been Romanized. Hitler stayed with Mussolini in Rome too long. Ah, the Romans, Germania's oldest enemy, the decadent cowards – and then Italy abandoned Germany! This time the blood of the Germanic peoples had come together. Germania's sons showed the German brothers and leaders the way to defend our people and our loyalty to the given word, to be or not to be.

"There the oldest was twenty-two years old – the Richtschütze. The youngest was not even eighteen. We trusted him with an MG 42 machine gun during training. Grootaers and I found it odd to train a recruit as an Oberschütze, as an MG-Schütze. 'Yes,' said Remy, 'as we heard during our training, the safety of the Geschütz depends on the MG-Schütze, he carries a great responsibility.' With a red face this young man performed his training and Remy himself looked out for this man, be it with camouflage or at the firing range. 'The MG-Schütze's job is to always secure the gun's position and to observe the field. He must immediately make a report if he notices something,' so said Remy to me and Grootaers. 'The man must be awake and confident and should understand how important his position is.' It was in this way that Grootaers and his Richtschütze had trained their men, the hardest group – the group that held together through every bit of bad luck.

"It was my first time at the front and I saw Russian tanks at distance of several thousand meters. Did the boys expect an attack? I sent Tollenaere to the Kommandeur. The Soviets were firing without the support of heavy artillery. A barrage of fire passed over our heads and grenades exploded in the field. In the distance I heard the rattling of machine guns, but our infantry remained calm. PAK Geschütz D'Hollander immediately fell out. D'Hollander blew himself and the gun in the air. A mistake by Kommandeur Rehmann? I didn't know. I still had my 2. Geschütz Reeb and 3. Geschütz Grootaers.

"Later I found out that there were hard words between Schrijnen and Rehmann. Albert Vincent came to me and told me they took Rehmann to the rear lines and were talking about a court marshal."

It was a bad start as the battle group's commander, Hauptsturmführer Rehmann, had ordered D'Hollander and his group to a position almost directly on the main

Fallen Officer: Shown at right is Untersturm-führer Jef Van Bockel. Van Bockel was a platoon leader in the 2. Kompanie under Untersturmführer Van Mol. He had just completed coursework at the officer candidate school Bad Tölz. It has long been reported that Van Bockel, along with Van Mol (Kp. Führer 2. Kp.) were killed in the command bunker on the first day of battle. D'Haese, first the Kp. Führer for the 3. Kompanie, later commander of the battle group, stated that the two were killed together in the trenches on the first day.

fighting line. This area was right in the middle of what would become the battle-field and would later be crawling with Russians. When the battle began, D'Hollander, knowing that his position would easily be overrun, was forced to evacuate his crew and blow his gun so that it would not fall into the hands of the Russians. D'Hollander was killed while setting off the charges[14] and the group lost their first gun. This was the beginning of the "suicide operation." D'Hollander was a brave soldier and respected by his men.

Despite the loss of one of the three PAK guns and the commander of the 1. Kompanie, the battle group was still quite strong. Their strength wasn't to last for long, unfortunately, as a string of bad luck was to rip through the ranks of Kampfgruppe's leadership. The first piece of bad luck struck on this very first day of battle, as the Russians laid a murderous carpet of fire on Orphanage Hill. During the barrage the command post (battalion bunker) received a direct hit. Many of the messengers and medics were killed or wounded. The commander, Hauptsturmführer Rehmann, was lightly wounded on the throat, and decided to evacuate to a field hospital. In the trenches in front of Orphanage Hill, the Kompanie Führer of the 2. Kompanie, Untersturmführer Van Mol and the leader of his sec-

---

[14] According to the veterans, D'Hollander must have chosen the wrong fuse to ignite the charges. Red fuses blew immediately and green ones went off after fifteen seconds.

ond platoon, Untersturmführer Van Bokkel, were both killed. The commander of the 3. Kompanie, Georg D'Haese, was also lightly wounded, but decided to stay at the front with the troops.[15]

As Rehmann was received at the field hospital, a doctor inspected him and ordered him to return to the front. Upon returning to the battle field, he ordered a foot messenger, Fons Van Broeck, to accompany him for a trip to Steiner's field headquarters. By the time that Rehmann arrived, Steiner had already been informed of the situation concerning the deaths of the others. He then began to speak with Rehmann about a renewed attack. Rehmann's answer must have disappointed him very badly, however, and he answered, "Rehmann, leave now! Stay in the baggage train! – Send D'Haese to me at once!" A short time after that, Rehmann sent a message to D'Haese telling him that he was to take over as commander of the battle group. From that point on, the Flemings were referred to as "Kampfgruppe 'D'Haese.' "

Dries Anseeuw, a loader in Unterscharführer Reeb's gun crew, wrote about his experiences on the first day of battle:[16]

> *As morning approached, we were finished with everything. But at the order of a Dutch officer, we had to abandon our position. We had positioned our gun near the house and to left of the road. The left side of the road belonged, however, to another unit, and so we were forced to find a position to the right of the road. The landscape was an open flat. In front of us was Orphanage Hill, to the right Grenadier Hill and behind us was Love's Hill. On the open flat was a beautiful position, and we had to drag our gun there quickly, since the nights were short, between 3 and 4 am it was a bright day.*
>
> *This position was excellent. The gun was protected by a "chest-plate" made of tree trunks. The length of the gun could comfortably be pointed to the right or the left. Along the "chest-plate" was a trench and outside of the position were a few single-men foxholes. This position was a dream and there were also a few munitions bunkers for our shells. In the meantime it became bright outside and therefore wise to disappearing our holes. At that time we*

---

[15] It should be noted that it has often been reported that many of the leaders were killed or wounded during a meeting in the command bunker. According to Georg D'Haese, at that time the commander of the 3. Kompanie, this is not true. As he reports, there was no time or reason for a meeting in the command post. The leaders were busy with their men in the trenches and were killed during the first attacks.

[16] Report from Dries Anseeuw dated Nov. 10, 1997.

Felix Steiner: Pictured above is Gruppenführer Felix Steiner, commander of the III. (germ.) Panzerkorps. Steiner was born on May 23, 1896 in East Prussia. In March 1914, at the age of 17, Steiner enlisted as an infantryman in the German army. By the conclusion of the First World War, he had earned the Iron Cross First and Second Class and had been commissioned as an officer. He was severely wounded on one occasion. He remained in the Army after the war and successfully completed general staff training. In 1935 he transferred to the SS-Verfügungstruppe (special purpose troops) as an Obersturmbannführer (Lt. Colonel) and served as the commander of SS-VT Regiment "Deutschland." On December 1, 1940, he was assigned to overtake the formation of SS-Division "Wiking" as a Brigadeführer. The "Wiking" division consisted of volunteers from Denmark, Finland, Flanders, Norway and Sweden. The division was formed around SS-VT Regiment "Germania" which consisted of German cadre. During the formation, Steiner was able to guide his men to overcome the cultural and language barriers, as well as any political differences, to form one of the best Waffen-SS divisions. As the Division's commander, he was held in high regard by all of the units under his command. On March 30, 1943, Adolf Hitler ordered the formation of the III. Germanisches Panzerkorps and Steiner was named its commander. The Corps consisted of various SS Nordic volunteer divisions, brigades and battle groups as well as several Heer and Luftwaffe ground units. Steiner was promoted to Obergruppenführer while leading the Corps during the battles in Narva and was awarded the Swords to the Knight's Cross after the conclusion of these battles. He ended the war as the Supreme Commander of the 17th Panzer Army. Steiner survived the war and the internment which followed. After his release, he became active in the Waffen-SS Veteran's Organization HIAG. He also wrote several books about Waffen-SS, including "Armee der Geächteten" (Army of Outlaws) and "Die Freiwilligen, Idee und Opfergang" (The Volunteers, Idea and Sacrifice). Steiner passed away in Munich shortly before his 76th birthday on May 12, 1966.

also had time to look over the area. Near Grenadier Hill there was another PAK in position, unfortunately we didn't know which gun it was.[17]

It was calm, we finished and were waiting for something to happen. But we didn't need to wait long. It came unexpectedly during the middle of the afternoon. Heavy dive-bombers flew above our position. The earth shook and the bombs ripped apart everything. We laid in our holes and pressed ourselves on the ground or against the walls.

The three hills had a quite difficult time with it all, and we, in the middle, received our portion as well. The attack from the air lasted a few hours and then it became calm again. It was one attack wave after another.

Finally we were able to stretch ourselves out and determine that our position had survived the attack. Thank God, everything was still in order and we had no dead or wounded. We had survived the first baptism of fire and we only had to await for the next attack. We all knew it.

The Geschützführer and the Richtschütze ran around the gun as the next attack wave came with a bang unexpectedly. Stalin Organs, light and heavy artillery, mortars, everything that could shoot was aimed at our positions. Orphanage Hill and Grenadier Hill had a tough time with it. Dirt, rocks, branches and trees flew all around the hills. We also had it tough, the Russians laid their fire further back, so that the open flat and Love's Hill were also hit. Grenades, dirt, fragments, rocks, everything was landing on us. Something fell in my hole. There was a large thud, like from a dud. It had come along my right side near my pistol holster and then past the heel from my right boot. I was very shocked and waited for the explosion, which didn't come! I was paralyzed and not in any condition to abandon my foxhole. After some time passed, I stretched myself out and searched for the perpetrator that had scared me so much. Then I saw it, it was a fragment that was twenty centimeters long and five centimeters wide. My belt was cut in half, and my pistol holster was almost cut apart. The heel of my boot was only scratched. One must have soldier's luck. With that it wasn't over, however, the hellish fire continued without calming down. Incoming after incoming, I never thought of leaving this boiling kettle. It was horrible. In the case that it was possible to quickly look out over the area and to see the three hills, we only saw dust and smoke from the exploding bombs. Almost all of the trees had disappeared, only a few thick stumps survived.

---

[17] This was most probably the gun of Jef Grootaers.

Wilhelm Rehmann: Shown on this page and opposite is Wilhelm Rehmann, pictured to the left as a Rottenführer in the Allgemeine-SS Standarte 53 (Heide) and to the right as a Hauptsturmführer in the Waffen-SS. Rehmann was born on March 15, 1912 in Hamburg. He worked as a salesman and later joined the Allgemeine-SS on June 6, 1933. During his career with the Allgemeine-SS, he held several positions in the Rasse- und Siedlungshauptamt (Race and Resettlement Main Office). Rehmann was commissioned as an Untersturmführer der Allgemeine-SS on November 9, 1938. While serving in the Allgemeine-SS, Rehmann also served with Infanterie Regiment 2 (Heer) from May 16, 1938 to July 16, 1938. He also took part in the Polish Campaign from September 1, 1939 with the 5./Infanterie Regiment 461 (Heer). For his part in this campaign, he was awarded the Iron Cross Second Class on March 22, 1940. In April he was promoted to Obersturmführer der Allgemeine-SS but remained in the Army and took infantry training from May to August 1940 at a Heeres Infanterie Schule (army infantry school). He was subsequently commissioned as a Leutnant d.R. on November 1, 1940 while serving with the replacement battalion of Infanterie Regiment 49. Before the beginning of Operation "Barbarossa," Rehmann was commissioned as an Obersturmführer der Waffen-SS on April 20, 1941 and was posted at the SS-Ergänzungs-Stelle "Rhein" (a recruiting post in Flanders) from April 20, 1941 until August 1, 1942. From there he transferred back to the Rasse- und Siedlungshauptamt where he received another promotion on November 9, 1942, this time to Hauptsturmführer der Allgemeine-SS. On April 1, 1943, he was transferred to the 10. SS-Panzer-Division "Frundsberg" where he served as a Zugführer and Kompanie Führer in a Panzer-Grenadier regiment. During his time with "Frundsberg," he took a course for company officers from July to August 1943. On November 14, 1943 he was transferred to "Frundsberg's" SS-Feldersatz-Bataillon 10 (field replacement battalion) where he func-

tioned as a Kompanie Führer. He served there until January 27, 1944 when he was transferred to "Langemarck" due to his "understanding of the Flemish mentality" (acquired during his service with the recruiting post there) and his Dutch (Flemish) language abilities. He arrived at the front during the second week of February. Before the end of February, Rehmann found himself commanding the 3./ "Langemarck" for Untersturmführer Demees who had been wounded in action. After the difficult battles in March, he was promoted to Hauptsturmführer on April 20, 1944. During the re-formation of the Brigade in the summer of 1944, he was slated to serve as the commander for the I. Bataillon and was chosen by Schellong to lead the Flemings as commander of Kampfgruppe "Rehmann" during the heated battles in the Blue Mountains of Estonia in late July. During the first day of the battle, Rehmann was lightly wounded and evacuated to a field hospital after which he sat out of the remainder of this intense fight (which lasted for some four days). This wound earned him the Wound Badge in Silver. During the Brigade's re-formation into a Division, he commanded II./SS-Grenadier-Regiment 67 and was commander of I./SS-Grenadier-Regiment 67 of the Reserve Kampfgruppe "Schellong" for the Ardennes Offensive. For political reasons, this battle group was never put into action. The last known report of Rehmann's whereabouts cites that he was wounded on February 17, 1945 while leading his battalion during the desperate battles in Pommerania (Germany). According to several reports from veterans, Rehmann had a mixed reputation. Among the veterans of the battles in the Blue Mountains, Rehmann was not well-liked because they considered him a coward who deserted them during their most difficult battles. On the other hand, Rehmann retained a good reputation among others who remained in Knovitz during those summer months of 1944.

Kommandeur D'Haese: Pictured opposite is Georg D'Haese, then an Unterscharführer and Gruppenführer within the 3. Kompanie of the Legion "Flandern." D'Haese was born on August 4, 1922 in Lede, Flanders. During his youth he attended grade school and later studied "Germanistik" (German Studies). D'Haese, the son of Flemish Nationalists, enlisted in the Waffen-SS on May 23, 1941, at the age of 18 and received the rank of Schütze (Private). D'Haese was assigned to the 8. Kompanie under Hauptsturmführer Kaiser of the Freiwilligen-Standarte "Nordwest" (volunteer regiment "Northwest") in Hamburg. In July 1941, D'Haese, along with the other Flemings of the Standarte "Nordwest," was sent to Radom (in Poland) where the Bataillon "Flandern" was being formed under Hauptsturmführer Lippert. The 8. Kompanie now became the 3. Kompanie and D'Haese and the men of his company were assigned a new Kompanie Führer, Untersturmführer Moyen. The general Waffen-SS training continued here and was moved to the training grounds in Debica in early August. It was at this time that D'Haese received his first promotion to Sturmmann. While in Debica, D'Haese was selected to train as a "Sturmpionier" (combat engineer) and was sent to Dresden where he trained alongside men of the Leibstandarte Adolf Hitler. There he took courses in explosives, flame throwers and quick bridge building. In early September the men were transferred to the training grounds in Arys (at that time in East Prussia). On September 24, 1941, the formation of the SS-Freiwilligen Legion "Flandern" commenced. D'Haese was once again assigned to 3./Legion "Flandern" under Untersturmführer Moyen. This was an infantry company, the Legion "Flandern" did not possess a Pionier unit. D'Haese was selected to be a "Gruppenführer" in charge of about eight men. On November 10, 1941, D'Haese departed with the Legion (now subordinated to the 2. SS-Brigade) east to Russia. "Flandern's" first action took place in Olonino on November 23rd. During the cold winter of 41/42, D'Haese was a member of a makeshift battle group under Obersturmführer Helmut Breymann. This was primarily a rifle company which consisted of his 2. Kompanie strengthened by parts of the 3. Kompanie and a heavy weapons company. This small battle-group of approximately 388 men fought in and around Koptsy and later along the Volkhov river. There the majority of the men were killed, wounded or suffered badly from the cold. Only about 100 of the men survived unscathed. These battles ended at the end of February. For his part in the battle, Sturmmann D'Haese received the Infanterie Sturmabzeichen (Infantry Assault Badge) in Bronze. D'Haese then fought with the Legion in the battles in and around Zyemptitsy from late February 28th through the beginning of the second week of March 1942. Thereafter, the Legion conducted reconnaissance patrols until April 15th. D'Haese, still with the Legion, took part in heavy fighting against thousands of Russians soldiers and partisans in the "Volkhov Pocket" from mid-April to the end of June 27, 1942. During these actions, the 2. SS-Brigade reportedly captured thirty-two thousand and counted over one hundred thousand killed Russians. By this time D'Haese had been wounded twice and earned the Iron Cross 2nd Class and the Wound Badge in Black. He was also promoted to Unterscharführer (surpassing the rank of Rottenführer). D'Haese was rightfully awarded the "Ostmedaille 41/42" for having taken part in the bitter cold battles that past winter. In late July 1942, D'Haese was with the Legion during the water trench warfare before Leningrad (now again St. Petersburg). He also fought with the Legion in the Neva Bend in northern Russia in October 1942. Finally, in January 1943, the Legion was relieved, but only for a short time. In February the Legion was deployed for the fighting in Krasny Bor, which took place from mid-February to late-March 1943. D'Haese noted that from the original 137 men in his company, only six returned with their commander, Untersturmführer Vogel. D'Haese was also wounded two more times during the fighting. The Legion was then sent back to the training grounds in Debica, where it received new equipment and an influx of new volunteers. D'Haese, a proven front-line combat soldier, who began as a simple "Schütze" (private) and later served as a "Gruppenführer" as an Unterscharführer, was ordered to attend the next class at the SS-Junkerschule Tölz. The course began on September 6, 1943 and completed on March 11, 1944. D'Haese successfully concluded the course during which he was promoted to SS-Standartenjunker and later, after completing the final examination, to Standartenoberjunker.1 D'Haese received his commission (Untersturmführer) on June 21, 1944 after arriving at the Knovitz training grounds, where the surviving remnants of the Brigade were to rest and refit after the battles in the Ukraine. In Knovitz, D'Haese was given command of Langemarck's 3. Kompanie. During the battles in Narva, Felix Steiner assigned D'Haese to lead the battle group after the fall-out of the majority of the officers and the battle group's commander, Hauptsturmführer Wilhelm Rehmann. After the battles in Narva, it was rumored that D'Haese was not awarded the Knight's Cross due to the fact that he was considered "politically unreliable" as it was known that he was a defiant Flemish-Nationalist and a member of the VNV. This rumor is still alive today. Due to his status as a combat veteran who fought in the trenches as a enlisted man, D'Haese was an officer that enjoyed great respect amongst his men.

The fire continued to last.. a long time thereafter!

We called to each other to find out if everything was still in order. We were happy that there weren't any dead or wounded to claim. Soldier's luck had not yet abandoned us. We were scared, but everyone tried to remain tough.

We didn't know how late it had become in the meantime, but it was certainly late-afternoon. The fire died down somewhat, but between the incoming we heard the howling of motors, and everyone, as if we had all just received an order, stuck their heads over the edge of their foxholes at once. The howling came from three German Panzers, which had stopped right in the neighborhood of our gun, and then went into position about twenty meters away from us. That didn't look that good for us! We patrolled the flat in the direction of the road which lay to the left of Orphanage Hill, but we didn't see anything suspicious. In spite of that we heard the Panzer men exchanging orders and immediately thereafter the first shot. It was hell, shot after shot left the barrels. We watched, but didn't see anything special. We heard orders again coming from the Panzers and they started to pull back driving backwards. Only the third Panzer, which stood next to our PAK gun, made a wide angle and exposed his backside to the enemy. He only managed to go 3 meters! A crack and the turret stumbled to the side. A red and black flame climbed into the air. It was a direct hit. I saw two men run in the direction of Love's Hill, then there was some screaming and then it was still. Only the burning and crackling of the Panzer could still be heard. As it became even stiller, we heard the incoming rounds from mortar fire, we still had to pay attention. How late it had become in the meantime, we didn't know, certainly it was already evening, because the day was long and the morning began early. We sat calmly in our foxholes or we ran to each other. Suddenly Panzer Alarm! A T-34 came full speed on the road in our direction. Now we were in the row! Everything happened lightning-fast. We called for the Geschützführer and the Richtschütze, I was already at the gun and I didn't see or hear anything from the two men. As it later turned out, the two men, who were located in another trench, were suffering from heavy shock from a round that landed in their direct vicinity. Since the two men didn't show up, I immediately took the place of the Richtschütze and adjusted the gun's optics to three hundred meters and called for Panzergranaten (armor-piercing rounds). The round was just in the chamber and everything had to happen quickly, because we had already lost too much time due to the fall-out of the other two men. I aimed, had the T-34 perfectly in my sights, and then I pressed the button. Hit! Direct hit! Just as it had happened with the German Panzer next to us, it happened exactly the same with this T-34. There was a huge flame, the turret stumbled to the side and red and black smoke came from the chassis of the tank where the turret had once been attached. We worried about the other two men, but we didn't have much time, as a second T-34 followed. I quickly set the optics to four hundred meters and then sent off another armor piercing round. Exactly as with the first T-34 there was a flame. Two hits in just a few minutes gave us a calm happiness. We maintained our view of the road. A third T-34 took a risk and followed behind the other two, and its speed was massive, it didn't appear too confident. Our gun was already loaded. I set the optics to six hundred meters. The tenseness increased as I followed the tank through my optics. I pressed the button and just like the two others, a red-black flame bellowed out from the tank. The third T-34 stood there burning like a flare on the road between the little house and Orphanage Hill.

Our victory over the three T-34s was worthless due to the fall-out of our Geschützführer and our Richtschütze, it was as if a black shadow stood over this victory. Everyone was irritated, but didn't know why or for what reason!

After knocking out the three tanks everything remained calm, we looked around, but even on Orphanage Hill it had become calm. We crawled back into our foxholes, with our eyes fixated on the open field left of Orphanage Hill. Everything remained calm and still.

Marcel Laperre continued:[18]

"I went to Grootaers' PAK for the first time and I immediately realized that Grootaers did not take the position I had chosen. I immediately inquired with Grootaers about his position and wanted to know why he did not take the position I had ordered. Immediately Schrijnen butted in, 'For the first and last time, only my men and I take the position! First we choose a small hill in the terrain, then we build it up and camouflage the gun's position.'

" 'My first lecture,' I thought. 'An order is an order,' was my answer, 'this small hill is an easily recognizable point on the terrain,' I continued.

" 'Untersturmführer, the Geschützführer and the Richtschütze decide on which position is the best and most secure, and which position will also be

---

[18] Schrijnen notebook.

successful in action. And when the opponent fires at us, he won't always hit us. Would you like to come along to the front?' replied Remy.

"We crawled a bit forward and it was there that the Richtschütze explained to me about his dangerous position.

" 'Untersturmführer, this Geschütz is so difficult to hit, camouflaged, dug in, only the blue sky and the forest are its background, barely noticeable for the enemy. But for artillery and fighter planes, you're right, it is a recognized position,' said Schrijnen.

" 'Untersturmführer, with this position Schrijnen has had success and barely any casualties. I mean, he is right,' said Geschützführer Grootaers. But I was even more astonished as the gun was shoved into position. The shelter quarters were laid out in front of the barrel of the gun, and blended with the rest of the gun's surroundings and were held down by stones on the left and right.

" 'Yeah,' said Grootaers, 'in this way as few as possible dust clouds form which would otherwise hinder the sight of the Geschützführer and the Richtschütze. And with no dust clouds, together with the fact that we used camouflage, it isn't easy for the Russians to determine from where the rounds are coming.'

"I swallowed the words of Kotlowski hard, 'most successful Richtschütze,' 'former foot messenger,' 'independent fighter.' I begin to scratch my head. I've already lost Geschütz D'Hollander, lost on the Orphanage Hill without even firing a round or being fired upon. Rehmann's mistake? If it was Schrijnen's decision, this gun would never have been positioned there. D'Hollander blew the gun in the air so the Soviets couldn't get it and was killed in the process. That's how a true soldier handles a bad situation. Later Rehmann talked about the wound he received just before he disappeared from the front. He was barely even scratched, everyone knew it. Even Steiner didn't receive him.

" 'Yeah,' said Remy, 'what is allowed for the gentlemen officers has never been allowed for the enlisted ranks. I spoke with Rehmann, who blew his truck and then ran with three or four of his men to the rear. He didn't even have more than a few scratches.' "

Geschützführer Grootaers recalled:[19]

---

[19] Schrijnen notebook.

"For our assignment, we arrived during a calm night. The following day, after our gun was set up, I saw several Panzers coming from the forest. I screamed 'Panzer Alarm, Panzer Alarm!' I gave the order 'Feuer Frei!' but Schütze Nr. 1 didn't even flinch. 'FEUER FREI!!' I screamed, but Schrijnen just gave me the barrel poker and told me to hold on to it. I looked out into the distance to get a better look at the Panzers, I noticed only three Panzers.

" 'Those Panzers retreating from the enemy are our Panzers. The enemy does not drive backwards, but attacks from the front side' Schrijnen said.

"I swore to myself, I then had a course at the Unterführerschule as well as a few weeks of front-line experience behind me, and I had to listen to someone tell me how to tell when a Panzer was driving backwards and how to tell the difference between our own Panzers and those of the enemy?

" 'The back of the Panzer is the weakest point and only our own men would offer us this weak point,' explained my Richtschütze 'and besides, if it was a Russian, no Ivan would do that because the back side, where the motor is, hardly has any armor. You should learn your tanks from all sides and memorize them.'

"A messenger came, D'Haese was the commander of the Kampfgruppe. A barrage fell on our positions. We had no other contact to the rear lines. The call was 'Panzers coming!' The barrage fell mostly behind us. Then five T-34s were attacking on the 1000 meter open field. 'Feuer Frei!,' I called. I observed the calm but serious look on the faces of my Schütze I and II, who didn't even release the safety of the PAK gun. Only the barrel cap had been removed. The chamber cover was still in place, 'to protect from dust,' said Horre. The Panzers came closer, the infantry men were becoming restless, they called 'the PAK, the PAK...' I said to Remy, 'Come on! Fire!'

" 'No, no – no shot,' he answered.

I swallowed hard, five Panzers and my Richtschütze didn't want to fire! My fever grew from my lust for action. From the side I saw Remy's hard face, and I could see a slight smile on his face. Finally he spoke to me.

" 'One thing you should never forget Unterscharführer,' he said, 'never give away your position too early – and this is no attack.'

" 'I am ordering you!' I said.

" 'No, wait,' he answered back, barely paying attention to me. Even Reeb's gun wasn't firing, or for some reason he couldn't fire. I swore softly to myself, my men were relaxed, they knew their no. 1 gunner. Then the Russian

Panzers were only three hundred meters away and my nervousness grew strong. The Panzers stopped and then they are pulled back, driving backwards into the forest. At that time I was a Geschützführer and the experience was important.

" 'Unterscharführer,' said Remy, 'this is a blocking assignment and there is no such thing as a blocking assignment against five Panzers. Ivan mostly attacks with masses. He knows no fear. He knows what a blocking assignment is... this famous blocking assignments, which really is a suicide operation, from which the majority of our soldiers will never return. The Kampfgruppe should definitely hold up the Soviets, that's why we are here.'

"A messenger, Juul Fieremans, came – sent by D'Haese. 'Grootaers, you did excellent, not giving away your position!'

" 'Yeah!' I exclaimed while I looked towards Remy. I then started to laugh. From then on I let Remy do as he wanted."

Meanwhile, at the commander's bunker, Marcel Laperre recalled the talk given by D'Haese as he took over command of the battle group:[20]

" '...I know that the simple men, the tried and proven, the Rottenführer or Sturmmänner, are all fighters with much front-line experience. The men of this proud battle group, all of them are ready,' said D'Haese. The men smiled upon him approvingly with camaraderie and proud respect. One of ours was Kommandeur, the first Fleming to be commander, as a young leader. Here one could see the eyes of the men light up. They knew him as a simple enlisted man, later as an Unterscharführer. We rushed on, quickly rambled on, as the eyes of D'Haese watched over the weapons with a dreamy sense of security. The plan of action had already been talked through in every detail with the men in their slick camouflage suits, a new thing from the Waffen-SS for a few years then. This was the day when Kommandeur Rehmann not only failed, but abandoned his men as a coward and Untersturmführer Georg D'Haese overtook the command of the Kampfgruppe. This 21 year old Kommandeur then stood in the way of a large Soviet offensive there in the Blue Mountains of Estonia. The Soviets were looking for a seam between the lines, a place where they could break through, and that is where the Kampfgruppe Langemarck stood. Reserves were not available to D'Haese. There were barely

---

[20] Schrijnen notebook.

any heavy weapons. The Kampfgruppe Langemarck was to blunt the lead units of the advancing Russian offensive and prevent a breakthrough at all costs."

Schrijnen's Geschützführer Jef Grootaers continued:[21]

"...The barrage of fire started up again and lasted for hours. Schütze I and II sat in their trenches in the vicinity of the gun, calm and quiet. Both of these men were so used to the barrages and they often took the time to sleep during them. This time, however, Remy started scribbling on a piece of paper. He drew and drew and then it became somewhat calm. Then Remy snuck up to the gun and prepared the cannon. Next I saw T-34s rolling out of the forest and watched them begin to approach our positions. PAK and Ratschbumm fired on our lines and the powerful tank motors were revving. Once again a short but hard barrage fell on our positions and the tanks continued to advance. Despite the incoming artillery rounds the men remained at their posts. It was then that I really got to know my men. Without issuing any orders the Panzergranaten began to spit out of the PAK's barrel. Already the first Russian tank was burning, Calmly, or better said, silently amongst the deafening noise I gave my orders, which were only partly carried out. The Soviets approached and I noticed that Unterscharführer Reeb was also attacking. The Ivans were shuddering and with a laugh they retreated from my gun. Four T-34s lay burned out along the road and numerous others were damaged. The Soviets, who had just a minute before had wanted to finish us off, then began to pull their tanks back. Then I looked with Schrijnen to see what he had drawn on the paper. I was astonished to see what I had not even noticed, how what I had seen before me was, in reality, quite different than I had thought. Remy showed me how Ivan was a master in the art of camouflage. This was definitely taught to us in the Unterführerschule, but Schrijnen taught me Ivan's tricks.

" 'Yeah' said Remy, 'I learned what camouflage means from the Russians.'

Then I heard and watched how the Soviets slowly crept forward, barely visible, but still the distance to them was constantly changing.

" 'That is front experience, Unterscharführer.' said Horre.

---

[21] Schrijnen notebook.

"Remy kept on drawing, placing the distance from the things he saw. 'The eye should be exercised – think about what I have drawn for the section of the forest, which is at a distance of about 1000 meters from us, and tell me what you see,' said Remy.

" 'Empty,' I replied.

" 'Yeah?' added Sobry.

"Now and then I held an eye to this section, I had to hold an eye on this section, to see what changed. Remy marked a cross at a point on his drawing, since it could have been a Soviet munitions dump or an assembly position. Without saying a word the men had already collected the empty shells and had hidden them in a camouflaged foxhole. Just at that time I remembered what Kotlowski and Fieremans had told me about my Richtschütze. I slowly began to understand what kind of men had been entrusted to me, men who could take care of themselves and could act. I then looked at the mostly silent Remy, he saw everything, said nothing, but grasped the situation. 'A formula,' he said, 'that is more valuable than any order.'

" 'The simple man should think and act independently, because you, I or Sobry could get killed or become wounded, and everything would have to go on,' commented Remy. I grasped the true meaning of Remy's advice from our training about the so-called carousel, where men traded places. It was then that I started to feel better about being around these men. As Unterscharführer I hadn't known anything and then I saw how everything centered around those that are able. The men's noses were in the dirt as the shells fell around our positions. The men carried shells and ammunition to our gun.

" 'Yeah,' said Sobry, 'for security there are Sprenggranaten.'

"Of course I already knew that we had three types of grenades: Panzergranaten, Hohlraumgranaten, special for heavily armed Panzers, and Sprenggranaten for unarmored targets, vehicles and infantry. We also had Panzerfäuste (German bazookas) and Tellerminen (plate mines). Everything was covered with camouflage in different trenches to protect against a direct hit so that not all the ammunition would blow at once."

Marcel Laperre continued:[22]

---

[22] Schrijnen notebook.

"...Grootaers' PAK was successful, Reeb's too, but Grootaers had a dangerous position, due to Schrijnen, no doubt, his old proven Richtschütze. Remy told me that his position had to fit the landscape, and that he would have to take the risk of being out there. And there it was again, his not well-liked, despised and even dangerous 'Kopfstellung.'

" 'The position,' said Schrijnen, 'right before the main fighting line, is the best observation post. There is no such thing as a safe position.'

"Of course his men agreed. 'Yeah, a PAK Geschütz should rule the enemy's entire terrain. Targets must be recognized and then smashed. That is the task of the PAK. The PAK directly supports our infantry, both against tanks and enemy infantry. The PAK must also take every risk to protect it from being discovered by the enemy,' they said."

Dries Anseeuw reported about the end of the day:[23]

It must have become very late, because it started to become dark. Unexpectedly we heard a voice: "Dries, pull everyone back, leave the gun where it is, take the optics and the firearm along with." It was Remy Schrijnen who stood at my foxhole and gave me the order from Untersturmführer Laperre. We came from our holes and followed Remy to Love's Hill.

In front of the hill stood a sand pit, I thought it was set up as camouflage for a machine gun. It was a beautiful and secure position. Untersturmführer Laperre was there, and told us that as soon as it was dark, we would have to manually pull the gun back. After talking and resting for a while, it was time. Untersturmführer Laperre, Schrijnen, a few comrades and I ran, one after the other, to the old position. We knew that the Russians were running about in small groups over the flat land and that with the high grass they had good cover. So we were forced to crawl. As we arrived at the PAK, we wanted to close the spread-out spars, but it was impossible since the end caps were bent by the incoming rounds from earlier that day. So we brought the gun back with spread-out spars. It was a difficult task. Untersturmführer Laperre hung on the barrel to even out the weight of the gun and would move to the left and to the right every time we would have to go over a bump. Sometimes he couldn't hold on and fell off, which made us all laugh!

---

[23] Report from Dries Anseeuw dated Nov. 10, 1997.

Dries Anseeuw: Above is Dries Anseeuw, who was a loader in Unterscharführer Reeb's crew. Anseeuw was born on August 17, 1925 and was just 18 years old during the battles in the Blue Mountains. Anseeuw survived the Narva battles and was awarded the Iron Cross IInd Class for his part in August 1944. Anseeuw continued with the PAK Kompanie of the Langemarck Division and fought with the active battle group until the final days of the war.

Finally we reached the sand trench on Love's Hill. It was then possible to rest.

The well-earned rest didn't last long. The Russians had probably had seen us and they were once again there with their heavy cannons. Just then came our Waffenwart Quisthout with his helper Achiel Taeckens from Torhout. As soon as the first incoming landed, Taeckens was hit and he died in my arms. I knew him from before, he was from the same area as me in Flanders. During the transport to Narva, we had talked about our homeland. He said to me: "Dries, where we're driving to now will be my death. Greet everyone in Torhout for me." It was over, what he had feared on the trip was now reality. He was just one of many that died and we didn't know how many would follow him. The bombing by the Russians continued, they knew where we had gone with our gun and the front part of Love's hill was hit hard. The gun could still be repaired for the continuance of the battle.

Second Day of Battle: July 27, 1944

Orphanage Hill remained in the hands of Battle Group "D'Haese." Grenadier Hill and Love's Hill were occupied by the Estonians and two companies of SS-Pionier-Bataillon 11 of the "Nordland" division. To the south, on the edge of the forest was "Norge."

A hellish battle began. The Flemings in the forward most positions heard the fire of battle in front of them, but were unsure what was going on. As it turned out, the fire was being exchanged between the Russians and fragmented groups of retreating soldiers from other units, including many of the Dutch who had been previously surrounded while trying to get back to the German lines. None of them made it through.

Marcel Laperre continued:[24]

"The men of the infantry didn't let themselves lose their calmness, there were no signs of panic. The PAKs protected them from tanks and the men still knew the PAK from Jambol. The stubble fields were now full of artillery and bomb craters. The fire road in the forest was no longer useable for the Soviets, since Schrijnen destroyed it with some direct hits. Our artillery would have been necessary to put the approaching Russians under fire. The road was full of Soviets who were advancing as if they were conducting field exercises. The mood was very good, the men could still laugh. The many casualties caused worries. There weren't many here. We had enough ammunition, though. I then found out that Geschütz Reeb was no longer in action. No one was killed or wounded, the gun was hit and damaged by shrapnel. Damn, it was my first time on the front and I had such bad luck. Too bad, because Frans van Mol,[25] Dries Anseeuw and the others were good men. PAK Grootaers needed no orders to attack, there stood the proven Richtschütze."

That same day, July 27, 1944, the Kampfgruppe lost its second of only three guns. Reeb's gun was dragged back behind the front lines and sent to be repaired, never to return. The men in the crews were split up amongst the infantry compa-

---

[24] Schrijnen notebook.
[25] Frans van Mol, who relayed many of the stories told to Schrijnen while in prison, had served as Schütze II in Unterscharführer Martens crew during the battles along the highway to Jambol. Martens, who commanded 1. Geschütz/I.Zug, was killed after receiving a direct hit in Jambol (early March 1944).

nies and fought with rifles for the rest of the battle. Only Grootaer's gun was left to hold the flood gates shut.

Elsewhere during the battle Marcel Laperre spoke to Georg D'Haese about the battle group's assignment and the problems of leadership. Marcel Laperre reported:[26]

"...the awesome goal before the eyes, these extremely difficult battles... There we were at Narva with our small Flemish Kampfgruppe fighting against the powerful communists. Our men held the highest goal in their eyes: victory. The Germanic volunteers there at those three hills stood deadly tired across from the Soviets. The question regarding what their motivations were, mostly all were simple workers or young college students. Our Western culture, life, spirit and freedom was threatened to be done away with by the East. The term communist East and West, these words are more than different than 'the West, north and south.' The Northern idea of life, our ideas of life, are eternally incompatible with the East. Our Nordic people, who are defended here with unimaginable hardness through the III. Germanisches Panzerkorps, here in Estonia, together with Germans, Estonians and many others.

" 'Laperre,' said Georg D'Haese, 'as I took over command of the Kampfgruppe Langemarck, I was worried about how my relationship with the other officers would take form. Some of the leaders are older than me and have a higher rank.'

" 'I wondered the same thing,' I answered, 'but now I have the impression that you enjoy a great authority with the other leaders and the men.'

" 'That's right, Laperre,' continued D'Haese, 'I also believe that I have found the right tone and have the same relationships with them as earlier. I have built a true trust with my new subordinates, officers, NCOs and men, because I know them and their abilities. That makes it easier to lead the battle group. Now, Untersturmführer Laperre, I wish you and your PAK Geschütz much success and soldier's luck, because many very difficult battles stand before us. It is great luck that many of the men have battle experience, hard soldiers from my time with the Legion Flandern, the rest of the old Guard which these hours depend on, as well as on the new men of the Sturmbrigade.' "

---

[26] Schrijnen notebook.

Jan Vermeeren reported:[27]

"...Standartenoberjunker Groenvinck lay on the branch of a tree and observed the edge of the forest and reported what he saw to his messenger. 'Go immediately to D'Haese and call in some fire!' he ordered. He observed the terrain and the edge of the forest through his field glasses. The promised signals troops never made it through to us. They just couldn't do it. They had to come from the signal's school but now the pocket was closed off. But there was no barrage of fire. Ivan had the infantry cannons, mortars and Stalin's Organs. The Reds covered us beautifully from all sides. They stripped our entire positions as well as the roads.

" 'Man! Man!' Groenvinck said to me, 'This isn't something that you hear about, it is as if we are on the edge of a volcano that is continuously spitting lava!'

" 'Strange,' I replied, 'have you ever seen a volcano eruption?' Groenvinck just started to smile. Then, without warning, a barrage fell on us. The howling became even more frantic. There was hot air and shaking earth, flying stones, dirt and grenade fragments. We all had a bad taste in our mouths. We lay or squat in the holes and the craters. Groenvinck was under the branch Now and then something hit us, steel or rocks, who knows. I heard Groenvinck flee, it was a baptism of fire. Everything seemed to be going well, but then the bombers and the fighter planes arrived and the bombs started flying and machine guns strafed our lines. From the forest came the Reds and the dance of death began.

" 'Pas Veux' said Groenvinck, 'that devil Ivan has to come over 900 meters of open land and they're getting their fair share!' "

During this day elsewhere in the fighting, Pioniere (combat engineers) tried in vain to close a gap in the main fighting line east of the positions in Tirtsu. The goal was to relieve the remaining portions of III./SS-Regiment 24 who were accompanied by SS-Gruppenführer und Generalleutnant der Waffen-SS Fritz von Scholz, Kommandeur of "Nordland." Von Scholz, who was known to always be at the front with his troops when they were in danger or experiencing difficulties, was

---

[27] Schrijnen notebook.

mortally wounded by a grenade during the fighting. He died the next day in a field hospital in Wesenberg.[28]

Towards the end of the day, the Soviets launched another vicious attack. At the time, the Flemings still stood in the forward-most positions. The Russian attack rolled over the remains of Kampfgruppe "D'Haese." After bitter hand-to-hand combat, his men retreated to Grenadier Hill in small groups. II./SS-Regiment 49 still held their positions north of Orphanage Hill. Counterattacks, supported by Sturmgeschütze (assault guns) were unsuccessful. The disputed points of the battle remained Orphanage Hill and later the threatened Grenadier Hill, which was being doggedly defended by Estonians and Flemings.

Jan Vermeeren continued:[29]

"...already one heard the uuuurrrrraaaaayyyy, uuuurrrrrraaaaaayyyy of the Russians. One waited for the screams to begin. The PAK began to fire. A mortar, machine guns and rifles started up. Groenvinck crawled from hole to hole. A medic bandaged the wounded and said that there were a few more dead. The old ones of the Legion and the Sturmbrigade took the Reds in the pincers like a horseshoe. The men had built up their positions without being ordered. No one needed to give orders here. The men with front-line experience did what was right. The attackers were stopped and ran into our flank fire. Handgrenades flew against the Reds. The first storm had been beaten off. Already the second storm began and then came a third wave. Groenvinck and three men fetched some ammo. It didn't take very long and the MG Schützen called 'Here! Here!...' Groenvinck brought us another ten men while the Reds continued their storm. The PAK fired uninterrupted and the Soviet mortars fell silent. The Russian Ratschbumm fired from the forest's edge onto our PAK, but it answered quickly and must have inflicted a direct hit since the three on the other side fell silent. Everything crackled: heavy machine guns, light machine guns, and rifles. The two MGs cut open the Soviet lines. They were above everything and shot over our heads. We dreaded this – even though the Red soldier fought bravely, the morale of their bad leadership must have

---

[28] Von Scholz, commander of the 11. SS-Freiwilligen Panzergrenadier Division "Nordland," died the following day (July 28, 1944) and was posthumously awarded the Swords to the Knight's Cross on August 8, 1944. He was the 85th soldier to receive this very high decoration. "Nordland," like "Wiking," was also a very successful division comprising of European volunteers. Von Scholz was a well-liked commander and was held in high regarded by his multi-national troops.

[29] Schrijnen notebook.

demoralized them, because they often fled back to the forest leaving their dead and wounded behind. Everyone shot until the fleeing masses disappeared into the forest. Groenvinck then went to get some supplies.

" 'Take them to the main dressing station,' I yelled, 'before the artillery fire starts up!' One of the men was done for, a shrapnel fragment cut open his arm pit and opened his artery. Two men carried him. The medic held his artery closed. Perhaps he would be able to save him. Then came more reports. The leaders had suffered many casualties and many had been killed. Hutten was badly wounded, Bottu[30] dead. Van Mol and van Bokkel were already dead. The majority of the leaders were out.

" 'The casualties here are bearable,' reported Groenvinck to his Kommandeur. Kommandeur D'Haese knew that it was Groenvinck[31] who was now in charge of an entire company. Fieremans came with a message from the Kommandeur. We were to go to a leader's meeting immediately. We left our lines with Laperre. Artillery fire began, but we arrived safely at D'Haese's post. Not including Dr. Hertgens, we still had four leaders. We took our orders. We had no heavy weapons, Laperre reported that we had only one PAK left, otherwise nothing.

" 'We can only praise the men,' said Groenvinck, 'filled with bravery, courage and prepared for action. They will hold out despite the heaviest casualties.' The morale was excellent in the midst of the heavy barrages. There was no sign of weakness. The men were proud of their young Flemish commander. The language of command was Flemish.

"D'Haese gave us the order to '...bring everything together. Group leaders are to have a free hand in the defense. You, Laperre and Groenvinck, stay in secure trenches. I want you to always be available for messengers to reach you. I can't afford to lose any more leaders. That is all gentlemen...' D'Haese ended the meeting formally.

Jan Vermeeren continued:[32]

"...I went with the leaders to see how they would split up our men. Quick but small 'alarm' groups were formed from old men who had a lot of front-

---

[30] Luc Bottu was killed in the flat land between Orphanage Hill and Grenadier Hill.

[31] Groenvinck started the battle as a platoon leader in the 1. Kompanie. After Untersturmführer Swinnen was killed, Groenvinck took over as Kompanie Führer.

[32] Schrijnen notebook.

line experience. They were to go from place to place and to wherever there was trouble. We three were to go forward with messengers, away from the Kommandobunker. Already we heard the droning of many planes. Everyone took cover.

" 'There!' said Laperre, 'in books it reads that an officer is never to lay flat and should never wear a helmet – as a sign of courage.'

" 'Yeah,' said D'Haese, 'a helmet just slows you down when you are running away from the fire!'

"The planes flew only about thirty meters above us. The two motors made an ear-splitting crack and then began to fire with their machine guns. I saw two trucks in the distance as they tried to disappear. One was erased by the plane and burned. The fire raged for fifteen minutes and then it was calm. The driver was wounded. The vehicle was burned out.

" 'Now the front calls,' said D'Haese to his men, his battle group. The road that goes in the direction of Narva was empty. The men kept their positions secret, nothing was noticeable, nothing moved, only the brown figures of the dead and wounded Russians in the field. Everything was calm. We crawled quietly into the lines.

"Groenvinck said to the Kommandeur, 'It's a wonder that anyone can live out here in these craters, with the stink and all.' Again we had to stay under. New planes flew over the terrain and searched for anything that moved. We saw the pilots and men sitting in their cockpits and saw how they made their signals. No more was to be seen. There was crater after crater and stripped sections of forest on Grenadier- and the Love's Hill. There were only shredded stumps left from the artillery rounds and bombs. Along side us ran the main road, the bridge to the Kampfgruppe 'Langemarck.' The Reds had to have it, but D'Haese and his men held it despite everything: the masses of infantry and tanks, the bombs and artillery. The front held. The Dutch, Danes, Norwegians, 'Nordland,' all of those Germanic volunteers made the sacrifice in the III. Germanisches Panzerkorps. They were an exception, tough and dogged. There was no difference. Here one couldn't name names. Every single man would stand and hold out to the end. Those that would survive knew what had been performed by every single man. With us was a young leader from Bad Tölz, Georg D'Haese. His leadership had everything in its hand: his leaders, their abilities to beat off all of the attacks, their worries, casualties – and no reinforcements. When the order was to shove a few men to the right or left, they didn't question if it is right or wrong, as one had to take risks. D'Haese was there when the storming Soviet troops tried three times to break through with their tanks. They all fell in concentrated fire from the infantry, a few mortars and a single PAK gun. The infantry stood ready with their handguns, handgrenades and close combat weapons. The stick grenades flew further than the egg handgrenades and threw the Reds back with such a rage that they ran back to their own lines as if they were lost. Fons Van Broeck, a motorcycle dispatch rider, made his way through the falling bombs. He left his motorcycle behind. He gave his message to D'Haese.

" 'Do you have any orders, Untersturmführer?' he asked.

" 'No, there is only thick air here,' he responded.

" 'Yeah,' said Fons, 'I brought ammunition with me.'

" 'Go,' said D'Haese to me and another. We three left and went from crater to crater with the ammunition.

" 'Vermeeren is shot! Go on!' I heard Van Broeck roar. Luckily I had only tripped. At the motorcycle we loaded all of the munitions into the compartments. We bent over to avoid being shot and we three managed without even a scratch. Later we brought back the badly wounded, the shredded flesh of our young comrades – reality was real. The Soviet Guard against the Guard of the III. Germanisches Panzerkorps. When I thought to myself, 'Give up,' I would roar back, 'no stay and hold out!' They say everyone thinks of their own head first and whoever doesn't think of his own head first is either dumb or stupid. In any case we were preferably dumb, I first thought of the others, and then myself. That was a fact that my comrades knew very well. Perhaps this was a side of the soldier that has luck and courage in unsure and unusual battles, to continue on without regard for himself. One called it heroism."

Marcel Laperre continued the story:[33]

"Next the Russian artillery laid their fire to the back of us and was decking our infantry. Then I heard 'uuurrrraaaayyyy, uuuurrrraaayyy,' the Soviets were attacking. They had to overcome a 900 meter flat before they could reach us, our casualties were bearable. As a platoon leader I could no longer look after my entire platoon. After the questionable casualty of Kommandeur Rehmann, I had to hold together the rest of the men from Unterscharführer

---

[33] Schrijnen notebook.

D'Hollander's crew. The success of Grootaers' PAK was known to me then. This team, everything was always all right by them. They were dependable: Grootaers, Sobry, Horre, Rubens, De Kessel and Schrijnen all had front-line experience and previous success, they didn't even need their gun. Hundreds upon hundreds of men formed on our lines and no one fired. I myself was actually a recruit – a platoon leader without any front-line experience. That day I saw the first Sprenggranaten of our PAKs in action, mortars, light machine guns and so on. Everything hammered all around us, I saw the rage of the men of Kampfgruppe D'Haese, under the command of a young Flemish Untersturmführer by the name of Georg D'Haese. The communists still thought that they could cash in these men. The situation was critical for us, but we remained. I heard a soldier say, 'us and D'Haese! We, the old Guard of the Legion Flandern, the last survivors of the Legion, have arrived.' Kommandeur D'Haese knew almost all of them personally, as he had spent years with them on the Leningrad front as a Schütze (Private) and group leader.[34] He knew what these men could accomplish. The inexperienced men melted like snow in the sun and there were no reserves to replace the killed or wounded. Therefore every man became three times as valuable. Hour after hour, in defense or in the middle of a barrage stood the Rottenführer and Sturmmänner of the former Legion Flandern, now the Sturmbrigade Langemarck. One could say that they were 'the backbone of the army.' These men carried out their orders better then a specialist. When I was at Bad Tölz, I never thought that theory and practice could be so different. In my platoon there was a Sturmmann, who possessed unbelievable capabilities while in action. Whether it was from front-line experience, courage or his calm decisiveness, he made the right decisions when we leaders could only shake our heads. Here I learned that one first needs to obtain front-line experience before he should be allowed to give orders in battle. A leader's decisions have an instant effect on the situation, for better or for worse. This is something one learns, not in leadership school, but only in the trenches before the enemy. There on the front it was proven that one had to leave the best soldiers to themselves. These men, the men that remained to the end were the patrol troop men, the men that were forced to wear an enlisted man's rank. Without these 'Frontschweinen,' you could forget it. I saw how these men carried out their duties, those men who knew each

---

[34] A group leader or "Gruppenführer," is similar to the "PAK Geschützführer" commanding several men, commonly holding the rank of Unterscharführer.

other so well. They were the exceptional ones, the ones that were seldom awarded higher medals. Here I learned how much a single man could accomplish, that a single man's performance could mean that our sacrifices were not for nothing. The 'Landser,' the one that fights so bravely and accomplishes so much, is barely ever even mentioned in the daily battle orders and almost never wins an award.

"I can't describe it, there I was for the first time in action at the front. I shot a man for the first time with a rifle that I had found with a fallen solder. I shot this Russian soldier from a distance of perhaps twenty meters. I saw the twisted face of this Soviet soldier. What was it? Hate? Fear? Courage? The desire to attack? I shot at this man, my first man and I realized that I had personally shot him and had killed him. I had pity for this courageous Soviet soldier. Perhaps everyone feels the same way when he kills for the first time.

"During a counterattack I saw how the men jumped out of their foxholes or emerged from the trenches and stormed the enemy. They won back a piece of land despite fighting against a tough defense and despite the fact that the Russians had an extreme advantage in men and weapons. Many of the brave gents of Kampfgruppe 'D'Haese,' as the men now call themselves, were killed or became wounded. The Russians couldn't take them all, the infantry carried out the most difficult tasks of the fight. My single PAK Geschütz supported them against tanks or the Russian PAK Riegel, and during infantry attacks as well. As soon as the communists broke out from the edge of the forest, my PAK began to fire at them almost immediately. Then came a tank attack... In every difficult situation our infantry mustered the task, in critical situations the men pushed their way to the front. I saw flames light up in their eyes.... what these infantry men could accomplish..."

" 'Yeah, Untersturmführer, your PAK men don't even realize that they are in battle,' said Unterscharführer Strooband[35] to me. I remember when Strooband said to me, 'ask the men calmly for advice, because that is the sign of an experienced leader. The men who have spent a long time at the front have an iron calmness which cannot be shaken by anything. They have a clear and daring understanding of action. They have an infallible feel for every situation in action and can recognize them lightning-quick. They know how to best take advantage of these situations. They have a heart for younger com-

[35] Unterscharführer Kamil Strooband had been awarded the Iron Cross IInd Class as a Sturmmann and infantryman serving in the 2. Kompanie of the Legion Flandern on June 26, 1942.

rades, because the men hang on to their favorite men, the men they recognize as role-models in action. These are your men, Marcel. Keep it up, Untersturmführer, the order is to hold your positions!

"A few leaders arrived and reported to the Kommandeur, gleaming. 'There is no breakthrough, the danger continued to be beaten back,' they reported. D'Haese remained calm and wished his leaders and men luck. Then came further judgments about the conditions at the front. Steiner chose D'Haese to be commander. The officers, NCOs and men were more than satisfied with their young Flemish commander. D'Haese said to his leaders that he would follow them into the trenches and dismissed them.

" 'Laperre, wait a minute,' said the commander. Then he got ready and went with me to Geschütz Grootaers. I warned him to be careful and to stay away from exposed positions. Grootaers reported that there was no new news. D'Haese looked over the PAK's position and the camouflage and took the opportunity to talk with the men.

" 'Stay under, please,' barked Grootaers, 'we don't want to reveal our position.' The commander looked at the craters within craters, which lay all around the gun.

" 'Laperre, do you think this is a good position? The gun is sitting here as if it were on a display tray,' said the Kommandeur with a somewhat sarcastic tone in his voice. 'Would a change in position not be appropriate?' he finished.

"I looked right at Grootaers and D'Haese's eyes followed mine. Grootaers became wide-eyed, stumbled and pointed at his Richtschütze, all while drawing his and everyone else's eyes to the smashed tanks strewn out across the field.

" 'My Richtschütze, a man with success and a lot of experience at the front,' barked Grootaers to his Kommandeur, 'is of a completely different opinion, an opinion I agree with!'

" 'OK..... Then everything is in order.' D'Haese answered, while looking at Remy skeptically.

" 'Jawohl, Untersturmführer!' answered Remy, 'this 7.5 cm long barrel has it in it and with my Zugführer and my Unterscharführer and such a group of men, this PAK can do it!'

" 'But the shells are falling somewhat thick here,' answered D'Haese, 'you know very well that we only have one PAK gun left and we are in an unusually dangerous condition and situation. Reserves are not available. These are words among men, open and honest,' he said to us. He wished the men well and then we left the gun to go and visit the infantry."

Marcel Laperre continued:[36]

"...the Grenadier Hill and Love's Hill received their share from the guns of the Soviet ships. The men had been laying in the ditches then for a couple of days, doing guard duty and bringing back dead and wounded. 'Yeah,' said one, 'even the Russians themselves are dragging their dead into bomb craters out there in no-man's land. They're burying them there because not even they can stand the smell of the corpses.' In such heat the dead began to rot.

"The men communicated with each other using signals which I didn't understand. The front had its own rules. I hoped my PAK would survive. The fire lasted for more than three hours. The sun burnt. Shell fragments and dust came from all over. There was rifle and machine gun fire, the bullets from which whistled on by while making an indescribable noise. Then came the Stalin's Organs. Their rockets went over my head and on by. Then I observed the men which were lying tense behind their weapons. I think I saw Kasper D'Haese.[37] The Russians would be coming soon and with their Stalin's Organs they would try to finish us off like heroes. Masses of tanks crept from the forest's edge, and with them were infantry men. 'There shoots the PAK!' exclaimed one. For the men of the battle group this was completely normal, that the PAK attacked so early, since our lines were so thin. If Sunday, July 30, 1944 ever came, we certainly wouldn't be able to take a Sunday's rest. I went and crept through the trenches. I had to see where we needed a few men. The lightly wounded lay behind their weapons. They were mostly 'alte Hasen,' positioned far from another in front of the trenches and the holes that were built at night. The men crept further forward towards the main fighting line. 'The Ivans don't play their drums there!' laughed one. Only the devil himself knew how these men could handle this. Someone made a sign and the infantry weapons immediately began to fire. Yeah, not even the Stalin Organs bothered the men. There was no hesitation, they shot and loaded, shot and loaded.

---

[36] Schrijnen notebook.
[37] Not to be confused with Georg D'Haese, Kasper was a Rottenführer in the 3. Kompanie. Kasper D'Haese was awarded the Iron Cross IInd Class after the battles west of Narva.

Others elsewhere shot as well. I was disappointed in myself, because everything was smeared together and started and continued without any orders from officers. No uncertainty could be felt. I came across a Sturmmann, a badly wounded Sturmmann, another man cared for him, his blood was squirting out of an open vein with every heartbeat. 'Lay a bandage on him, Untersturmführer, I must go to my MG,' the man said and then he was gone. I did what I could. The Sturmmann could still laugh, 'perhaps a ticket home,' he said. He seemed to remain quite sure of himself. 'The arm is finished,' he said, 'it isn't so bad on my leg.' I then tied off his arm. He wouldn't bleed to death now, I hoped. This man definitely needed to be carried out of here, 'leave it for later, Untersturmführer,' he said. I thought to myself that the valley, Grenadier Hill and the Love's Hill were still in our hands. Our infantry was still holding out and was successful. 'Untersturmführer, go on,' said the Sturmmann, 'they'll get me later.'

"I didn't have any worries about my PAK Geschütz crew, they were good men, very able. No, we had to learn that the men had more of a sixth sense than we officers thought. The men trusted their superiors and the men knew that commanders should have other abilities. The criticism of Hauptsturmführer Rehmann was more than correct, but we had to be silent that Rehmann made so many mistakes as well as about his miserable attitude. Schrijnen said it even more frankly. On the other side of the coin is Kommandeur Untersturmführer Georg D'Haese, calm, sure and able, as if he had always been a commander of a Kampfgruppe. D'Haese, who was an experienced patrol troop leader from the Legion Flandern, was known by the old ones of the Legion personally. He was one of theirs. D'Haese knew the morale of these men, he knew what they could accomplish. Perhaps no one thought of these men far behind the front. I continued to listen to the noise of the incoming bombs, the smoky fires, and the Stalin Organs. Artillery and bombs continued to rip through the air. Perhaps the fragments hit the men. Every time I witnessed a hit, I was happy that I was still alive. Lightning and thunder and roaring bursts incensed the soul. The soldiers reacted calmly and sober behind their weapons. The rest of the Kampfgruppe closed the seam of the entire battle group. D'Haese's word had meaning: 'The front will hold.' Now and then we heard tank noise, but no one tried to look any closer. We only dared to look to the edge of the forest. I searched for my PAK Geschütz and wanted to order it to begin to fire a bit early this time. The men with front-line experi-

154

ence were calm at this moment. I knew the whipping bang of the Geschütz and the iron calmness of these men. These men were as hard as steel, there were no apathetic faces, only dirt-smeared faces. They were smiling. A bond brought these men together. The 'brothers of the front,' as I had heard. It was a small society. Only they knew who didn't belong. I heard it was made up of only men who concentrated on victory. There was a strong camaraderie and no big shots. It was a silent group. 'First let's win the war and then we'll talk,' they said, because big words were just BS. We were all exhausted from the heat and the overpowering stink of the dead. The men were always ready and had been so for days, day and night. Despite this, the men knew that Kommandeur D'Haese still had three leaders on the front, Standartenoberjunker Groenvinck, Untersturmführer Van Leemputten and myself, Marcel Laperre. Every man in our platoons had become an independent fighter, one could say. In hedgehog positions the men stood with their machine guns. Bullets swept over the field, one machine gun's fire crossed another. These men were not easily defeated. The infantry remained the best of all weapons. The heaps of dead enemy soldiers was the proof of the performance of these men. I could see the destroyed and damaged Russian tanks in the field. With my binoculars I could see the shredded anti-tank guns and their dead at the edge of the forest. I saw the Russians running, perhaps they would gather around another one. On our side there was a calmness, a certain tranquillity among the men. 'Yeah, Untersturmführer,' said one soldier to me, 'one gets used to it over time.' I understood this man, he meant it like he said it. One learned the hard facts of reality, whether officer, NCO or enlisted man. Everyone had and was forced to have trust for the others and with the others. I continued on. 'Stay down!' I heard someone call. This was no exercise place where one could go for a walk, a realization that brought peace to me. The men observed the landscape despite the fire-waltz. Let the world call us what it will, Nazis or Fascists, we were definitely not communists. Germany had a lack of natural resources which prevented it from becoming a world power and they wanted to annihilate this Germany and the entire North with it. For the first time in hundreds of years the Germanic people were together in a struggle, perhaps to be or not to be. The hypocrites and the political know-it-alls all wanted to bring an end for the empire in the middle. Here stood Germanic volunteers, brave and modest, they paid a high price in blood for the freedom and security of the North. In an extreme emergency we found ourselves as members of a society that no one in Europe or anywhere else had ever seen.

"I looked forward to another place on the front. On the landscape lay crooked bodies and forgotten dead faces. Next to them were blown-up tanks, some of them had men hanging out of them. The smell of dead bodies and of burnt flesh was overpowering, we couldn't carry these decrepit bodies anywhere. Someone said to me, 'Untersturmführer, the Soviets leave their dead and wounded and some of them have been laying here for days.' The smell when the wind blew a draft in our direction was quite noticeable. Now and then we pushed one of the dead Russians into a crater, because these swollen bodies were an unbearable sight. We had no relations with death anymore. Neither the stink nor the disfigured bodies bothered us. Between the Soviet's equipment lay dead Soviets everywhere. Our dead were retrieved during the night. The flies loved the horrible stink. 'Be careful of epidemics when with the wounded,' said the old ones. Then came Leo Tollenaere, as if he had something to report. 'No, everything is OK,' he said.

" 'Untersturmführer, look over at the PAK,' called Strooband. It was barely noticeable from 100 meters, and only then because we knew where it was. One could think that it was further towards the edge of the forest when it was firing. The positions were camouflaged by a Sturmmann who knew what he was doing. Everyone knew Remy who fought before Leningrad as a foot messenger with the Legion. He fought as a PAK Richtschütze with the Sturmbrigade in the Ukraine. His good reputation continued in Narva. 'He is a very dependable man, Untersturmführer' said Strooband. As a young leader I was happy to hear only good things about my platoon."

Marcel Laperre continued:[38]

"What was a name or a rank in that place? There at Narva for the first time was a reality, a holding-together, a union between the men. It was the indescribable law of the fighter. The outsiders will never understand the strength, the will to remain, or the morale of the Germanic peoples. Good times, bad times, life and death, these things will never be separated from us front-soldiers for our entire lives. That was the brotherhood of the front, an organization without a symbol, only the men will ever know who belonged."

"The thundering incoming shells caused the earth to shudder all around me. D'Haese had come to the front again and it let loose, there were crashes

---

[38] Schrijnen notebook.

and deafening noise. Then came Kamiel Horre and Valeer Janssens, crawling, throwing themselves, jumping through the craters with the rhythm of the incoming shells. The brave runners were then with D'Haese, he took them in his cover. 'One leader and fifteen men have fallen, not to mention the numerous men that have been badly wounded,' reported Janssens. 'Steiner called,' continued Janssens. 'Now we have get back,' said Horre, 'and Remy needs more ammunition!' In spite of this we saw that the PAK was still shooting. 'Now we can't look after the old ones, be it my name-partner Kasper, Strooband, Jan Vermeeren, Salien Sapunski or all the rest,' said D'Haese.

"I saw Remy, the former foot messenger, his face before me... the light spotty traits of his face – a smile, I would say. These were hard gentlemen. When they go down, then they'll go down in good company. Nowhere could panic be seen. Only Rehmann split, said the men. It was true but we leaders had to keep hush. We couldn't forbid the men from talking about it, only warn them, but even a German platoon leader called Rehmann a cowardly swine. It appears as if there was no more organized defense on the front. But that was a deception in itself. The men were where they needed to be. One jumped in for another. Supply lines were also under heavy fire and Soviet bomber formations were on the way to make sure that no supplies or reinforcements arrived, at least during the day. A shell landed three steps in front of Untersturmführer D'Haese, but the grenade lay stuck in the ground. It could have exploded at any second. We immediately pushed ourselves in to a crater and put our arms over our head.

" 'Marcel,' said D'Haese to me, 'I think it is strange that everyone covers their head when a bomb falls, the head is the central command post, but I just realized it must be a dud, out of this hole and on!'

"Along the way we saw a badly wounded man with a bandage on his upper thigh. His pants were shredded and he was bleeding. We dragged him with us to Dr. Hertgens. D'Haese and the rest of our group took off to the command post, the wire connection was out.

" 'The men call themselves Kampfgruppe D'Haese,' said Valeer Janssens along the way.

" 'Yeah, but I don't feel like a victor, the casualties are too high for that. But our assignment, we will complete it,' commented D'Haese.

"The connection was restored and the telephone immediately rang. Steiner wished the Kampfgruppe the best of luck against the overpowering infantry and tanks. 'You all have done more than your duty with this defense. I know of the hellish barrage of fire and the bombing your group has endured, and it isn't over yet, the Flemings must continue to hold.' he said. I received my new orders from D'Haese and rushed back with Fons Van Broeck. At the front raged a volcano of gray smoke. There were exploding bombs and grenades, stinking streams of smoke, dust and the dead. The men had a hard task which they had to master. Schörner and Steiner trusted it to the Flemings to hold the crossing of two powerful forces, here in Estonia. There were still four as far as I knew.[39] I sent a messenger, who was to report on casualties. The messengers came and went. At the PAK Horre and Sobry were wounded and stayed with the wounded Schrijnen. It's only scratches, they said. I thought of Rehmann... The composure of these men... I knew it was against all rules of the officer, but here at the front in action it was not those with rank that played the main roles, it was every single soldier. It was also those that didn't even ever get to see an officer. One had to simply be there to be able to be able to judge what every single one performed – not what a platoon, a company or a regiment performed. Because it was the men that had the fullest trust in their leaders and carried out their orders. This day was a success. Then the night came. I went to my gun. Only Leo Tollenaere and Miel Sobry were there.

" 'Where are Remy and the others?' I asked.

" 'They are on patrol – no one knows what the Soviets could try. They could send out small patrols to penetrate our lines in this darkness. We have to do a little bit of night work ourselves,' responded Leo.

"There was a small shoot-out during the night as Strooband discovered a Russian patrol troop. He discovered them as he noticed a flattened section of wheat field. With machine guns and machine pistols he and his men finished some of them off while the rest of the patrol fled. The next morning all of the men returned.

" 'Nothing special to report,' said Schrijnen.

"Then came the Kommandeur, a twenty-one year old who looked much older. He looked around at everything, the cratered landscape and all.

" 'What bad luck, Laperre, I mean about your platoon, but this gun makes everything equal again,' commented D'Haese.

---

[39] That would be Untersturmführer D'Haese, Untersturmführer Van Leemputten , Untersturmführer Laperre and Standartenoberjunker Roger Groenvinck. A 'leader' was not necessarily an officer.

"D'Haese saw the gun's smashed protection shields, covered with holes from bullets and shrapnel. The men were already trying to fix up their camouflage. This was the last PAK gun in an uneven fight against the giant tanks.

" 'I counted over a dozen tanks laying out in that field, blown up or damaged. And the help against the infantry...' D'Haese then began to slightly smile. 'You all have accomplished something.' 'Man, Laperre..' continued D'Haese, 'my men, my infantrymen, these boys...this is a chapter in history, this bridgehead is, a battle of unknown hardness. It is our luck that we have only a few men that have never been on the front before.' D'Haese then ran his finger over the dried spot of blood on Schrijnen's smock, 'Without the men with front-line experience we never would have been successful. Because when this fire-waltz lasts for hours and teeters back and forth you have to be able to hold your nerves and not run stupidly into death. Yeah, Laperre, I know this feeling and I am happy that there are still a lot of old ones with us. Yeah, today we leaders can learn a lot that one could never learn as well in a leadership school, but what one has to learn in combat. You and I see it here at this single gun, every single man knows his duties and carries them out without orders.' "

By the end of the day the Flemings were positioned on Grenadier Hill. Many of the men had been killed or wounded. Unfortunately about fifty men of the battle group had remained in the Orphanage itself. Georg D'Haese reported long after the war:[40]

At the end of the day on July 27th, there were still about fifty men located in the shot-up orphanage. With a patrol troop of about thirty men I tried to free those that remained there. We crawled forward, meter for meter, and after about twenty meters we came across some of our previous positions, which were annihilated. We heard the men who were still located in the Orphanage call to us. Then we couldn't advance any more. Thereafter came a barrage of fire during which we pressed ourselves against the ground. The barrage wounded and killed some of my men. Some of them crawled back, others waited for darkness to come. We had seen the hands of our comrades reaching to us – but couldn't grasp them.

---

[40] Letter to the author from G. D'Haese dated March 24, 1997.

The "**Kinderheimhöhe**": This is a picture of Orphanage Hill in the summer of 1944.

The "**Grenadierhöhe**": This is a picture of Grenadier Hill in the summer of 1944.

A View from the Trenches: This picture was supposedly taken from the trenches around Orphanage Hill in the summer of 1944.

During the night – with Steiner's approval – I put together a new patrol troop, some Estonians and men from other units came along as well. It was an evil slaughter – man against man. There were calls and screams. The surrounded men in the Orphanage tried to break out – but for nothing. Everything for nothing. After two hours we were back, dead tired, sad and depressed – as well as wounded. We hadn't reached our goal.

Third Day of Battle: July 28, 1944

The Russian General Govorov wanted to force the decision. Eleven infantry divisions and six tank brigades stood before the "Tannenberg" line. Eleven against four. Obergruppenführer Steiner was a feared opponent. His method was to place all of his fire power at the right position. But even this experienced soldier was no magician. The bled battalions and regiments would not be able to offer resistance to the massive storm of Russians much longer. In the early morning the battles erupted once again. The focal point of the battle, as the day before, was Orphanage Hill, where the Estonians and Russians were fighting in hand-to-hand combat.

The Norwegians prepared a new attack after a short German artillery barrage. As soon as they advanced from their positions, the Russians decked them with artillery fire. Then came the enemy dive-bombers which shredded them. Even the Estonians had to retreat and pull back to Grenadier Hill, where they took position with the Germans and the Flemings in the trenches. At 1000 hours the Russians stormed Grenadier Hill with tanks and a mass of infantry and attempted to break-through the lines along the Chundirnurk-Kirikukula highway. The German artillery then laid down an intensive barrage and a few of the Russian tanks were annihilated.

The only remaining PAK with its leader Grootaers and his no. 1 gunner Remy Schrijnen stood in a very dangerous position as several Russian tanks rolled onto the terrain. Grootaers screamed not to move from their position and Schrijnen's nerves were again strong. Schrijnen did not flinch until he had the most dangerous tank in his sights. And then it was fire, fire, fire. Four Russian tanks were burning and those that remained took aim at Grootaers' PAK. All the German guns began to fire and as the Russian tanks turned to flee, the others followed. Grootaers' PAK remained undamaged. His PAK continued to serve as the look-out post for the remaining infantry. The landscape built an important defensive position, especially for fighting against tanks, since on the one side of the road was the Finnish Gulf and on the other side was a large swamp. The only secure land was a strip about four kilometers wide which was guarded by the German forces. This is where the Russians continued to concentrate their attack. The attack was supported by a continuous wave of infantry units and Russian tanks. Wave after wave came and after each attack remained the survivors who only had to wait for the next attack. The attacks continued, supported by fighter planes and naval artillery.

The fighting in Schrijnen's section lasted uninterrupted and the Russians continuously attempted to break through the trenches held by Kampfgruppe "D'Haese." The Russians would often have to be beaten back with pistols and shovels, but the battle groups managed to hold their positions.

On this third day of the battle, five more T-34s were defeated by Grootaers' PAK. By the end of this particular phase of the battle, the PAK sat surrounded by craters left by the misses from the Russian's T-34s, naval artillery shells and artillery. The gun itself, however, continued to remain intact. A *Nebelwerfer* battery was rushed into the battle and gave D'Haese's men some relief, but just before the burden placed on Grootaers' PAK was about to be slightly relieved, the Russians renewed their attack. During the initial phases of the advance, Schrijnen was wounded in the shoulder. Grootaers, worried about his Richtschütze's health, retreated to fetch a medic. As he returned with the medic and several other men, a Russian a naval artillery round killed him and the others. They were just a few meters away from the gun's position. Two other soldiers were wounded and Schrijnen was also wounded a second time, this time receiving shrapnel in the face. Now Remy was left to act as both Geschützführer and Richtschütze.

Marcel Laperre continued:[41]

"...this man, a simple Sturmmann, then lead my only remaining PAK Geschütz while at the same time being the Richtschütze. He was a specialist for these suicide operations, be it in retreat during 43-44 or with the rearguard destroying the Russian Pakriegel. I knew from my Kompanie Führer, my Spieß, our Kompanie war diary and from stories that the men surrounding this Sturmmann from the past did not like to talk about their doings along the road to Jambol. No one ever mentioned how these men dug in along the road and fought. Then I was on the front for the first time as an officer and leader – in the thick of it with this Kampfgruppe. I watched how every single man stayed calm, whether under massive attacks from Panzers or infantry. No one abandoned their post. I sensed my own doubts as I watched the men remain behind weapons until they were killed or wounded. One after the other they held out for hours under pressure from heavy artillery fire and dive bombers. The men beat off the attacks and without receiving orders, they attacked themselves when they had to, death and the devil beside them. The inexperienced noticed during this heavy action what kind of determination these brave men and experienced warriors possessed. They had the determination to decide every situation. For these men this was nothing and they always arrived at my post with 'nothing special to report.' Despite the many grim situations, the men still took the opportunity to smile. I happened upon a severely wounded man with a smile on his face. He said to me, 'perhaps a ticket home.' Such an experience cannot be described in words, especially when one knows that he may be saying 'good-bye' forever. The men in this inferno of thick, stinking smoke and columns of fire remained in their positions as deafening bomb explosions surrounded them. A Sturmmann came to me and said to me with a look of conviction, 'Yeah, Untersturmführer, the climax of the battle has been reached and we're staying!' I looked out to the forest and saw a very gloomy

---

[41] Schrijnen notebook.

situation. All of the young soldiers were dead or badly wounded. These men battled everything to the ground, infantry, anti-tank guns, tanks, trucks, all in calm heroism, all while under fire from bombs and grenades. The air thundered, the ground shook and bullets from dive-bombers nailed our positions shut. I saw the remains of shredded men laying in craters and foxholes. The Red Army responded to their defeated infantry and tanks with firestorms launched from Stalin Organs and masses of rockets with their disastrous effect. Our men were right in the middle of it. The pressure in the air from the stink of burnt gunpowder was intense, but our men stayed in their trenches, unshaved, unclean, with two hours of sleep at the most. The men carried out the heaviest burden of the battle. We officers gave the orders, the men carried them out. The effect of Rehmann's failure as commander had little effect on the men. In the middle of February he came to Langemarck with a replacement company to fight at the front. The years he spent in Antwerp and Brussels had turned him into a coward. In contrast to him, the troops knew their commander, Georg D'Haese, and had the fullest trust in him, they knew which leaders could and could not.

"Then there was something going on over by the PAK, Remy must have seen something. I looked through my field glasses and viewed the edge of the forest. The barrage of fire had started up again. Everything was flying all over the place. Schrijnen once told me, 'to attack is sometimes the best defense – but only at the right time, Untersturmführer.' I also remember that he told me that we were on the street of death. When I think of all the badly wounded that Tollenaere brought back and when I see all of the Russian's knocked out tanks, trucks and their dead and wounded, I thought to myself that Remy was right, it was the street of death. I looked out to the edge of the forest once again and I saw a Russian anti-tank gun with a crew member working feverishly with his poker.

" 'Yeah,' said Adrian Heusdens, 'Remy said that the luck of a Panzerjäger only lasts until he comes across a better one.'

"Fons Van Broeck, one of the oldest Kradmelder (motorcycle messengers) from the time of the Legion, came along and told me that I was to report to the Kommandobunker. Everything at the bunker was thrown all over the place. I reported to the Kommandeur and told him of my gloomy experiences. D'Haese replied that he is proud of his Kampfgruppe. I knew that this primitive command post would never fail. The commander was surrounded by four men, three of which were messengers.

"Fieremans came and stood before the commander, 'nothing special to report, I just got done loading wounded with Tollenaere, the worst of which we brought to the rear lines. Now we want to load some ammo for the PAK,' he said.

" 'Good,' responded commander D'Haese, 'bring it to the cannon.'

" 'Yeah, Marcel,' continued D'Haese, 'you have had a lot of luck with this single PAK Geschütz. Such men, that fight so bravely.'

" 'Yeah, Kotlowski told me, let Schrijnen do as he wishes,' I replied, 'he takes on every risk and has the courage to say what he thinks, always the truth, he's a go-getter and acts on impulse. The men stand behind him without any recognition. This group of men, they know what is expected of them.

"I didn't dare say what Schrijnen said about Rehmann, and as if he was reading my mind D'Haese replied very officially, 'Yeah, Untersturmführer, the Landser who can always look death in the eye on this stage also tends to have quite a snout and almost never holds a piece of paper in front of his mouth.'

"I agreed and thought that Remy's frankness could cost him his head one day, but I noticed that other men of the Legion could swear up a storm. But I knew what went through the heads of these men, thoughts of betrayal and lies were not even possible, these men loved the truth. I spoke with Sturmmann Albert Vincent, D'Hollander's driver, and he told me how Schrijnen had sent Rehmann away from his gun. This report made me sure that brave soldiers like Vincent told only the truth, even about a higher officer.

"D'Haese interrupted my thoughts once again: 'Now Marcel, all men fight to the last bullet, it is not we leaders that are the role models, but the men, the men who carry out our orders. Even though we are officers, everything works fine without us, we can't be everywhere at the same time. It could be that the men and their doings are what make us leaders. Sure, we can send men here and there, help them on occasion, but the average man must remain alone. He can't console himself or scold himself, as before him stands the enemy. In battle he can't refuse to act. We can be leaders, but the men are the followers. Whether the enlisted man looks to his officers as leaders or not, his duties are difficult, the fate of the rest of the men often depends on him. As leaders our responsibilities are more important. Our orders determine the life and death of our men in victory or defeat, and then we flee when something is not successful. I mean, everything depends on the men, and we never ask ourselves under what pressure these men operate, since because of our ranks and because of our positions, we don't operate under the same conditions. Be it the building of positions, trenches, bunkers, or in battle, in heat, rain or frost, without a single night's sleep, the men are mostly under extreme pressure. Yeah, Marcel, I personally did it myself as a simple soldier, I know what I am talking about, we leaders always think that without us the men are really nothing. But isn't it really the other way around? The man in action must fight, act, and must be able to react lightning fast. In new situations he must adapt quickly, as a leader is never around to help him out. Our responsibilities determine the fate of many men and it is up to us leaders to try and understand every situation correctly. Luck also plays a large role in everything. Yeah, nowadays, since the beginning of 1944, we have no more aerial reconnaissance and it hasn't become any easier to lead, but it is even more difficult for the small group leader and the Landser.'

" 'Yes, Untersturmführer,' I replied, "it is men that I now command, everything is different than we were taught at Bad Tölz.

" 'Yes, Marcel,' D'Haese responded, 'school has never been the front. What is taught at such a good leadership academy really has to be learned at the front. One has to learn within the walls of reality, change things around and make them fit, far from all theories of the war schools. Here everything is different, here no one is allowed to refuse, because to refuse on the front costs blood, valuable blood, that of all the best men. You will still yet find out what a simple Sturmmann, Rottenführer or old NCO is worth. They are it, the so-called 'back-bone' of the army, the men, the do-ers, those that are always at the front of the battle without any leaders. A platoon leader or company commander cannot be everywhere. It is here that one has to know how to act with forty or perhaps with only twenty men, against an attacking enemy. There are no more exercises to be conducted in the field, no more sand bags, just danger – and still worse, having to operate despite heavy losses of dead, wounded, and even material. As far as I know the men, no one plays the role of 'hero.' These men act depending on the situation. They are volunteers and every man fights according to his own method. These men are heroes, men without nerves, may I say, because even today no man has run away from the fight. Men like these are rare. So many men have seen their comrades become killed or wounded. Now, Untersturmführer Laperre, off to the front with my orders."

Marcel Laperre continued:[42]

"Later I said to Remy, 'Too bad that Unterscharführer Grootaers fell.'

" 'One should not speak about death,' said Schrijnen, 'there is already too much death, life goes on.'

"The men behaved excellently, even though we had only one gun left. The soldiers lay in the craters, not carelessly, but definitely unconcerned and unimpressed. New formations continuously attacked. I heard the noise of the fight and watched as the poor infantry bore the brunt of the battle. I heard someone call to me, 'nothing to do, Untersturmführer, only peace could save us,' he said with a smile. Something like that I hadn't imagined for my first action at the front – for me everything was still a puzzle. Schrijnen was an experienced man, who had already proved himself often while with the Legion and the Brigade. I saw his laughing dark and daring eyes light up under his helmet. They called him a 'lone wolf' when he was a foot messenger. His lively eyes let others know that he was different, he knew no limits. If he thought he hadn't understood something correctly, he was always there to ask questions. Or if he felt that initiatives hadn't been carried out, he was always there to explain. 'What do you think?' he would constantly ask. Kotlowski had advised me well, said Paul, Juul and Leo. Remy is very careless with his life, but in difficult situations he was bound to all of the laws of reason. He always said, 'I am not the only one that can ignore the beating fire of the incoming artillery or the shower of bombs, I am not any better, all of you lie right in the middle of it all.' I remembered when Schrijnen said to me, 'Yeah, Untersturmführer, the time of the sandbags is over, now you must deal with reality, because now it isn't a game anymore. The life and death of your men are at stake and it is victory that you must achieve.' It was difficult to judge such a man, especially if you didn't know him. During training he was very tough on himself, especially during combat training, and he required the same from his comrades. At first I thought that he must be a soldier with a sense of adventure, a go-getter with no patience. While on the front I tried to understand this man, he had no pity for himself. I heard him say, 'When it comes down to it, a soldier must only think and act in a soldierly way. That means put everything into it, your own life as well.' This was a man who accomplished so much. He didn't even know how he exposed himself to danger. He was a

---

[42] Schrijnen notebook.

man who jumped in for another. His comrades belonged to him, not one of them wanted to be transferred to another Geschütz or group. Remy said to me 'a go-getter is a man that doesn't let his feelings be shown in critical situations and can't become weak.' The men looked at his face, he was trusted and had luck, that was the most important thing. Grootaers said to me on the second day that Remy had not 'stolen' his reputation, but that he was more than dependable. In just a few days I had learned more than the entire time I was at Bad Tölz.

"Then there was the men of the infantry. They crept around silently during the night, switching posts back and forth, and were experienced men. Rubens, Fieremans and Oberscharführer Blaha, my second in command, all talked about Hauptsturmführer Knorr. I had read the company's action reports, and there appeared 'Geschütz Dahlhoff' again and again, how hard and bitterly these men had fought during those early months in 1944.

"Then came Fieremans with new orders from Kommandeur D'Haese for the leaders and the troops. More attacks were to be expected and he wanted to know what was up with the PAK Geschütz, since it was very important, very important for the infantry as it was used to support them with Sprenggranaten. I wrote my response about the situation at the front, about what was going on at the PAK Geschütz and how the PAK smashed the Soviet's anti-tank guns and Ratschbumm on the edge of the forest and also about our remaining strength. There was nothing to keep secret, we had heavy casualties. But the success of the battle group against the overpowering Soviets weighed heavier than everything else. The spirit of the men there was definitely a one-time occurrence. The Kommandeur wanted to know what was still available, that was Georg D'Haese's order. I sent Fieremans off to the Kommandeur. Fieremans, the old man, was no longer with his leather motorcycle overcoat. I followed him with my eyes as he passed some wire strippers (signals men) who lay dead. They had been smashed during a barrage.

"Through my head ran thoughts.... a few days at the front and I had gotten to know some of these men very well. One shouldn't get to know their names or write them down, 'but they should,' said Remy, 'one should know which man was where and when and what he did.' As Schellong saw me off he said to me, 'Damn, for the first time I am not going to be with my men of the Legion and the Sturmbrigade.' Now I knew what it meant to say 'my men.' I had heard so much about Schrijnen, Spieß Wallow himself had said

'Untersturmführer, that is the man you can trust with everything. I have known him for a long time personally since the time of the Legion. An order is an order for Remy, and he carries it out, sometimes in his own way, he has a seventh sense, Untersturmführer, you know.' In the middle of this thought I heard the crackling of grenade shrapnel and strong machine gun fire, the men took their positions and readied themselves for the defense. The rage of the attacks were beaten back with an even bigger rage. As a young leader I was astonished at the intensity of my own baptism at the front. It wasn't as easy as I had thought. Many times I had to swallow hard. The men were outside day and night. There was rocky ground, shot up bunkers, dead and wounded comrades all over. A good a third of the Kampfgruppe was at that time dead or wounded. I climbed the Grenadier Hill, I had to think about my boys and help was not to be expected. As a leader I knew I had too little front-line experience, the men with front-line experience, my own men, well I was happy to have them. Men like Tollenaere, Van Broeck, Fieremans, Rubens, Vincent and so many admirable men, all in my platoon. During the night came the Russian artillery for hours, it would be a sleepless night for many. There were huge detonations and noises from the dying wounded, a combination which perhaps killed my men deep inside. I went to the Geschütz. Excluding the guard, many of the men were in a dead sleep – despite the noise – but were immediately awake at the first hint of danger. The inner instinct of sensing danger had long ago been awakened in these men. I knew then that being scared and fear were not the same. Schrijnen had explained to me that fear is inside and can turn a man into a coward, and render him unable to react when threatened. 'I have never known fear,' said Remy, 'but when I am scared, I swallow those feelings hard.' Astonishing thoughts from the daredevil himself, a man who was known to have no fear and proved himself in every situation. Not insane courage, but well thought-out planning, this was how I got to know Schrijnen, a man who maintained the trust of his men, a man from which calmness and confidence streamed, a realist, a soldier, a political fanatic. I later spoke with D'Haese about the group.

" 'Yeah,' said D'Haese, 'Laperre, you had barely become a recruit and then were immediately shipped off to officer's school, never having fought at the front, never suffered at the front, never in winter, summer, snow or rain. You have been with the Kampfgruppe for a few days, in the middle of some of the most difficult battles ever – and you have the best men – men who you don't have to worry about. They are fighters, they build bunkers, positions, stand guard, you know Laperre, as a leader you should have done these things already, because the little men in the forward-most trenches and foxholes, they carry the main burden of the war, it is they that have to lay in the hurricane of fire, continuing the fight, some while wounded. When I think of Rehmann, the man that left with only a scratch, I have to change my impression of the leader. This image, that only the best go to the leadership schools, is somewhat false. Yes, I noticed that at the leadership schools that 99.9% were college students. When I think of men like Fieremans, Tollenaere, Saelein, Vormeveren, Strooband, Kasper D'Haese and Lafronski, I think that these men could be strong, excellent leaders. So many capable men go to the front direct from the leadership schools and then have to depend on the 'alte Hasen.' I thought about it and I think that I will let Schrijnen continue running his crew, I don't want to assign an Unterscharführer to his crew.

"At the PAK it was calm, there was only a shell here and there. While creeping through the trenches I heard good things about the PAK. The men didn't know that I was the PAK's Zugführer. Strooband and Vermeeren, who both knew Schrijnen well, told me, 'Yeah, Remy, back then he was with the Sturmbrigade on the retreat along they highway to Jambol. So many battles were fought by the 3-ringed Geschütz along that highway. He shot the highway clear, be it against anti-tank guns or infantry. The men had guts. Today, on the Narva front, it this man once again who is holding out.

"Dive-bombers combed the landscape, but everything was calm. Hands and faces were in the dirt. In the vicinity of the PAK fell bombs and rockets from the Stalin's Organs. My driver, Leo Tollenaere, approached me, 'Geschütz Schrijnen, everything in order, Remy is lightly wounded, but they survived though, Untersturmführer. War reporters were there and Remy told them that they should go see the platoon leaders or the infantry. 'Yeah' said the war reporters, 'no one sends us there!' ' The war reporters always made fun of the enlisted men, I thought. Leo then continued 'Remy was so quiet and barely said a word, but Horre and Sobry wouldn't shut up.'

"What struck me as a leader is that whenever I spoke about the commander, every man named Untersturmführer Georg D'Haese, no one named Hauptsturmführer Rehmann. Remy must have been right when he said that Rehmann was a coward and that the men would walk through the worst fire for D'Haese. I had to go on. I saw a man run out of the enemy barrage with a

Laperre's Driver: Pictured above is Leo Tollenaere, who served as Marcel Laperre's driver for the battles in the Blue Mountains. Tollenaere had enlisted in the Waffen-SS after his older brother, Dr. Reimond Tollenaere, was killed in action. Tollenaere was approximately 28 years old during the battles, an old man in comparison with the majority of the others. In contrast, his platoon Leader, Marcel Laperre, was only 21 during the summer of 1944. Tollenaere survived the battles and the war.

ripped open stomach, pushing his intestine back in. He was running to the rear, I hoped he would make it. The strength of the men touched me deep inside, I had so much to learn here on the front, everything was new. Character, calm heroism, everyone was just a young man. Despite this they could still smile and be happy when someone called to them. Normally the men took every risk in battle and wanted to live. None of the men I spoke with felt special. The heavy desire of the storming communists brought about our desire to remain. The Soviets were bloodily beaten back while their new replacements kept coming into the fire. That day was tough, although our PAK did what it could. I went with Groenvinck here and there, there and here, ordering men here and there. Kommandeur D'Haese held his head high despite the continuing casualties of his battle group. With great desire and strength, with a healthy trust of himself, he knew the old ones of the Legion. His confidence was not guarded. The men in this dangerous situation knew each other, some being men used to being alone, who acted just as the other hundreds of thousands of other men in the same uniform. The order was above the man. On both sides stood brave soldiers; on our side quality, on theirs quantity. The casualties of the masses of attacking Soviets were shocking even for our leaders. There were too many men available on the other side, and the Russians continuously threw them into the fire. Was it a worthwhile price that they paid?

"I saw two or three men join the battle without being ordered. 'An order from within,' Untersturmführer D'Haese said to me, 'and also an unclear law of the soldier. The boys are holding their nerves, Laperre. At one time they reported as volunteers because of this order from within, an order that was more like a war, just as it is today. Only now the comrades have become harder, tougher. They have seen too much in Russia. The suffering and hardship of the Russian people.... The men volunteered and knew why and for what. They are clever, brave and modest men, too modest. They experience the brutality of war for the first time on the front. The single PAK gun of your platoon fights without receiving orders. An old legionnaire, a Sturmmann, leads there, ably and successfully. There are also such men in the infantry companies and platoons. They do as I order, holding out and fighting. The old experienced men creep around to wherever they feel that the fire of the battle could return. They pay close attention when they are out there. It is from there that they report to me what the men say or recommend. These men carry a certain responsibility on their consciousness and they can do it, for there is only victory or death. The men, Laperre, they have trust in you, in Groenvinck and in their Kommandeur, they are sure that we are able on our turf, we have our own opinion about tactics and strategy. I know that I now have the name of a commander, with which one can never get used to. I must behave hard and without compromise above you all, I must maintain the decisiveness and the toughness to be a shining improviser on this battlefield. I was with the men earlier and they said to me, 'we'll do it Untersturmführer!' Yeah, Laperre, they are my comrades from the Legion, I am one of them, their Kommandeur who cares for everything. I am the right man, an able leader who can grasp the situation and make his orders clear and understandable for everyone. I think the men take me seriously because I was with them from 1941 to 1943 with the Legion in the trenches as a simple soldier. You know Marcel," he said, "I am a man who was spent much time in the trenches and who sees clearly and judges impartially. You, on the other hand, have only now seen such fighting for the first time – and indeed as a young officer. Sometimes you take part, when the battle teeters back and forth for hours. And when I give the order not to take a step back, it is then that the men must rule a field full with the enemy and hold their line. These men are necessary – these independent fighters who make their own decisions. They are brave and sacrificing soldiers and comrades. Ask them for their advice calmly and that will be a sign to them that you are an experienced leader. The men with front line experience have knowledge and an iron and unshakable calmness – a clear understanding in action,' finished the Kommandeur.

"A dry crack called me back to reality, my PAK Geschütz called me to the fight, I crept forward over the hill. It was Panzerjäger against Panzerjäger and grenades whistled incessantly on by. I heard grenade fragments thunder against the armor plating of the PAK. The 7.5 cm Geschütz unloaded itself and the rounds echoed on the edge of the forest. I then saw how mixed-up everything operates with the men. A group of them had been formed almost a year before this great battle: Kamiel Horre, Paul Rubens, Miel Sobry, Leo Tollenaere, Schrijnen – these were the experienced men. These men had strong nerves. The fire cannon then swelled and grenades and bombs exploded against it for hours. I had to go on, I had seen enough of these men. Adrian Heusdens enlisted with me in 1943, Van Dem Beamten too. The attack came and we immediately heard the energetic bellowing answer of the Russian PAK. The incoming rounds made this place look like hell. Bomb after bomb shook the ground. Dirt and rocks flew high in the air. There was a lot of smoke and the stink of burning gunpowder was intense. D'Haese's men were standing on the edge of annihilation. The falling bombs cracked hard and brought death with their explosions. We were still there. We remained with conviction on that battlefield. Where did these men get their hardness? Their relaxed attitude astonished me. There was the trust that every man had when I came with new orders. For me, as an inexperienced young leader, this was something astonishing.

"The men spoke freely. 'Untersturmführer, we'll do it, the order will be carried out,' they would say. This is impossible to describe, this character, unclouded by jealousy or rank. One knew and followed these men, their advice and their orders. I talked with Paul Rubens, Juul Fieremans and Fons Van Broeck, all who had known Schrijnen since 1942 when he was a foot messenger with the Legion Flandern before Leningrad. I also spoke with my driver, Leo Tollenaere, who had known Schrijnen since 1943. They all told me about this unusual soldier and his behavior. Whether in the barracks or at the front, he was always the same. Remy was the best comrade that there was. According to Rubens, Remy was at home on the front, he was happy to be there and made sure that the others did not stray. He took part in every dangerous assignment or carried it out himself. Schrijnen had the capabilities to understand the situation and knew how he had to act. He wasn't a know-it-all that didn't ask others for advice, but he made up his mind lightning-quick.

" 'I was with Dahlhoff and Schrijnen from the end of 1943 until March 1944. We were the team with the three-ringed Geschütz. We were known and requested again and again,' said Rubens, 'be it to smash the Russian Pakriegel or to cover a retreat. Now we are together again, Remy as Richtschütze and Geschützführer here at Narva.'

" 'He carries out his duties as if he was playing a game,' said Paul and Leo, 'Remy has a higher sense of responsibility, and in action he is hard on himself and he acts without regard for his safety. And he expects the same from his comrades.

" 'Yeah,' said Fieremans, 'that's how we know Remy, Untersturmführer.' I was naturally very happy as a platoon leader about the success of this last remaining Geschütz."

Marcel Laperre continued:[43]

"Then came Albert Vincent, 'Untersturmführer, could you come to our group?' We crept and crawled away from the Geschütz and before us stood a platoon in defense of the attacking enemy infantry. A small hill protected these Ivans from the PAK and after about twenty minutes the men beat them back across the field from where they came. 'Untersturmführer!' called one, 'we need ammunition!' Albert Vincent was already on the way with three other men without even asking. Yeah, Sturmmann Vincent was a good six or seven years older than me. Schrijnen had told me 'Vincent, Paul Rubens, Jan Withaegels[44] and Leo Tollenaere aren't good drivers but can fight like the devil himself.' I remembered that Remy had told me a story how Vincent had driven up to the highway where burning vehicles were, despite Reeb's orders not to. They had Remy in the back, who was badly wounded, and were taking him back to our medics. Reeb cried for Vincent not to drive on the highway, he was afraid that one of the burning Sturmgeschütze would blow, but Vincent didn't listen. Reeb jumped off and ran along the highway, keeping his distance from the burning Sturmgeschütze and shouting to Vincent to get off the

---

[43] Schrijnen notebook.
[44] During the battles in the Blue Mountains Withaigels served as the driver for Unterscharführer Reeb (2. Geschütz). Withaigels had fought in the battles to Jambol in early 1944 where he served as the driver for Geschützführer Unterscharführer Chantraine.

highway. Since Reeb was faster than the truck he got ahead of Vincent and waited up ahead past the burning vehicles. There he watched Vincent, the poor driver he was, as he almost smashed into a burning Sturmgeschütz. Fortunately he managed to just graze it. As he approached Reeb, he didn't slow down to pick him up, but just kept on going.

"Ah... Remy. I could say, with him only the eyes in his brown face move. But his men knew his ice-cold voice. He sat on the spar of the gun, a foxhole wasn't there for the Richtschütze, his hole was distanced from the gun for security. Because in action the Richtschütze sat on the spar or bent over with his eye on the telescopic sight. He had to be able to move freely while the barrel recoiled.

" 'It comes right down to the second,' Remy advised the boys. 'Think about Unterscharführer D'Hollander,' he said with a stern look in his eyes. Then we knew it could get serious.

"Later we watched as Remy came from the trenches and jogged towards the gun. Then from out of nowhere came a few Soviet fighter planes, hammering behind him. The Red fliers, who often whipped everything into a mess, fired cross shots onto boulders. Then Remy changed directions and rushed away from the Geschütz position towards the dummy position. Lightning quick he would appear again and again, and besides being strafed, nothing else happened to him. Such luck.

" 'My own stupidity, I should have stayed somewhere in a foxhole,' said the Richtschütze and Geschützführer. 'But then again, that's how I diverted the dive-bomber from our position,' he quickly added thereafter.

"Then I heard a rumbling... 'Untersturmführer, get in our dug-out or out to the men in the trenches! Those are Stalin's Organs, a few batteries of them,' a man said. Already it was cracking from every side, all around us. There was the stink of burning gun powder and one could barely breath. 'Gun still in order!' called the Geschützführer to me. I was stunned. 'Yeah,' he said, 'instead of shooting in waves the Russians shoot these things all at once. Their mistake, because in the mean time we can take a break and breath some fresh air.'

" 'Yeah,' said Schrijnen, 'that's how they waste all their ammo.'

"The men suffered from nausea from the stink of the burning gun powder and had no chance to recover. Schrijnen continued, 'When the Russians begin to retreat we continue hitting their infantry with everything we have, because this finishes them off and demoralizes most of the survivors. The remaining soldiers become insecure – I know this feeling but have overcome it.'

"The Bolsheviks broke out from the edge of the forest. Here and there they made small advances, but it seemed as if they never came to any kind of decision concerning an attack plan. After a while the Soviets began to probe the front.... and with much confidence. I said to my Richtschütze, 'Na Schrijnen, let them dance!'

" 'Untersturmführer, it could be too early, do you think this is really an attack or a trick? – Because they aren't storming as they usually do,' answered Schrijnen.

"The advances were easily intercepted by our own infantry. The PAK was calm, the Soviets didn't do anything further. The experienced infantrymen could feel the danger and crept into forward positions. Then the Soviets gave it a try with a crowbar. Even to the right of us it appeared as if all hell had broken loose. The Norwegians, Danes and Dutch and part of 'Nordland' stood there ... those troops felt the heaviest brunt of the battle. Then I heard the crackling... Artillery, mortars and Stalin's Organs raged for hours over our positions on the Grenadier- and Love's Hill. Men lay deep in there foxholes. 'Damn!' I thought to myself, 'I can't get out of here!' Then and again steel would hit steel. 'The gun is still OK,' I heard someone call. 'Almost ready for action,' called Adrian Heusdens. The fire-waltz was a few kilometers long and a few hundred meters deep. Suddenly everything stopped, but one could hear the humming of the Red Air Force. Then bombs were falling. I didn't know how I was surviving this... I looked out of my foxhole and I saw that Schütze I, II and III were already at their places. The planes were dive-bombing but nothing moved.... Then the Soviets streamed from the forest, the dive bombers took the rear terrain. The Wehrmacht's artillery fired, but only for a short time. Then I was at the PAK and got a chance to see how everything worked there. Shot after shot... I noticed that the machine gun must also secure the gun from the rear – against the dive bombers. 'Jawohl!' called Van Dem Beamten. Wave after wave attacked, the battle teetered back and forth. Rubens, Tollenaere, Fieremans and Van Broeck dragged PAK munitions to the gun. 'We're running low,' said Leo, 'but what luck, Spieß Wallow brought up more rounds during the night.' What a man, I thought to myself, such a Spieß.. even during the night there was heavy fire that fell on the supply roads. Luckily these roads don't lead through the swamps as most did. The battle waged for hours. 'Undecided' said Vermeeren. Then I was one of three leaders there at the front. Kotlowski had said to me, 'Laperre, you have the lead platoon and the lead gun – a man with success and luck. Trust him calmly, because Grootaers and his men are dependable. I have just enough front line experience to just about see through the men, even though Schrijnen makes me wild. But he can take a lot of abuse and admits it openly and honestly when he makes a mistake.'

"Kotlowski's men were then my men and it was the very same Richtschütze that secretly agonized me, although I didn't let anyone know it. Schrijnen, with his damned 'Kopfstellung.' And then he took over the leadership of the Geschütz and I was not needed there.

"The PAK bellowed into wave after wave of attacking soldiers. 'Hopefully we won't lose this last PAK gun, it's the cornerstone of our defense,' said Strooband. The strength of our battle group sunk. From more than 400 men in action in the trenches there were perhaps only 200 men left. The remaining 200 were dead or badly wounded, the lightly wounded stayed or came back to their comrades at their own will. I was astonished at such toughness. At the Junkerschule we thought, 'it could never be as hard at the front like it is here at Bad Tölz.' And it was I who got the lesson: Bad Tölz was a rest home compared to those few days with the Kampfgruppe. The troop's desire to hold out stood far above the level of intensity of the leadership school. I then knew that the battling troops fought for something real, the holding of the front. At the leadership school we fought to become officers. It was a big difference. We were ready to go day and night at the front. There was no time for rest. And as soon as you were half asleep, someone would call, 'wake up!' Patrols crept here and there. I had to continually tell myself to be calm, and not to listen to the fire.

"It was the end of July and the Russian Navy decked the Grenadier Hill and the Love Hill with heavy artillery rounds. They were shooting at us, but luckily our men in the bunkers, in the Kommandobunker and in the Medics bunker, had dug in deep enough so that there were no dead. The infantrymen praised the work of the PAK since it could attack the storming Russians at a distance of nine hundred to one thousand meters. Here the PAK had to risk everything, even our camouflaged position. To beat up the tanks and the infantry was the task of the PAK. It had to immediately attack the masses, our infantry had already bled so much that the PAK could only help somewhat.

The violent numbers of Russians and material against this section of Langemarck in Estonia's Blue Mountains....

" 'A proud feeling to lead such men. I know for myself the life in the trenches and I know what these men can withstand,' said Kommandeur D'Haese himself.

"On the day when Kommandeur Rehmann not only failed, but abandoned the Kampfgruppe as a coward, Untersturmführer Georg D'Haese overtook the command of the Kampfgruppe. The 21-year-old, as commander, stood in the way of a large Soviet offensive there in the Blue Mountains of Estonia. The Soviets were looking for a seam between the lines, a place where they could break through, and that was where the Kampfgruppe Langemarck stood. Reserves were not available to D'Haese, there were barely any heavy weapons. The Kampfgruppe 'Langemarck' was to blunt the lead units of the advancing Russian offensive and prevent a breakthrough at all costs. The condition of the Kampfgruppe was not very rosy. D'Haese stood slender before me and took my message. There was a smile on his lean face, he was also a Fleming.

" 'Now I am worried,' said D'Haese, 'whether the thin defensive front will hold, looking at the latest reports. The casualties in the last few days are damned high for my Kampfgruppe.'

"The sunburned faces of the men were hard and glazed like leather. The faces looked me straight in the eyes, I could only see determination in them. There I get to know men with more character than I had ever known. These men knew of the face of death, how the features of the face change. These men had seen the dying already too often, the dying that got shot or took shrapnel. They saw how death came to the dirty, distorted and twisted faces, how their eyes wilted. The battle went on, the front knew no mercy.

"The man next to me said, 'Death is no longer a puzzle for us.' But in this inferno of violence and death I saw eyes that shined in a lively glitter – the front has its secrets, its magic, it was a part of life for these young and hard youths. In spite of this, these men were more human than humanity itself. These men, I simply cannot judge them. They belonged to an organization where snobs and show-offs were not wanted. We knew that none of our names would ever be engraved in stone, that only happens with the brave men.

"Then came the Kommandeur... 'Hold your nerves!' someone said just before he stepped into the trenches. Kommandeur D'Haese had to be concerned with every single man, since the front was then so thin. D'Haese's personal and energetic leadership alone prevented the Russian bridgehead from expanding. The Soviet breakthrough had been avoided. The main thrust of this great attack continued anew, the Soviets sent their air force which took everything under fire. Tanks appeared at the edge of the forest but didn't roll any further. That showed that their effect had been reduced by our PAK. Then the Soviet infantry broke out from the edge of forest and crossed a terrain littered with corpses. The Russian tanks fired on our positions over the attacking infantry men. Even here our men had the advantage on the slightly climbing terrain. The storming opponent had it even tougher. Wrecked Russian tanks were littered everywhere, be it cooling heaps of glowing hot metal or slightly damaged tanks. The front held. Then it was our turn. One of the old ones gave the sign and it let loose.... machine guns, rifles, pistols, our infantrymen defended their positions and inflicted heavy losses. Small break-through positions were beaten off and the Soviets were destroyed.

" 'That was a tactic of an old legionnaire, which will always remain a risk,' said Kasper D'Haese, but the Flemings know no pity.' And so it was that D'Haese's order was carried out."

Kamiel Horre reported:[45]

"The Soviet attacks came daily, the Soviets fought so bravely, someone told them it would be an honor to be the first to step over the border into the Reich. The Germans fought with victory in mind at Narva. The bombs were hurled against the edge of the forest. I heard Sobry say 'Remy, it's burning, we need more Sprenggranaten!' We saw a group of vehicles together and our grenades hit them. German bombers weren't in this section of the front, the Russians ruled the air. The black smoke and the high-reaching flames were proof of the PAK's success. The men called, 'it's a direct hit' and then it stopped and burned. We knew what would follow. Schütze I and II covered the gun with camouflage as well as all of the holes. A little bit later we heard the droning of the motors, bombers, fighter planes flew in. The bombs then began to fall. The plane's machine gun bullets whistled on by. All of the bombs fell behind us in the direction of Love's Hill. We thought about Remy's 'Kopfstellung' and hoped that they would leave us alone – but all for nothing, the main fighting line was being shot up. Perhaps the PAK was a picture for

---

[45] Schrijnen notebook.

their eyes as they looked out of their foxholes. Bombs exploded, stones flew and dry earth and bomb fragments whistled by. The annihilated T-34s were marks where troops could be found. We couldn't do anything, only give away our positions. Light splintering bombs were being thrown then. 'The infantry had to carry most of the burden,' I said, 'but the old foxes of the Legion Flandern and Langemarck know how to survive!' Kommandeur D'Haese knew how too, his task was more than difficult, nothing more was available. Numerous vehicles were shot in flames, they were the ones transporting the wounded. The burned wrecks of our Red Cross ambulances lay left and right of the road and burned in the forest. The drivers continued to drive despite this, whether being fired on by from artillery or by bombers. Leo Tollenaere, Juul Fieremans, Fons Van Broeck were tired and dirty, but they did what they could. They had to get through this hell.

"The next morning Van Broeck said to me, 'In the bunkers we fell into a deep sleep. Nothing disturbed us, neither bombs or artillery, a deep healthy sleep.' D'Haese came from the forward positions with Laperre and Groenvinck. Their faces were serious and we were immediately awake and fresh. Juul snored lightly.

"D'Haese showed a slight smile around his mouth, 'How securely the man sleeps! That is the morale of the troops. They didn't teach us at the leadership schools, the confidence of the men, that is a thing of their character.' "

Marcel Laperre continued:[46]

" 'The morning concert is starting now,' said Horre, and already the first detonations of all calibers exploded around us. An impenetrable wall of shell fire and smoke. The men didn't hear it, they barely even ducked, but no head went above the edge of the trenches. I ordered that someone should look out and see what was going on. None of the men obeyed and Schrijnen refused. Schrijnen could put up with a direct hit, but a splinter during a pause in battle he couldn't stand. Such stupidity, I thought. Schrijnen sure could be nasty. My most agonizing threat for the men was 'he who does not obey will be sent away from the gun.' That would be a blemish for any man.

" 'When it has to be, then only one man is to look out, and only occasionally,' said Schrijnen hesitantly.

---

[46] Schrijnen notebook.

" 'I feel useless at this gun,' I said to D'Haese, frustrated.

"D'Haese laughed and said to me, 'Laperre, Laperre, the simple soldier has the experience of the battles which are behind him. Your men carry out your orders which says something to me. The men do not fear death, they have overcome this fear in a dozen hopeless situations. Their lives are indeed important, but in this case not an obligation. The lives of the commanders and the leaders are important, they carry the fate of the others and the result of the battle depends on them. We say that the little man has to fight, and is ordered by capable officers. We know that their fate depends on our actions. It is a battle of to be or not to be, here at this front. The men are ready and so many of them volunteer for the most dangerous tasks to save their comrades – yeah, loyalty means more than death. I had laid in the trenches with so many of these men, many from the Legion Flandern, and we watched many a barrage of fire go over our heads and together we beat off attacks. Now I am their commander. The action reports cause me many a worry. There are many casualties of leaders and men. I have looked at the casualty reports and many of the men I knew personally. I was at the main dressing station twice. I saw men with shredded bodies and many dying comrades. I greeted them and I saw that they were unshaken in the beliefs of their convictions. Many knew that this was their end, but I did not see any fear in the eyes of these men. I have to get back, I have gotten a good overview of the conditions here, even Groenvinck proved himself well.' D'Haese rushed back, there was still a lot to do."

D'Haese reported:[47]

"I had to get through this. Everything cracked here, swirls of sand, dust and stones. The noise increased more and more. I jumped here and there and ran where the paths go under. The incoming shells from the navy guns shredded everything. I gave the list to my helper and he shook his head. He was to care that the names and facts were recorded so they could be reported to family members. The post was secure enough, dug deep into the ground. The entrance ran like a running trench. Despite this I was not calm. Hours went by. An attempt to attack by Steiner wasn't successful. One of his staff officers said to me that he wasn't there and the orders hadn't changed. One of the commanders of 'Norge' stopped by and brought a bottle with him. He had the

---

[47] Schrijnen notebook.

same worries – the same worries he had had for the past three months. He had been waiting for a fresh battalion to relieve his men.

" 'Damn,' said the Norge commander, 'your section is getting more than its fair share, all without heavy weapons. We still have Panzers and Sturmgeschütze as well as the Dutch, a regiment from Nordland and the Danes. But these days it is the Flemings that everyone is hearing about. The reputation of your legionnaires is great within the III. Germanisches Panzerkorps.'

"After a few factual conversations he retreated to his bunker. I gave an order to my messenger for the Kompanie- and Zugführer to meet near Laperre's wagon. I was the first one there, it appeared to be a calm corner. The men arrived. It showed that the men had had little sleep and their faces and uniforms were smeared with dirt from crawling through the fire. With a short handshake I greeted the men and Valeer had glasses and a bottle with him. I began the discussion:

" 'A small drink in this chaos of annihilation. We can all see how everything is sinking together in the heavy punches of the Soviet artillery. One could say, where those bombs go, no more grass grows. The hills are still in our hand, as well as the road and the railway. Our supply is impossible during the day since Soviet fighters prevent it while their artillery bombs it at night. During the night it can come to battles with single enemy patrol troops. These are taken care of by the older ones right away because the men are clever. They leave their foxholes and crawl forward into no-man's land and lay in craters, waiting. Laperre, you and your PAK Geschütz make sure that you have enough ammunition. The PAK must give uninterrupted support to the infantry and continually bring on and annihilate the Soviet PAKs. We all know those dangerous 'Ratschbumms'[48] well enough. Until now our single PAK gun has completed its assignment bravely and loyally and has also managed to beat back the tank attacks. Now what these fighter plane attacks mean, well defense against them is almost impossible. More than 3/4 of the battle group has fallen out, be it by death or serious wounds. The fact that no one has been reporting in sick is a sign of the robustness and health of the men. The wounded stay at the front lines even though normally the men have to be cared for at the main dressing station. But these men have a sense of responsibility and stay in action. One doesn't learn this in books, even though they teach it at the lead-

---

[48] "Ratschbumm" was the nick name for the Soviet anti-tank gun. It was nick-named for the sound it made.

ership schools. The men, however, find it normal that one should continue despite his wounds. I call these men 'leaders' because that is their character and responsibility, a living task. Despite all of the lice, difficulties and mistakes, the men must still have the energy to make decisions while in battle and the trust they feel from top to bottom must remain unbroken. The men operate most often independently, my gentlemen, and as leaders we have much to learn in this respect. The simple man can recognize a situation quicker than we can. That was the meaning of this battle, to inflict as much damage as possible on the enemy, it is their duty to stay out of the shadow of fear and not to bear regret. My gentlemen, off to your posts.' "

Marcel Laperre continued:[49]

"The talk had ended, the Kompanie- and Zugführer left their Kommandeur. D'Haese knew all too well what was waiting for him. The size of the dugout for the wounded increased. Only the wounded in the field hospital were shipped off, even though so many sunk into the side of the road or lay shot-up, burned out. Sometimes there was no saving these boys, only the field hospital could save them. Dr. Hertgens had to make difficult decisions... Even Leo Tollenaere drove through the fire in Laperre's VW to pick up the wounded. He had had good luck, because everything that moved was attacked. The Soviets came thinking that every single bunker had been destroyed. However, some of the well-equipped bunkers for the wounded were still there, nothing was hopeless, everyone just needed to bite their teeth together."

D'Haese continued:[50]

"My men at the front with their unshakable hardness, the Officers, NCOs and men, none of them thought about saving their own skin. As commander and young officer, one was a different person. I had to change myself as the responsibility of my orders had changed. My tone of my voice had changed, I knew that when my orders could not be carried out, that I could just blame it on someone else, just as Albert Vincent and Schrijnen had said about Hauptsturmführer Rehmann. Those words made me think that 'what the fight-

---

[49] Schrijnen notebook.
[50] Schrijnen notebook.

ing soldier is not allowed to do should also be enforced on the gentlemanly officers,' as Schrijnen once said to me openly. 'A coward,' said this man to me, 'is most often a lowly man, he forces others to be brave but refuses to do the same when things get hot. He tries to portray the enlisted men as the cowards, the same enlisted men that carry out his orders in trust.' I knew from my experience in danger that the troops should have respect for their commander, but at the same time be able to freely express their opinions. The commander that understood this was successful, his assignments were carried out. These were not men which trotted after the lead sheep, or had fear in front of men who wore silver or gold stripes. In all those days there had been no reports of cowardice. Instead of being awoken with a trumpet's reveille, the troops were woken with a fire waltz. Again and again, over a stretch of four or five kilometers, waltzed a wall of fire over my Kampfgruppe. Positions and shelters were crushed, foxholes were buried and there were spiraling corpses and trucks blown to the side. Again and again the earth was not cared for. Again and again it was hell. Then came the warming sun. It was as if this four kilometer wide flat of earth would break open and that everything that could move would be thrown about. For hours the barrage went back and forth, even our neighbors got their fair share of the steam. Then the Soviet infantry and T-34s appeared at the edge of the forest. Together with the Soviet PAK, everything fired on our assumed positions. Could anyone still be alive in this ripped open earth? Without stopping, the Soviets attempted to penetrate our lines. As our PAK fired on them, the Kampfgruppe's MGs, MPs and rifles clenched their teeth together hard. Our infantry and PAK ripped large holes in the forward streaming Soviet masses. Even the Wehrmacht's artillery was decking the Soviet lines with bombs. Messengers came and went. The casualties were bearable and the advance into the open land was worth it. The men knew how to help themselves. Those devilish chaps at the PAK had luck. Despite all their courage and fortune there was still no victory. That is what they were saying over there at the gun. The attack stalled somewhat. From our positions it continued. The edge of the forest was then on fire. The Russian PAK and trucks burned, their tanks pulled out of the danger-zone, or pulled back from the attack. The word then came to me – we'll do it. Our artillery was still firing into them, they were beautiful shells and made our defense easier. Then came the fighter planes over our section. They were coming for the artillery. The Kampfgruppe was still standing and the men beat off the second attack. I departed for the Kommandobunker with Valeer, then I heard several bangs. The clouds from the detonations prevented us from seeing. The unforgotten lay again in this hour in the massive fire from all the Soviet cannons, Stalin's Organs, tanks and mortars. The Red Air Force dropped their bombs with no danger for them in sight. A deadly dance swept through the Kampfgruppe. The men set out to perform their tasks. Valeer was so worried about me. 'Valeer, just think what is lying about out there. The alarm posts, it is there that there still exists a paradise,' I said to Valeer. My men...., we all carried these days with a heavy heart through this hell, whether officer, NCO or enlisted man, everyone had to swallow his fear hard. One can't call this fear. As Schrijnen said to me, "two times I looked a coward in the eye, one time Unterscharführer Kirmse, one time Hauptsturmführer Rehmann. I saw it in both of their eyes, the cowardice, the naked pitiful cowardice.' Schrijnen told off Rehmann and after the battles when Rehmann appeared again and tried to mix in with the men, he wasn't successful. Hypocrisy was not an admirable trait among front-line soldiers. They knew the scent of the coward."

The battle raged on and on July 28th, for some unknown reason, Schrijnen decided to change positions and moved his PAK five hundred meters to the left of his previous position. Schrijnen was barely finished making the move when his old position was completely destroyed by a Russian naval artillery round. Who can say what made Remy change positions? Perhaps all the things the men said about this simple man's sixth sense were true.

Marcel Laperre reported:[51]

"I saw during counter-attacks how the men jumped out of their foxholes and out of the trenches and stormed against the enemy. They ran back with the communists, and won back the land – despite a strong defense and despite the fact that their opponent was widely superior in numbers and weapons. A portion of the men were killed or were wounded and our opponents didn't retrieve all of their weapons. The infantry carried the heaviest burden. My single PAK Geschütz supported the infantry against tanks, PAK Riegel or infantry attacks. Already on the edge of the forest where the Bolsheviks broke out, the PAK took them under fire or stopped a tank advance. In all difficult situations our infantry managed their assignment. In critical situations the men advanced

---

[51] Schrijnen notebook.

to the front. What these infantry men could perform! I could see the fire in their eyes."

" 'Yeah, Untersturmführer, your PAK men are not aware of their actions,' said Unterscharführer Strooband. 'They are more than stubborn. The fact that they haven't been smashed," he said, "is definitely because of their camouflage and the luck-child Remy. He takes responsibility for the attack, which the life and death of the entire crew depends on. He risks everything.'

"I replied, 'Strange for me, Remy said the same thing about the infantry: '...they, and no other branch of service carry victory and stand uninterrupted in the heaviest danger and attacks.' ' I had told this to the infantrymen gathered at the PAK and they then began to laugh, but the gun's crew just bit their teeth together.

"Once again the Russians attacked, wave after wave. Enemy bombers threw their bombs on our lines and artillery of all calibers and Stalin's Organs overwhelmed our section for hours. We had experienced this for some days at that point. We had no air force for defense against the bombers, and this disrupted the supply lines. Our little bit of artillery could only shoot now and then, mainly because as they did, the Soviet pilots were immediately there to nail down their positions. In this barrage we laid as good as defenseless, worthless against the shower of bombs. Then came another barrage, the entire infantry of the Kampfgruppe D'Haese heard the order: Hold out! Then the communists attacked wave after wave from the forest standing at a distance of eight hundred to one thousand meters away. From the forest it stormed, and aimed shots of a few remaining heavy machine guns began to fire. For an instance the enemy was successful in coming within the vicinity of the PAK Geschütz, but the PAK's crew beat the attack off in close combat and by that time the infantry men had stormed to the help. No, we still needed their PAK. The infantry men mopped the communists back into no-man's land with their machine guns and machine pistols. 'The PAK...' thought the men, and with well-trained aimed hits the rounds covered both sides of the street where the enemy infantry was preparing to attack. Next the PAK hit everything that moved on the edge of the forest. Even though our infantry forces were vastly inferior in strength to those of the Russians, our desire to fight was stronger. Ivan was unsuccessful in his attempt to take control of the main fighting line, however, but the lion could still show its claws. Despite the fact that Kampfgruppe D'Haese was surrounded and on its own, it stayed put.

Kommandeur D'Haese knew the situation, but so did the men of the old guard, who didn't ask questions, but just continued to fight and have trust. Heavy barrages of Stalin's Organ fire fell and there were new craters on top of the old craters. 'A wall of fire,' said Tollenaere who had brought a message. He watched as the firestorm fell on his comrades. As my volunteer driver he had to wait for orders. New moon-like landscapes were everywhere. Again and again the cracks of incoming bombs, grenades and Stalin's Organ salvos sounded over the battlefield.

" 'It was ugly,' said Leo Tollenaere to me, 'the incoming rounds were nearing my foxhole, where I waited for Fieremans and Van Broeck who were to bring me messages. All alone I squatted there, once again the end of the earth went on by me.'

"Finally Fons Van Broeck came with a message for myself and Groenvinck. The message – it was almost over, we were going to be relieved soon. One thought only of the difficulty to retreat from the Stalin's Organs... The message was also sent forward. Yet another difficult day was almost over. Then Tollenaere brought another message, Schrijnen changed positions. Dammit! Without my permission! I then again thought of the words of Kotlowski about Remy.

" 'Yeah,' said Leo, 'a few minutes later a ton of bombs fell on the old position, just about right where Remy stood. Damn, a few of us had to carry the gun a good piece of land away, forward into the main fighting line, and since we couldn't operate the gun it fell silent. Therefore we brought ammunition immediately to our new position. The mood was good at the gun, the men said that as always, Schrijnen had sniffed out the situation. Otherwise it would have been the end for us – for us all – since all over our old position was mass of craters – crater upon crater. We also had some prisoners, they were talking about the thousands of dead and wounded and how the their officers and men were fleeing this piece of flat land. The tanks apparently didn't trust themselves and the swamps were impassable. Sometimes the Russians thought of putting in the 'Du-Gerät' into action. This beast is a sort rocket which fires lung-irritant[52] into enemy positions. The prisoners freely stated that the troops along with their officers would have fled unless their superiors didn't promise

---

[52] This would be poisonous gas - as used in the First World War. One often wonders why the German soldiers continued to carry gas masks during the war as the use of gas was forbidden by the Geneva convention. The Soviets had not signed this agreement and the threat of the use of gas lingered.

to bring this weapon into action to answer our attacks. The prisoners say that we have a lot more to expect. They can't believe that we are still hanging here, they were told that the III. Germanisches Korps was finished.'

"At this late stage of the battle, Kommandeur D'Haese had more than worries. His Officers, NCOs and men disappeared to the front. He knew that it wouldn't last much longer. He once again went to the front, to his surrounded infantry. He knew that he only had one PAK Geschütz, but the men would hold out. The men had very strong nerves. The infantry had been carrying the main burden, all the men knew that they came here to sacrifice themselves. The successes were honorable for the spirit of the front-proven men. The men without front-line experience paid the most amount of blood. As the first one fell in battle, we thought that the years he had spent in the concern didn't protect him. He had led a Rottenführer, at first they were successful, but then the men were killed.

" 'A lesson for me,' said D'Haese, "as a commander one should know to lead such newcomers against the enemy and not let them lead others against the enemy, surely not in such a fight as this.

"D'Haese had to go back and watch the continuous attacks from the air, mortars and artillery. The Soviets were once again attacking from the edge of the field."

Jan Vermeeren continued:[53]

"After every attack I saw the dead and wounded. Some were hit with bullets, others with grenades or bombs. They were shredded and ripped apart. Some badly wounded, but still alive, I tried to help them wherever they went as everyone does, because the medics here don't have enough hands. We didn't feel that we were heroes, only soldiers that did their duty or more than their duty. There were enough heroes, be it in romance novels, cowboy books or war stories. I refused this word as a front-line soldier. Every soldier that did his duty in grave danger belonged to a heroic fighting troop. We received orders and they were carried out. Yeah, one could say that there at Narva that the majority of us were acting independently. When the floodgate of hundreds of grenades was opened, and bombs of every caliber rained upon us and our neighbors for hours, we did our duties. The bombs drummed again and again

---

[53] Schrijnen notebook.

in the torrent of fire, and we laid there hungry, tired, and pressed to the ground. None of us thought of cowardice or of running off, there was no panic. Everything was calm and sober. I wondered about myself, because as I was with the Legion and earlier the Sturmbrigade, I had never seen a fire-waltz such as this. And as the Russians attacked in masses, the front of survivors stood, not softer, but harder. No one fled to the rear, no one refused to bloodily beat back the heavy attacks from the widely superior enemy infantry and tank forces. The desire to live flickered back time and time again, and if it was that only our will to fight to the last bullet was what saved us, then so be it. With every shot and every saving day, we held out every hour, and remained true to our oath and to the order of our Kommandeur Untersturmführer Georg D'Haese. 'To live is to fight, and that means to survive,' and so we fought on. Others will say that we were heroes, our officers, NCOs and enlisted men, all of the Flemish chaps. No one here thought about a Knight's Cross or an Oak Leaf cluster. It was not like a Fleming to think of an award in battle as most award winners were not gentlemen, but rather someone who wanted to be noticed by the officers when they were in the vicinity, someone who wanted to play the hero. What we could bring back in the way of wounded... The dead stayed for the night, and sometimes we could smell the sweet stink of the dead Russians in the field. It was especially bad when a breeze blew in our direction. Even the hardest soldiers had to stuff something in their noses, but that barely helped. The tanks, yes, that was a feeling for itself, and when it had to be we let the tanks run over us and then we annihilated them in close combat from the rear. At this late stage of the battle, the Kampfgruppe still had only one PAK gun that defended it. There was renewed rumbling from the Stalin Organs and we crept further forward in the field. There were enough craters and dead Russians lay all around. Once in a while, if we didn't pay attention, it would come to a shoot out with a wounded Russian, but for the most part we felt secure. We cursed Hauptsturmführer Rehmann who had abandoned us as a coward. Yes, this jackass from the Race and Resettlement Main Office, he didn't have anything more than a scratch when he left. Other badly wounded soldiers stayed in front of the enemy, be it a shot in the leg, arm, shoulder or whatever. No, there weren't any cowards among us and we all knew what a coward Rehmann was. Hopefully someone would charge him and he would be court-marshaled. To be an officer means to set an example, the part where you were supposed to be the first do die was only a part of it. He ordered that we were to fight to the last bullet, to perform a heroic defense, an unforgetful contribution to our assignment to build a defensive front and save the Western world. The rest of the men were forgotten knights who lay about during those days, hour for hour in a massive barrage of all the Soviet guns, Stalin's Organs, tanks, mortars – and this Mr. Hauptsturmführer Rehmann flees from the danger to let the others die. Untersturmführer Georg D'Haese, just twenty-one years old, led the battle group driven and able, unbroken. He was an example of the best Germanic loyalty and soldiership.

"The survivors held on to anything there in the Blue Mountains. Throughout their heroic action, the strongest Soviet forces and troops from the Leningrad area were prevented from marching right through to East Prussia. The massive artillery attacks were aimed almost perfectly. A messenger ran on, that was his job, he was an independent fighter. Most of them were stubborn dogs, those foot messengers. He didn't come to us, we saw an incoming shell and that was the last we saw of him. It hit like a large fist and smashed him flat on the ground, right in the middle of other detonations. Later we found him shredded, a boot with his leg, a part of his head and torso. We wrapped it all up in a shelter quarter and dragged it back to the rear. So ended the life of this young messenger.

"The wall of fire wandered on further, it went on by the PAK's position. The supplies were to remain covered below. The wounded were bandaged in craters left by the Soviet guns, I pressed my face against the cool butt of my machine gun. The incoming artillery salvos wandered here and there, it was a landscape of craters. Our mortars decked everything. With calmness and doggedness the survivors worked their way back to their positions. The machine guns came back out of the forward terrain. I could still see Kasper D'Haese. The flames and smoke came down on us. In our foxholes and in the craters were our dead comrades lying together with the dead enemy. The dead bodies laid like shields against the bullets and shrapnel. Even the dead were useful to us. Then hell passed us by. We were used to the shaking of the ground and had known it from 1941-1944, but here it was worse, these overpowering heavy weapons were tough. Then came the attack planes, they hurled small and large bombs so that one could barely breath. One after another came the Red fighters over the terrain, there were no German dive-bombers to ward them off, but still, the front held. Those few of us who survived would talk about this for a long time, about the Kampfgruppe 'Langemarck' under the leadership of

Untersturmführer Georg D'Haese at Narva in the III. Germanisches Panzerkorps under Obergruppenführer Felix Steiner. We would speak of the last battle between the West and East, the battle of the Germanic volunteers in Estonia. It was a gleaming example of Germanic manhood for the boys yet to come. Heroism was displayed day and night for four eternally long days. Officers, NCOs and men were thundered by the incoming bombs and grenades. Then came the squeaking of tank tracks and the revving of the tank motors. Everywhere where the volunteer Germanic peoples stood, stood the firemen mostly at the focal points of the battle. Their loyalty, comradeship and preparedness for action was already heard of by all the German comrades in the Greater German Wehrmacht, independent of political ideas or feelings. In this northern pocket in the Kurland in the Baltic countries bled the blood of the Germanic youth against the Soviet avalanche of tanks, artillery, fighter planes and infantry. The Germanic peoples would proudly say that we did not refuse our duty there at Narva. In the west the Allies occupied city after city. No one knew what was happening with their parents, brothers and sisters, wives and children. We couldn't think about that, just fight to the end, I said."

Marcel Laperre continued:[54]

"I went to the gun, it is our only heavy weapon. Luckily Schrijnen changed his position, it was the 28th of July. 'The position is prima,' said Schrijnen, 'but we don't have the time to build it up correctly.'

"Already the grenades were exiting the barrel. Man, it was an open firing position! Fieremans, Rubens and Horre came with rounds. I saw how the rounds fell into Ivan and hit him. Then the PAK was under fire, grenades cracked, the men loaded and fired on. They weren't listening, there was no time. I knew that Remy was responsible for this nightmare. The incoming rounds fell near the PAK, the enemy battered the gun, the salvos landed ten meters in front of the PAK.

" 'Doesn't Remy notice this?' I asked Fieremans.

" 'Remy grins whether incoming or outgoing, the men don't notice either way,' he replied.

"The PAK lied in the middle of exploding Salvos, five meters next to the gun. Splinters whistle, the men laid flat. Already the Richtschütze was above,

---

[54] Schrijnen notebook.

'LADEN!' was his call, and on went the dance of death. Tanks prepared themselves at the edge of the forest.

" 'They can only be pigs who want to finish us off,' said Horre.

" 'This damned storm attack,' I thought as I rushed to the infantry. Every single man stayed with or laid behind this weapon. Every man then had his own ideas on how to fight and how to survive. Every grip of the hand was tough during this defense, and every hand would not let go. One could say that this battle group hadn't really made any mistakes. The men with front experience played a large role here. To wear down our defense the Soviets sent barrages of bombs. But still, the life of the remaining row of the Kampfgruppe's leaders and men remained normal. Untersturmführer and Kommandeur D'Haese was a solitary man, you could see it in him. He knew that there were only a few men and strongpoints left. Dr. Hertgens, Groenvinck, Van Leemputten and I were still with him as leaders. D'Haese decided about life and death, victory or loss, D'Haese and his men fought bitterly. The front wavered, but held, no one could talk about the brave one or whatever, whether leader or little man, every one gave his best. I saw Jan Vermeeren, Strooband, Casper D'Haese and others. Then there was a raging jump: they came out of their foxholes with their machine guns at their hip firing, belching fire against their enemy to stop him. These were admirable soldiers, seasoned veterans, who were prepared to battle to the last man. This glass stem, the most important point of defense on the whole line, was defended and held.

" 'The Soviets must be placing cannon next to cannon, you can tell by watching the incoming rounds,' said Jan Vermeeren, 'but until now the calm and clever remainders of the Kampfgruppe have been able to beat them off.'

"Even where the Russians stormed the PAK, our infantry men, together with the PAK's crew, beat them back with shovels and rifle butts in a bloody hand-to-hand battle and chased them here and there. The edge of the PAK's position must be held. Fieremans, Van Broeck and Tollenaere fetched the wounded and the dead, no wounded were left unattended, all at the own initiative of the two messengers. Our sacrifices were great. But the enemy's sacrifices were still even greater because the Russians had enough reserves while we had none. During a break-through over Love's Hill and Grenadier Hill we were still able to win them back, the flat still held. Kampfgruppe D'Haese held its defensive position for days as the fire department. The Soviets thought that they could easily lock up this battle group, but they were wrong. The

Flemings in the III. Germanisches Panzerkorps had corps spirit, they held and beat off every attack. Like wave-breakers the men stood against a power twenty times stronger than themselves, be it in tank attacks, infantry attacks or the barrage of fire from the Soviet artillery. Powerful waves of attack planes dropped bombs in every quantity and of every caliber, strafing the landscape. The Stalin's Organs covered everything, the Soviets were now trying to out-smart us, and slowly, very slowly, the Soviets crept forward. It was difficult for the infantry men to see them as they laid in the barrage. Both hills were hell, but over the flat terrain came the attack again and again. The Soviets had done everything to smash this single PAK gun, reality looked grim for the PAK.

" 'Yes, in your section it looks much worse as the Soviet planes are cov-ering you with bombs. You men who laid one hundred to two hundred meters away from the Russians in no-man's land suffered the dance of the death,' I said to Vermeeren.

"The Soviets were soon bombing empty lines. We could only laugh with disgust during these moments. Kommandeur D'Haese was still able to report to Steiner that the front was holding. Still, the initiative remained with the few survivors, a word and the front still held. So it was on this piece of land. A shredded, overturned and bombed piece of land. Here lay hundreds of dead in the field. A stink that one cannot describe. The last grenadiers were far to the front with their machine guns, laying in the bomb craters, with only a single 7.5 cm PAK supporting them. In this last episode Kommandeur D'Haese knew that his Kampfgruppe was as good as finished. Only his few leaders, NCOs and men were still there. In this eerie fire it was only the PAK that fired into the edge of the forest where the Soviet PAKs set up.

" 'I heard Strooband say to Kasper D'Haese, Vermeeren and Salien with-out envy, 'Remy is worth his money.' This Sturmmann and his men have carried so much on every piece of land, the Soviet commissars must have often fled his gun. It shot the forested section into fire, while holding up tanks and annihilating their PAKs. On this street we saw trucks flee back from this burning inferno that only the forest could save. Even at 1000 meters, that PAK could do a lot of damage, but after that it couldn't do much more. This section of forest had been a deadly place where everything burned to the ground. Tanks, trucks, what a loss for the Soviets. A single PAK Schütze who could shoot targets at one thousand meters without order, had success, yeah, Remy himself said that one must also have luck in life.

" 'For us,' said the rest of the men to me, 'your presence has had an honorable effect, we fought along during this unbelievable battle. Even in this barrage we were able to attack and to survive, smashing tanks and infantry. The tanks, with their grim humor, instead of continuing they just drove away.' "

Laperre continued:[55]

"Tollenaere and Juul came to give the order for another retreat. I rushed to the PAK to relay the orders. With a heavy heart I gave the order – but I am happy that I would be leaving with my men alive. But what a shock, Schrijnen would not obey my order.

" 'I am staying here until I'm finished. To leave here would be like letting the Ivans loose,' said Schrijnen.

"The men obeyed, and Schrijnen took my threat for a court marshal with a grain of salt. He continued alone.

" 'Not for the first time,' said Kamiel Horre to me.

"We arrived safely at our new positions without Schrijnen."

The Russians then prepared another attack. 30 T-34s as well as 4 Stalin Tanks arrived for the attack. Schrijnen loaded, aimed and fired continuously, one Russian T-34 was in flames immediately. The Russians could not have expected that Schrijnen's PAK was still active. Remy then cleaned his barrel and he had to push out the shell from the last shot with the poker since the gun wasn't working properly, something which exposed him to enemy fire. Schrijnen claimed the fate of three more T-34s and three of the four Stalin Tanks as the 4th Stalin fired on his position from a distance of just 20 meters.

What happened next is best recalled by Georg D'Haese:[56]

Schrijnen, at the last gun, loaded, aimed and fired upon the colossus that stood before him. A grenade got caught in the gun's barrel and the tanks rolled closer and closer to him. He quickly jumped to the front of the gun and boxed the grenade back with the poker. "LADEN!" roared Schrijnen, a Russian tank standing only a few meters in front of him. He fired and hit. The air froze stiff. He then smashed the turret of the next tank while a third Russian tank aimed

---

[55] Schrijnen notebook.
[56] Letter to the author from G. D'Haese dated March 24, 1997.

Untersturmführer Walter Van Leemputten:
Van Leemputten was the battalion adjutant and had just completed his coursework at the officer candidate school Bad Tölz and promoted to Untersturmführer. Van Leemputten was shot during an attempt to retrieve surrounded comrades in the orphanage on Orphanage Hill and later died of his wounds in a field hospital on August 15. Before he died he was awarded the Iron Cross IInd Class.

exactly at Schrijnen. Its shot, together with the shot Schrijnen fired, exploded at the same time with ear-shattering violence. The tank's crew was either dead or badly wounded.

Remy himself was thrown some twenty meters away from his destroyed gun and lay wounded for hours. The Russian advance continued and after some three days of continuous fighting the Russians overran the Kampfgruppe's old positions and Remy was left for dead.

The battle continued and that evening Sturmbannführer Scheibe, with his thunderous roar, called together another group to try and win back Orphanage hill. The group consisted of the 5th and 6th companies of "Norge", 6th and 7th companies of SS-Regiment 24, and the remains of Kampfgruppe "D'Haese." This fifty man group, among which there were twenty Flemings, once again lead a counter attack against Orphanage Hill. There was a short preparation on the south side of Grenadier Hill, the direction of attack was northeast.

Georg D'Haese reported:[57]

---

[57] Letter to the author from G. D'Haese dated March 24, 1997.

> *After advancing twenty meters Untersturmführer Van Leemputten was badly wounded. He was shot in the stomach with an exploding bullet. The attack bogged down as the enemy returned violent fire.*

The Soviets beat off the attack, Kommandeur D'Haese and many others were wounded. Sturmbannführer Scheibe didn't return. That was the last attempt to win back Orphanage Hill.

Fourth Day of Battle: July 29, 1944

General Govorov wanted to finally force the decision. This was to be the decisive day. As usual, an ear-splitting hour long artillery barrage was laid on Grenadier and Love's Hills, and further back, into the German artillery positions. Enemy attack planes fired on everything that moved. Russian bombers carpet bombed the entire battlefield, nothing was protected. The focal point of the attack was Grenadier Hill, which looked like a glowing inferno as the bombs fell on it.

On the highway to Tirtsu more than one hundred Russian tanks rolled onto the German positions. The German artillery fired salvo upon salvo uninterrupted on to the storming tanks, but they continued to advance, despite heavy casualties.

The remaining Norwegians from the 2nd Battalion, the remaining Flemings, the Estonians from the 20. SS-Grenadier Divisions and the remains of a Marine Battalion continued to fight on in small groups. Germans, Flemings, Estonians, Norwegians, Danes, all who had previously not known each other, laid together in shot-up command posts, bunkers and bomb craters. They fought on, completely dependent only on themselves. There was no contact with each other, nor did they expect any more orders. Everywhere there was an inferno burning, from incoming grenades and bombs. From the east side of Orphanage hill the Russians crept upon their positions. Just as everything looked as if it was lost, the German artillery suddenly laid some of their rounds on the Russians. Panzers and Sturmgeschütze from "Nordland" mopped everything up. It wasn't masses of personnel and material that were decisive here, but courage and respect for death. Obersturmbannführer Kausch's Panzers (SS-Panzerabteilung 11 "Hermann von Salza") decided this battle. They hunted the retreating Soviet tanks as they rolled back to their lines. During the attack they found the smashed gun of Remy Schrijnen and nearly a dozen knocked out or damaged tanks. Remy was spotted by the crew of Paul-Albert Kausch's command tank. They pulled the wounded man up from the ground and laid him on their Panzer and brought him back to the field hospital in Toila.

Paul-Albert Kausch: Shown above is the leader of the unit that saved Schrijnen's life, Sturmbannführer Paul-Albert Kausch being greeted by a General of the German Army in early 1944. Kausch, who held the rank of Obersturmbannführer when his unit discovered Schrijnen on the battlefield, was nicknamed "Peter" by his comrades and had joined the SS-Verfügungstruppe in 1933 at the age of 22. The first unit that he served with was the Leibstandarte Adolf Hitler where he distinguished himself and was recommended for officer candidate training. Kausch visited the SS Junkerschule Braunschweig from April 1935 to January 1936 and thereafter he attended several Army and Waffen-SS courses in machine gun warfare. He then served with the SS-Totenkopfstandarte "Oberbayern" which would later be incorporated as an infantry regiment into the 3. SS-Panzergrenadier-Division "Totenkopf." While serving with this division Kausch won the Iron Cross 1st and 2nd Class. Thereafter he became divisional adjutant for Felix Steiner, then the commander of the 5. SS-Panzergrenadier Division "Wiking." From there he served as commander of SS-Artillerie-Regiment 5 (Wiking) until being transferred to train as a Panzer commander. From there he enrolled in a regular German army course for Abteilungskommandeure. After successfully completing this course he was posted to command the SS-Panzerabteilung 11 "Hermann von Salza."

Soon the Soviets noticed that they would be able to advance no further and they abandoned their positions. But before doing so, they combed through the east side of the cratered Orphanage Hill. Here they found only dead and wounded. Whoever couldn't walk was shot and killed.

This bitter defensive battle, which brought enormous casualties for both sides, was, for the most part, over. In four days 113 Russian tanks were knocked out of commission. Fifty Flemings had been taken prisoner and from this group only four would return in May 1962 after being imprisoned in Soviet gulags for eighteen years. The Soldier's Cemetery in Jöwi (near Narva) was the final resting place for many Flemings.

Later Marcel Laperre reflected on the end of the battle:[58]

"As a platoon leader I couldn't understand why Remy refused to follow my order to evacuate his position. His men said that what he did was something more than simply not following my orders.

"Fieremans said to me, 'Untersturmführer, what Remy did had nothing to do with heroism, Remy covered the retreat of 'Das Reich,' the LAH and 'Langemarck' from February to March 2, 1944 as we were boxed in by the rows of Soviet PAKs. For Remy, it was his duty to cover his comrades. For Remy his PAK was there to defend us until the end. We were happy to have had Remy on the front, this stubborn 'go-getter,' as he was called. Back then, in Jambol, we would never have made it if it wasn't for him. In action Remy has no time to think of fear, in danger he can only think about the task at hand. Call him a hero to his face and he will laugh. His trust and his luck are the most important contributors to his success.'

"Remy himself said that he imagined a front-line soldier to be 'a man without nerves, without fear, a go-getter, who isn't allowed to anything disturb him in critical situations, and isn't allowed to be soft.' The men looked me in the eye.

" 'Trust and luck were the most important thing in action, Untersturmführer,' said Leo Tollenaere, 'and Remy trusted you during your first action at the front. His refusal to obey your order, as you see it, was not a refusal in reality. Remy defended an exposed position, a position that should normally have been given up. But that was impossible for this man. The PAK secured, the PAK fought, and battled the Soviet PAKs and tanks to the ground, not to mention their infantry attacks. Without making a sound, he fought with his men in close combat as the Soviets attacked, like possessed men, with a wild rage. Ask Casper D'Haese, Salien, Vermeeren, Strooband or others. Ivan was not able to beat these men and the men in Schrijnen's crew were in the thick of it with him. No, he is a soldier, a soldier with responsibility. Place him before a court marshal and he won't admit it, Untersturmführer, that he didn't follow your orders. Whether or not he will come back is more than questionable.'

"His men looked to the ground. They felt that an order from their platoon leader was to be obeyed and only their Geschützführer stayed alone, ignoring

---

[58] Schrijnen notebook.

the barrage of fire, at his PAK to protect us during our retreat. What do these men feel? As a leader I don't know. Later in conversation with Schrijnen I began to understand him.

" 'The men don't need me very much, Untersturmführer, and when I lose this party, a surrender it is not. I lost my gun, yeah, but you and this brave PAK crew are still alive. The goal is above the man, this goal has been reached and if I would have been killed, nothing would have been lost. Others would have stood in my place. Everything is possible and nothing is impossible. Look at your men, none of them are big talkers, but gentlemen that are experienced and independent enough to grasp their own initiative.'

" 'What did you think of me when you didn't see me for many hours at a time?' I asked.

" 'Either dead or badly wounded in action. I never think of a man as a coward unless I see it myself or another man tells me that someone is a coward.'

"For Remy it didn't matter what rank or position a man has, 'nobody is born a hero or to stand above the rest. Everyone is placed according to their abilities,' he said. So simple and correct Schrijnen was. We 'intelligent ones' should take the time to think that the little man was at least equal to us in spirit. During the calm in Toila I had the chance to talk with Remy and really got to know this enlisted man. He was open and honest, and stated his opinion man to man, without trying to appease anyone or trying and gain their trust. For me Schrijnen was a courageous and admirable soldier and stayed that way, not jealous and satisfied."

And what happened to the Kommandeur? Everyone had assumed that he had been killed because he wasn't with the troops ready to depart. They were about to leave without him, no one had seen him. Valeer Janssens, a good friend of D'Haese, went back to Love's Hill to find him. There he was, staggering about, also looking for wounded men.

As D'Haese saw him he said to Valeer:[59]

"Valeer where were you? And why do you have that shelter quarter with you?"

---

[59] Letter to the author from G. D'Haese dated Feb. 9, 1997.

"At the train it was said that you also laid in the trenches, shredded, and I wanted to bring what was left of you back with the shelter quarter to the forest camp and give you a proper burial."

With that the tenseness eased – a smile – it was a small and unforgettable occurrence. Janssens then brought D'Haese to Toila to meet with Gruppenführer Steiner. There the two soldiers shook each other's hand, long and hard, and looked deep into each other's eyes. Steiner knew what had become of D'Haese's battle group. After Steiner eased the grip, he took of his German Cross off his tunic and pinned it on D'Haese's breast. Steiner asked D'Haese to write up a list of soldiers that had especially proved themselves during the battle. He didn't want any reasons for the award. Everyone was awarded what D'Haese had recommended. If a soldier had the Iron Cross IInd Class, then he was awarded the Iron Cross Ist Class. If he had no awards, he was awarded the Iron Cross IInd Class or the Infantry Assault badge. On the list D'Haese had also written Rehmann's name. But in this case Steiner wanted a to hear a reason for the award. D'Haese's told him that he had set up the new line of defense after the first attack. This explanation did not convince Steiner and he turned the recommendation down.[60] After the meeting, D'Haese returned Steiner's German Cross in Gold to him.[61]

The battles west of Narva would continue for maybe a week and a half, although there were only local skirmishes after July 29th. By the end of the battles, the Germans registered 113 destroyed Soviet tanks. Despite this relative success, the casualties were very high, and besides the completely annihilated SS-Freiwilligen-Regiment 48, many officers and their men were killed. Among others, Obersturmbannführer Arnold Stoffers, commander of Regiment 23 "Nordland," Obersturmbannführer Hans Collani, commander of Regiment 49, "De Ruyter," Sturmbannführer J. Sooden, commander of the I. Bataillon of Regiment 47 and Obersturmbannführer Hermenegild Graf von Westphalen zu Fürstenberg, commander of Regiment 24 "Danmark," were all killed. Also, the commander of the Division "Nordland," SS-Gruppenführer und Generalleutnant der Waffen-SS Fritz von Scholz, died after receiving mortal wounds inflicted by an attacking T-34.

---

[60] Rehmann was awarded the Iron Cross later by another officer. It was rumored that Schellong awarded him the Iron Cross after returning to Knovitz. In Rehmann's personnel file, it indeed states that he was awarded the Iron Cross Ist class in 1944.

[61] Steiner never made sure that D'Haese received the German Cross in Gold and D'Haese only received the Iron Cross Ist Class. Rumors have it that D'Haese would have been awarded the Knight's Cross if he had been "politically correct."

That so many higher officers were killed in battle is a testament to the brutality of the struggle and the even worse fate of the average soldier.

The Flemings themselves also suffered a devastating fate. Of the approximate four hundred men that comprised the battle group just a few days earlier, only some 37 survived without serious wounds. One thing was certain, the memory of those few days would remain with the survivors for the rest of their lives.

The Aftermath

On July 30 & 31, 1944, the Russians advanced once again with tanks and infantry, but Grenadier Hill remained in German hands. The Soviet attacks died down. The bunkers on the north side of Love's hill had been destroyed by bombs or were burned out. A stink of rotting flesh came from the bunkers. Killed German and Russians soldiers laid all about, one upon the other.

On August 1st the front was calm. The German Army leadership thought that the Russian's next attack would come from the Gulf of Finland. Countermeasures were conducted, since a heavy ship traffic was observed. This operation was termed "See Lion." On August 2nd, a small break-through southwest of Chundinurk was beat back by the Estonians. The attacking Reds were Mongolians. On August 3rd, the German artillery was strengthened by SS-Werfer-Batterie 521. On the front it was calm. On August 4th, the German artillery prevented an attack by a Soviet division by firing on their starting point.

The great Russian offensive against the Tannenberg line was lost. Chundinurk was given up, the front line was evened out. Due to their great performance, the soldiers of Strafkompanie 103 (Penal Company 103) were given back their previous ranks and their badges. They were then subordinated to Regiment "Danmark." All the units used the time to bring everything back in order and to improve the defensive line.

During the week, the remaining men of "Langemarck" had taken a break and was once sent back to the front lines. Georg D'Haese recalls:[62]

> *I and the remaining 37 men (from about four hundred) went to Toila on the Gulf of Finland (Steiner's headquarters) to rest and serve as a coast guards. There it was exceptionally calm.*

---

[62] Letter to the author from G. D'Haese dated Feb. 9, 1997.

We looked after our wounds, exercised a bit and received our awards from Steiner. There was a visit from Schörner. Some wounded returned from the hospital. We were strengthened with a company of soldiers from the Kriegsmarine.[63]

During this calm time D'Haese was approached by Rehmann who instructed him that now would be a good time to hold several talks on National Socialism. D'Haese refused, pointing out that the talks would do the soldiers little good, and that it would be better to do combat exercises.[64]

During their rest, the PAK men received two of the French PAK guns for further action. At first Unterscharführer Eduard Reeb and Remy Schrijnen were the Geschützführer. They were positioned on the coast of the Finnish Gulf for coastal defense. During their two week stay, Unterscharführer Chantraine showed up and took over Remy's gun as Geschützführer. During the two weeks on the coast things were calm had time to go swimming and exercise.[65]

After a while the men were ordered to go back to the front. They were positioned along a railway, to the left Chantraine, to the right, Reeb. This position was held until the order came to evacuate the position.[66]

D'Haese continued:[67]

After a few days Steiner sent me and the healthy soldiers back to the front. Nothing much was going on. We were soon again relieved. The battle group was then transferred to Reval and from there we took the a ride on steam ship "Gottland" to Swinemüde (Pommerania).[68]

During the trip, D'Haese stayed with his men below in ship while Hauptsturmführer Rehmann chose to remain above. Wanting a breath of fresh air, D'Haese went up and ran into Rehmann. Rehmann then asked him why he remained with the enlisted men below and told him that it would be better to remain above with the other officers. D'Haese just smiled, excused himself and returned to his men.[69]

---

[63] Letter to the author from G. D'Haese dated Feb. 9, 1997.
[64] Interview, Georg D'Haese, conducted on Oct. 2, 1997.
[65] Letters to the author from R. Schrijnen dated Nov. 28, 1997 and (via Toon Pauli) D. Anseeuw, dated Dec. 12, 1997.
[66] Letters to the author from R. Schrijnen, dated Nov. 28, 1997 and (via Toon Pauli) D. Anseeuw, dated Dec. 12, 1997.
[67] Letter to the author from G. D'Haese dated March 24, 1997.
[68] Letter to the author from G. D'Haese, dated Feb. 9, 1997.
[69] Interview, G. D'Haese, conducted on Oct. 5, 1997.

The Blue Mountains of Estonia Today: These are a few photos taken in the Blue Mountains in the 1980s. The orphanage (Kinderheim) on "Orphanage Hill" had been completely destroyed during the battles and a new one was later built, however not on the same place as the previous one. The memorial on the lower left was put there by the Flemish veteran's relief organization, St. Maartensfonds. The stone bears the words, "Here rest unknown yet unforgotten soldiers from Flanders." The stone has these words printed in Russian, Flemish and German. Although the famous three hills are located in Estonia, only Russians live there.

As the men arrived in Swinemüde, they all lined up outside the ship and waited for their leader to lead the march. As Rehmann stepped forward to lead the men, the cook, an Austrian by the name of Franz Waldthaler, went forward and grabbed Rehmann by the collar and dragged him to the back of the ranks, telling him that that is where he belonged. Due to his refusal to fight along side his men, Rehmann's reputation amongst his men had been badly damaged.[70]

On August 10, 1944, the commander of the III. SS-Panzerkorps, SS-Obergruppenführer Felix Steiner, was on hand in Hitler's "Wolfschanze" in Rastenburg to personally receive the Swords and Oakleaf Cluster to his Knight's Cross for the battles in Narva from Adolf Hitler himself. The commander of Army Group "North," Ferdinand Schörner, had recommended Steiner for the award and it was quickly approved.

During the party after the award, Hitler spoke with Steiner and told him about his decision to evacuate Estonia. With that, the fate of Estonia was sealed: Estonia would be the first country to be re-occupied by the Soviets. The Estonian people would be left to fend for themselves, while the Estonian Waffen-SS units would continue to fight outside of their homeland alongside the Germans until the bitter end. Steiner immediately returned to Estonia to begin to organize the withdrawal and help the Estonians themselves escape the fate of Soviet occupation.

Remy Schrijnen is awarded the Knight's Cross for Bravery

After the battles west of Narva had concluded and the Flemings had been evacuated, word got way to the higher corps about Schrijnen's heroic act. Schrijnen was awarded the Iron Cross 1st Class and the Wound Badge in Gold on August 3, 1944. Ten days later, on August 13, 1944, Obergruppenführer Felix Steiner, the commander of the III. SS-Panzerkorps, submitted a recommendation for Schrijnen to be named to the "Honor Roll" of the German army. If approved, Schrijnen would receive the *Ehrenblattspange des Heeres* (Honor Roll Clasp).[71] The recommendation was officially submitted on August 28, 1944 and the recommendation was later changed in favor of the Knight's Cross. The following is a translation of the award recommendation:[72]

---

[70] Interview, G. D'Haese and F. Van Broeck, conducted on Oct. 5, 1997.

[71] The *Ehrenblattspange* or Honor Roll Clasp was awarded to soldiers named to the Honor Roll of the German Army. There were other Honor Roll Clasps for the other two branches of service, the Kriegsmarine and the Luftwaffe. The clasp was awarded to those who distinguished themselves in combat situations and was first instituted on January 30, 1944. The prerequisite for the award was that the bearer hold both the Iron Cross IInd and Ist Class.

[72] A copy of the original document is in the appendix.

Award Ceremony at Knovitz Training Grounds: Shown above is Remy Schrijnen parading before the men of "Langemarck" shortly after being awarded the Knight's Cross. Behind him are Kommandeur Conrad Schellong and Schellong's adjutant, Untersturmführer Willi Teichert.

On 7/26/44 at 0900 hours the Russians attacked with three T-34s along the "Narva-Reval" highway. Schrynen knocked out two T-34s at a distance of 400 meters. During the afternoon at 1500 hours the Russians attacked again with infantry forces, and was supported by artillery and heavy grenade launchers. Schrynen again knocked out two T-34s and a single "Stalin" tank. A further T-34 was damaged. It's crew disembarked. The damaged tank was probably dragged away during the night. On 7/27/44 at 0400 hours the Geschütz Schreynen moved to a position 400 meters north of the Hill Kinderheim, left of the "Narva-Reval" highway. Schreynen recognized a position where eleven Soviet tanks were preparing to attack. Under the protection of two T-34s, six T-34s and one KW II approached the highway from the north. At a distance of 700 meters, Scheynen knocked out a T-34. The two T-34s in position to attack the others shot at the anti-tank gun. Schreynen cleared a jam in the gun and 5 minutes later he knocked out a KW II. Immediately thereafter the Geschütz was knocked out by a direct hit. Sch. was named in the Wehrmacht reports that followed the battle.

A New Knight's Cross Winner: Shown above is a studio portrait of Sturmmann Remy Schrijnen shortly after his award of the Knight's Cross.

Another Recipient of the Knight's Cross: Shown above is Obersturmbannführer Paul-Albert Kausch after receiving the award of the Knight's Cross. Kausch was awarded the Knight's Cross on August 23, 1944 for the battles west of Narva. After his unit rescued the wounded Schrijnen on the battlefield, Kausch fought on until he was badly wounded. According to a press release, Kausch had gathered survivors of his battle group and initiated a counterattack which closed a dangerous gap in the front. It was during this attack that Kausch was badly wounded.

Long after the conclusion of the war, Schrijnen disputed the accuracy of the formal recommendation. According to Remy, he never knocked out any KW IIs during the battle.

It wasn't until September 21st that Remy was notified of the award and received his preliminary award document. At this time he was also promoted to Unterscharführer, skipping the rank of Rottenführer. Thereafter there was a party with friends, during which Remy and his friends had plenty to drink. Later that week he received a letter from the leader of the VNV, Dr. Elias Hendrik,[73] congratulating him on his award.

During the beginning of October 1944 the official award ceremony took place at the troop exercise grounds at Selschau-Beneschau near Prague. Conrad Schellong personally laid the Knight's Cross around Remy's throat. This was a gala affair and all officers of Langemarck and the exercise grounds were present. Remy was then ordered to Hilvorsum, Holland, where the Panzerjägerschule was located. Remy first went to the offices of the De Vlag movement to meet Jef Van Der Weile. There was also a Catholic priest there, whose function was to persuade boys to join the Waffen-SS. Remy didn't want anything to do with this and refused to help the De Vlag organization. As he put it, he "stayed loyal to the VNV."

As a Knight's Cross winner, Remy was told that he would be sent to Bad Tölz and thereafter become an officer. This was common for low-ranking Knight's Cross winners, just as Gerardes Mooyman who had won the Knight's Cross in the same way as Remy, for exemplary performance as a Panzerjäger. Mooyman completed the course at Bad Tölz and was commissioned an Untersturmführer. Remy, who considered himself a member of the working class, refused to go to Bad Tölz, since "99.9% of the officer candidates there were college students." He did not feel qualified to become an officer. Due to his refusal, he was then sent to Berlin to see the Reichsführer-SS, Heinrich Himmler. Himmler wanted to know why Remy did not want to attend officer candidate school. He told him that as a Knight's Cross winner and officer, that he would be a great inspiration to the men of "Langemarck." Remy explained his opinion to the Reichsführer and as a final statement answered that "the Führer" had only been a corporal while in the army. Himmler acknowledged that he understood Remy's position and after a half-hour visit, Remy was again on his way.

Indeed, Remy was promoted to Unterscharführer (senior corporal), skipping the rank of Rottenführer (corporal). The rank of Unterscharführer was considered

[73] Staf De Clerq, the leader of the VNV during the early years of the war, had passed away.

a non-commissioned officer rank and not an enlisted man's rank. Because of this, Schrijnen's uniform was decorated with NCO tresse. Schrijnen, however, reports that he was not a proper NCO, as he had not even attended courses at an NCO school. Therefore he states that he was a *Tapferkeits-Unterscharführer* or "Bravery Senior Corporal." While this may seem "arrogant," in reality it is not. Schrijnen considered himself a *Tapferkeitsunterscharführer* because he received his promotion, not because he had completed the necessary training, but solely because he had won the Knight's Cross. This is Schrijnen's way of stating that he did not consider himself a properly qualified NCO.

As a Knight's Cross Winner, Schrijnen was required to speak to various groups, including Flemish workers working in Germany, members of the Organization Todt, N.S.K.K., and the Flemish Allgemeine-SS (General-SS). The purpose of the speeches and talks that Remy was to give were to try and persuade members of these groups to enlist in the Waffen-SS. But Remy refused to spread propaganda or try and persuade members of these groups to become front-line soldiers. In his opinion, it was a personal decision that had to be made independent of persuasive recruiting tactics. The vast majority of these men had no desire to serve at the front and did not enlist. During his trips to visit the various groups, an old battle wound began to give Remy some problems. Apparently he still had shrapnel in his back and this caused inflammation which had to be attended to. That was in December and by the end of January, Remy was allowed to leave the hospital and returned to Langemarck in February.

During his time "on tour" as a Knight's Cross winner, Remy was treated with awe, he was deemed a hero. Wherever he went he was shown special courtesy and respect. Schrijnen himself admitted that this was one of the most marvelous times of his life.

• • •

At the end of 1944 the war was drawing to a close. The Germans did everything in their power to hold on as long as possible, but for nothing. In 1945 the war in the East was fought for a different reason: to save the fleeing German population trying to escape the wrath of the Red Army. Amongst the fleeing Germans were also Flemings and other foreigners who were working as volunteers in Germany.

The atrocities committed by the Russians on German soil motivated the Germans and their foreign comrades to fight even more bitterly. New methods of warfare and improvisation helped the German units slow the inevitable end of the war and save as many civilian lives as possible.

In the end, all was lost. The Flemings, once considered heroes by much of their homeland population, were returned to their native land as outlaws. It was then that new forms of oppression against the Flemish nationalists began.

5

The Bitter End

Langemarck's final Rest, Refit and Redesignation

Due the numerous contingents of Flemish youth and other activists in Germany, it was decided that a complete Flemish division would be formed. Obersturmbannführer Conrad Schellong was designated to lead one of the three foreseen infantry regiments and initially was in charge of the Division's formation until it's new commander, Standartenführer Thomas Müller, arrived. The Division was to consist of the following: three thousand Flemings who were at that time actively serving in various units of the Waffen-SS (this included veterans of the Brigade as well as those serving in the "LAH," "Das Reich," "Wiking" and other units.) Three thousand men from the *Vlaamse Wacht*, a nationalist/militia-type organization in Flanders. Two thousand men active in Flemish para-military organizations, among others the Flemish Allgemeine-SS. The remaining seven thousand were a combination of young boys from the Flemish National Socialist Youth, the N.S.K.K., the Flemish Arbeitsdienst (Labor Service) or Flemish workers working in Germany. Despite the seemingly exact distribution outlined here, reports indicate the strength of the Division was between fifteen and eighteen thousand men. The structure of the 27th SS Volunteer Grenadier Division was foreseen as follows:

27.SS-Freiwilligen-Grenadier-Division "Langemarck"

Divisionsstab[1]	*(Divisional Staff)*
Division Kommandeur –	SS-Standartenführer Thomas Müller (G)
Adjutant –	SS-Obersturmführer Friedrich Seidel (G)
SS-Grenadierregiment 66[2]	*(SS-Grenadier-Regiment 66)*
Kommandeur –	SS-Obersturmbannführer Conrad Schellong (G)
SS-Grenadierregiment 67	*(SS-Grenadier-Regiment 67)*
Kommandeur –	SS-Sturmbannführer Otto Hansmann (G)
SS-Grenadierregiment 68	*(SS-Grenadier-Regiment 68)*
Kommandeur –	SS-Hauptsturmführer Hans Stange (G)
SS-Panzerjägerabteilung 27	*(SS-Anti-Tank-Battalion 27)*
Kommandeur –	SS-Hauptsturmführer Ekkehard Wangemann (G)
SS-Artillerieregiment 27	*(SS-Artillery-Regiment 27)*
Kommandeur –	SS-Obersturmbannführer Holger Arentoft (G)
SS-Pionier-Bataillon 27	*(SS-Combat-Engineer-Battalion 27)*
Kommandeur –	SS-Hauptsturmführer Heinrich Bauch (G)
SS-Nachrichtenabteilung 27	*(SS-Signals-Battalion 27)*
Kommandeur –	SS-Hauptsturmführer Karl Kauss (G)
SS-Versorgungsregiment	*(SS-Supply-Regiment 27)*
Kommandeur –	SS-Sturmbannführer Heinrich Scheingräber (G)

Although on paper the Division appeared as a full-strength combat unit, ready to continue with new found strength, reality was, in fact, quite different. Former battle group commander Georg D'Haese took the time to characterize the true situation:[3]

> *The 27th Infantry Division Langemarck was for the most part an impossible effort to form a defense against an overpowering opponent with the last available reserves. The division consisted of:*
>
> *1. The still remaining experienced front-line combat soldiers placed in*

---

[1] The Divisional Staff had the following at its disposal: two grenadier battalions, an infantry gun company, an assault gun battery, a FLAK (anti-aircraft) company, a Panzerjäger (anti-tank) company and a supply column.

[2] Each Regiment consisted of only two battalions as opposed to the usual four (one heavy) battalions.

[3] Letter to the author from G. D'Haese dated Aug. 20, 1996.

Regiments 66 and 67 and the Panzerjägerabteilung 27 commanded by Hauptsturmführer Wangemann.

2. The transport columns, combat engineer units, building troops (foreign workers who had come from Belgium and were working in Germany) came from the occupied areas of Belgium and were received by the Division's formations.

3. Members of the Flemish youth movement (youths approximately seventeen years of age).

4. Belgian servicemen who were more or less serving with the Luftwaffe, Heer and Kriegsmarine (German Navy) and who would have otherwise only had to wait to be pursued in their native Belgium as German collaborators.

During action they were spread out among various villages in the Lüneburger Heath. The majority of the them, in contrast to the earlier units, could not speak German and served without completing sufficient military training.

Besides the lack of experienced manpower, the Division also suffered from an extreme lack of material goods. Weapons, rations and all other necessary equipment required to train a combat division were severely insufficient.

It should be noted that at this time the political make up of the unit changed again. Most of the new members were more sympathetic to the Germans and there was a greater portion of members who had been members of the Flemish Allgemeine-SS or the De Vlag movement.

Remy Schrijnen would have belonged to the SS-Panzerjägerabteilung 27 under Hauptsturmführer Ekkehard Wangemann. Wangemann was an experienced officer and had served with various units of the Waffen-SS throughout his career. The battalion was structured as follows:

SS-Panzerjägerabteilung 27
Führer: SS-Hauptsturmführer Ekkehard Wangemann

Abteilungstab:	(battalion staff)
Schreibstube	SS-Hauptscharführer Jaus (G)
Stabsschirrmeister	SS-Oberscharführer Jan De Wilde (F)
KFZ-Werkstatt (I-Staffel)	SS Unterscharführer Igosse (F)

1. (PAK) Kompanie *(anti-tank)*   SS-Untersturmführer Anton Kotlowski (A)
2. (FLAK) Kompanie *(anti-aircraft)* SS-Obersturmführer Xavier Dillinger (G)
3. (SIG) Kompanie *(heavy inf. cannons)* SS-Untersturmführer Ernst Fischer (G)
4. (Stg.) Kompanie *(assault guns)*   SS-Obersturmführer Willi Sprenger[4] (G)

The following men served under Anton Kotlowski as platoon leaders:

I. Zug   SS-Oberscharführer Dahlhoff (G)

II. Zug   SS-Untersturmführer Hugo Mortier (F)

III. Zug   SS-Untersturmführer Marcel Laperre (F)

During the final phases of the formation of the Panzerjägerabteilung, Schrijnen was laid up in the hospital, where chunks of shrapnel were being removed from his battered body.

After the Division was deemed "ready" for action, it was subordinated as a reserve unit to the 6. SS-Panzer-Armee, which was stationed in the West. This occurred in December 1944 just prior to the German Ardennes Offensive (The Battle of the Bulge). Before the offensive began, high-ranking Flemish officers were asked about a Flemish role in the possible liberation of their homeland. The officers declined to take part in the battle as they preferred that the unit only be engaged against communist forces.[5] A factor in their decision could have been the fear of harsh reprisals from the English and American forces. In any case, the unit was kept in reserve in the event the offensive was successful, so that they could be used to march back into Flanders in a parade, which would have been a political coup.

During the initial successful offensive operations of the Battle of the Bulge, a battle group was formed from the combat-experienced men of the Division. The Kampfgruppe was commanded by the former commander of the Sturmbrigade, Obersturmbannführer Conrad Schellong, and consisted of the following:

I./SS-Frw.-Regiment 66 commanded by Sturmbannführer Johannes Oehms

I./SS-Frw.-Regiment 67 commanded by Hauptsturmführer Wilhelm Rehmann

---

[4] Sprenger was later killed in action on April 19, 1945 and replaced by Untersturmführer August Heyerick who survived the war and passed away on February 12, 1996.

[5] This was one of the dictates of the original Flemish Legion, that the Flemings would never be put into action against the Western Allies and only against Communist Russian forces.

Commander of SS-Panzerjägerabteilung 27: Pictured here is the commander of the SS-Panzerjägerabteilung 27, Hauptsturmführer Ekkehard Wangemann. Wangemann was born on November 29, 1908. In 1930 Wangemann studied theology until receiving his degree in 1934. From 1934-1935 Wangemann was a Pastor in a church in Mecklenburg. From 1935 to 1937 he worked as a helper in the Reich's Internal Ministry. In 1937 he joined the Allgemeine-SS as a Sturmbannführer. During his time as a student, Wangemann received NCO training in the "black Reichswehr" and continued this training in the new Wehrmacht. After the war broke out, he fought in northern Norway where he won the War Merit Cross IInd Class. From there he was posted as a platoon leader in the 5th Totenkopfregiment in Prague and Warsaw in 1940. After being transferred back to "Nord," he served first as a platoon leader and then later as the Kompanieführer of the 7. Kompanie in 1941 in Finland. He was first wounded in the battles in Karelien. It was there that Wangemann was awarded the Iron Cross IInd Class and the Finnish "Mannerheim Order" as well as the Infantry Assault Badge. At the end of 1941 he received a post at the "Germanische Leitstelle 'Berlin,' " and at the end of 1942 he was transferred to the staff of the SS-Volunteer Division "Handschar." It was Wangemann's task to make sure that the Muslim's requests considering their religious customs were respected. Several Muslim officers later brought it to the attention of Wangemann that the German officers in the Division were not following the rules concerning the consumption of pork and alcohol, and after a disagreement with General Sauberzweig (German leader of the Division) considering this matter, Wangemann requested a transfer to another unit. This transfer took place in early 1943 and Wangemann was sent to the Sturmgeschütz school in Burg near Magdeburg where he was trained to be a commander. After the conclusion of his training, Wangemann was transferred to the staff of the then forming Stumgeschützabteilung 11, which was training in Grafenwöhr. From there he was transferred to the divisional staff of "Nederland" which was fighting in Croatia and would later fight in the Oranienbaumer Pocket. In 1944 he was transferred to the Sturmgeschützabteilung "Das Reich" and took part in the battles on the Normandy invasion front. There he won the Panzer Assault Badge and the Wound Badge in Silver after receiving his second and third wounds. After the conclusion of the invasion battles he was finally transferred to SS-Panzerjägerabteilung 27, where he would serve as commander until the end of the war. During the battles in eastern Germany (now Poland), he won the Iron Cross Ist Class. Wangemann survived the war and now lives with his wife in Kiel.

SS-Panzerjägerabteilung 27 commanded by Hauptsturmführer Ekkehard Wangemann

The Kampfgruppe was readied for battle during the initial drives and was deployed for defensive operations, should this be necessary. Later, as the German Bulge advance was halted, the men returned to the rest of the units training in Soltau. During the beginning of the second week of January, the Flemings were moved to Lüneberger Heath to get ready to depart for the Eastern Front. In the end it was only the previously mentioned battle group commanded by Obersturmbannführer Schellong that would depart for the front. Finally, after some initial confusion, the battle group found itself the city of Stettin in Pommerania. It was the end of January 1945.

And so began the final chapter of the war. Unfortunately it would be by far the most gruesome chapter for the Flemings and the Germans. As the Russians entered German territory they inflicted heinous atrocities on the civilian population. Gang-style rapes were committed by Russian soldiers on children of all ages. Old

PAK Company Staff: Pictured here is company commander Anton Kotlowski and several members of his staff. This picture was taken in the Fall of 1944 in Knovitz. The runes on the breast signify full membership in the SS or German citizenship. Notice that only the soldier to the far right is not wearing the runic patch, as he is a Fleming. From left to right: Heinz Schubert (who supposedly succeeded Hans Wallow as Spieß- this is not confirmed), Platoon Leader Kassberger (which platoon he led is unknown, he may have been a reserve platoon leader), Kompanie-Führer Anton Kotlowski, Kompanietruppführer Freese and Oberscharführer Raes, a Fleming.

men and women were murdered. The Germans and their foreign volunteer comrades continued to battle on, although all hope for final victory had been lost. Now the soldiers would be fighting to hold open the roads so that columns of fleeing of German civilians could escape to the West. Amongst the civilians were also foreign volunteer workers, which included many Flemings.

Langemarck's Panzerjägerabteilung was deployed between Stargard and Zachan after some transport delays. Close by was the 28. SS-Division "Wallonien." Members of the 23. SS-Division "Nederland" (Dutch) were also in the vicinity. Also in the vicinity were the "Panzer von Salza," (SS-Panzer-Abteilung 11 "Hermann von Salza" from the 11th SS-Division led again by Obersturmbannführer Paul-Albert Kausch) and the 4. SS-Polizei-Division. At this time many soldiers for the III. SS-Panzer-Korps were returning from the retreats from Latvia and were immediately put into battle on the front lines.

Sometime later, after several positional changes and suffering through very adverse winter conditions, communication between elements of the battle group became strained and contact with one of the infantry companies was lost. Schellong and his men were facing an enemy that enjoyed a numerical superiority of six to one. All this, not to mention the Russian's extensive supply of equipment and tanks.

Many local battles took place during this time period and in some cases the German forces were able to continue to ward off the Russian pursuit while at other times they were not. The will to continue to fight despite the desperate situation was fueled by the conduct of the Russians on German soil. The German soldiers and their comrades from the near West were witness to the aftermath of gruesome attacks on civilians as older men lay murdered and women raped. Corpses, dismembered and sometimes hacked into little pieces, lay scattered all around.

During attempts to maintain some kind of organized defense against the Russians, it was Untersturmführer Fernand Laporte who led his company against a threatening Russian force which was trying to rip a hole in the lines. Laporte and his men retook portions of the village of Schwanenbeck in a storming attack where the men used bayonets and hand grenades. The answer was a Russian artillery barrage which pinned the men to their positions. The alternative (doom for thousands of fleeing refugees) was worse than reality, and so it was that Laporte motioned for his men to attack in the midst of the Russian artillery fire. Laporte and his platoon leaders attacked while leading at the front of their men, and despite their superiority, the Russians began to flee. Laporte was killed during this attack.

Fernand Laporte: The picture of Schrijnen shown below was given to Laporte on February 7, 1945 at his request and was removed from Laporte's uniform after he was killed in action defending the German village of Schwanenbeck in Pommerania just ten days later. (The dark blotches are blood.) The picture of Laporte at right is a studio portrait taken at the Junkerschule Tölz where Fernand had attended officer training courses. Nand (Short for Fernand) Laporte was born on March 30, 1922 in Blankenberge, Flanders and had just turned 19 when he volunteered for service in the Waffen-SS in May 1941. Laporte was fluent in French, Dutch and German when he volunteered and had successfully completed the Flemish college entrance examination, which qualified him for university studies. Laporte was also a leader in the VNV. It is unknown in which unit Laporte fought in the early years of the war but he was enrolled at the Bad Tölz officer candidate school from September 1943 until March 1944 and left there as a senior NCO. From there he was transferred to Sturmbrigade "Langemarck" during the rest and refit period in the Summer of 1944. Laporte was commissioned as an Untersturmführer on June 21, 1944 and did not take part in the battles in the Blue Mountains of Estonia. Laporte went on to serve as company commander for one of infantry companies in the 27.SS-Freiwilligen Division "Langemarck." Laporte, surely a brave leader, had earned the Iron Cross 2nd Cross during his time on the front.

By mid-February Langemarck's Panzerjäger Battalion was placed in reserve in Stargard while other units were positioned elsewhere or continued to fight at the front. During their absence, "Langemarck" had fought several defensive battles and had managed to hold back numerous penetrating Russian units trying to expand bridgeheads on the Ihna river. By March 1st, the Russians had brought up a ten thousand-man strong division. They then began to advance in a northwesterly direction towards Stettin. The Flemings, along with their Dutch and German comrades on the front, tried in vain to hold the Russians back. The Russians penetrated the line in several locations. That same day, SS-Panzerjägerabteilung 27 was brought back from Stargard and it was immediately subordinated to the remaining remnants of I./SS-Rgt. 67. The Battalion's commander, Hauptsturmführer Wilhelm Rehmann, had been wounded two weeks earlier, so Hauptsturmführer Ekkehard Wangemann took command of the combined unit.

As Schrijnen returned to the front from the hospital in late February, he was not sent to serve in the battle group, but was employed in a PAK platoon that was to be used for "special purposes" by the III. SS-Panzerkorps. This platoon was to deployed at hot spots along the crumbling lines of the German defense. Several of his old comrades, among others, Kamiel Horre and Paul Rubens, would serve in a gun crew under Schrijnen's leadership. An Unterscharführer Notrupp served as *Zugführer*. Schrijnen picks up the story in late February 1945.[6]

...so in 1945, we were retreating in the direction of Kösslin and there were very long columns of refugees all over. Someone called and said, "boys don't wait too long, hundreds of Soviet tanks are on the way," but we answered that the "Führer's order" was the "Führer's order," hold out as long as possible until the columns of civilians were out of danger, we did this gladly for the women and children, it was our duty. The columns of civilians continued and an old lady stopped to speak with me, "poor boys, we flee while you boys are killed." We saw Fallschirmjäger (parachutists) also on the retreat. An Oberst from these units arrived and told us, "boys, you can't do anything about it, come with us." I answered to him, "Herr Oberst, it won't get as bad as it has been for you and your men." He saw my Knight's Cross and we began to converse. I told him that I was from Flanders and had been in the Kurland battles. At the end of our conversation he said, "I can only wish you

---

[6] Letter to the author from R. Schrijnen dated Sept. 10, 1996.

*all success..." Then the T-34s rolled into our positions with out any security.
When they reached a distance of six hundred meters, we gave them fire. The
first T-34 burned almost immediately and then they all began to retreat. By the
time they were all gone, two of the tanks had received direct hits and five were
damaged and immobile. The MG-Schütze had counted thirty-five attacking T-
34s. We had to retreat and it was then that I heard that Untersturmführer
Marcel Laperre was also in the vicinity with his PAK platoon. I hoped that we
would meet up. It is barely believable, said the officers.*

*Our Zugführer (platoon leader), Oberscharführer Notrupp, sent out one
of our motorcycle messengers, Thor Petersen (a Dane), who now had a Puch
motorcycle (Italian) instead of a BMW. "Yeah, Remy," I thought to myself,
"once again our platoon has been sent on a suicide operation." Attack and
defend, what luck, the 7.5 cm PAK was mobile even on this terrain. The 8.8 cm
FLAK was an extremely strong gun, but the requirement of a secure position
and its heavy weight made it not as maneuverable or mobile as our PAK and
everything had to happen fast. Engels came with food, to the left of us came
Fallschirmjäger and Navy men, the PAK platoon waited and listened, all of us
were ready to fire. Messengers arrived and informed us that we were to await
a large scale attack of tanks and infantry. I believe it was the 22nd of February 1945, before Kösslin. We fired Sprenggranaten into the Soviets and the
enemy turned away and moved to the left which offered us their flank. A messenger arrived, we were to retreat immediately. We fired our guns a bit more,
but we had to follow orders because we were in danger of being surrounded.*

On March 2nd, Kampfgruppe "Langemarck's" Panzerjäger guns were placed
in positions along the Ihna river in the vicinity of Zachan. At this time there was
much confusion among Langemarck's leaders and after much debate it was decided that the troops would retreat towards Stargard while leaving a small battle
group of one hundred men at Zachan to cover the retreat. Remy and his gun crew
remained near Kösslin. Schrijnen recalls:

*There we were with platoon leader Notrupp, an Unterscharführer. To the
right was Unterscharführer Stamm as well as a commander of the army, who
also had a 75 mm PAK gun. We then heard an evil rumble and it began to
thunder like a coming storm. The Stalin's Organs ripped the earth apart and a
yellow wall of fire stood there, flickering. Lightning shots fired at us, red tongued*

flames, more rumble and our feet felt the shaking of the ground. The large attack had come. Luckily I still had a few Pervitin tablets which the doctor gave me, he told me not to take them too often. Only with them was I able to stand up straight. At least I tried to relieve the men from a part of their drudgery. I could hear the soft rumbling of the battling infantry. We still stood before Kösslin, it was March 2, 1945. The Stalin's Organs still didn't touch our positions, they were somewhat too far to the front, luckily. We beat off the thousands of attacking Soviet infantrymen. Also our PAKs and MGs joined the fight. Then began the dance of death. Our "Nebelwerfer" brought relief but the air became lively with fighter pilots and bombs. And they hunted us, trying to break our resistance. We reached the highway and while crossing it we received heavy fire. I warned my men that whoever lost their nerves and ran away would be dead. There was only one thing to protect us, our trenches, narrow and deep, and a few groups of Fallschirmjäger. The Soviets then came out of their trenches, already we began to storm forward, not looking up or to the right or left. Then our rounds started to fly. It finally came to close combat with pistols, shovels, my specialty, the shovel. The Soviets broke off the attack and began to flee, we immediately went to our PAK and took the fleeing Soviets under fire. We shot trucks into the air and the Soviets received a punishment that they had not anticipated. We took a Soviet Major prisoner, a Jew who could speak good German. He told us that the Soviets would be attacking with all fierceness all the way to Stettin, over the Oder and as far as possible into Germany, they wanted to penetrate deep into the West. This Soviet Major was amazed at the number of non-German volunteers. He had heard we were forced to join, he didn't think that anyone would be compelled to fight with the German Wehrmacht, still less the Waffen-SS. He then asked us if we were anti-communists or fascists. We told him we fought for our homeland, within a greater German empire, not as less, but as an equal and after the war our countries would be independent and be able speak our own language and have our own culture. He shook his head. We just sent him to the rear. We behaved as soldiers and departed as soldiers.

In our section we had seventeen men dead and many were wounded. We decided to change positions, four or five hundred meters to the left and near the infantry from the crossing to Kösslin. In this way I could cover the flanks and the crossing and rule the highway to Kösslin. Kösslin was soon a village of gray.

*A regiment, some two hundred men of the III. Germanisches-Panzerkorps,
Volksturm and Army, now made up the front. The regimental commander, a
Hauptmann, brought us rounds for our PAK. There we were, some of the old
"Oostfronters" of the Legion "Flandern" and the Sturmbrigade
"Langemarck." I looked next to me and I saw amongst them a battle group
from the Kurland, from the III. Germanisches-Panzerkorps, only some of which
are "alte Hasen." These men, who had been on the Eastern Front for some
three to four years by this time. They had volunteered to fight against the
Soviet Union in 1941. At that time we all knew that we were fighting for the
German people and our people, but in 1945 we were fighting to protect the
women and children fleeing the murderous onslaught of the Soviet soldiers.*

In the sector of Pommerania where Panzerjägerabteilung 27 was fighting, the
soldiers remaining in Zachan were attacked by a Russian patrol and a battle for
Zachan erupted. The battle lasted through that afternoon, but the Russians were
forced to retreat. Shortly thereafter the Russians rained shells on the town, but
since the Flemings were located in a small sector of the city, they were unharmed.
Meanwhile, the Divisional staff and the remaining elements of the Division had
stopped in the villages of Groß and Klein Schlatik. Since the Soviets did not take
Zachan, Hauptsturmführer Wangemann devised a plan to retake the village that
night. Unfortunately the Russians spotted movement and began immediately to
attack the Flemings with mortars and rockets. During the attack three officers were
badly wounded and had to be evacuated. The attack on Zachan was canceled and
Hauptsturmführer Wangemann and his men were forced to retreat.

On March 4th, the Flemings began a retreat through several villages and the
Russians were right on the Fleming's heels. Kampfgruppe "Langemarck" then
erected defensive positions around the village of Stargard. The strength of the
battle group had now been reduced to some 500 men, a quarter of its original
strength. The battles had also taken their toll on the PAK units. Kotlowski's unit
had been reduced to a mere platoon, only three guns still functioned. Wangemann's
Sturmgeschütz company, like Schrijnen and his PAK unit, were on permanent loan
to the III. SS-Panzerkorps.

On March 5th, the Russians had surrounded Stargard on three sides. The vil-
lage contained members of several other units from the 11. SS-Division "Nordland."
The Soviets continued to move to the West as did "Langemarck" as well. The
Division ended up in a small village named Grimme. The weather during the fol-

lowing days then turned favorable for the Germans. What had previously been a boon to their offensive operations, was now welcome: the Spring weather softened the ground to mush, making it difficult for the masses of Russian tanks to maintain mobility. This allowed the Flemings to take a much needed five-day break. Remy Schrijnen recalled:

> *In Pommerania the Soviets had a more than 5x advantage over us with regards to all weapons. We were there anyway. Munitions were low and next to us fought companies of the Artillery School. The Fahnenjunker (officer candidates) from Großborn, young courageous men of the Army, who were expected to fight as infantry men. Our battle group, made-up of Germanic volunteers, we got along very well. Now we were only fighting for the refugees, women, children and older people from East Prussia. We were under the command of an Oberst Schneider and a Hauptmann Bruns (Knight's Cross winner) we fought good and hard.*
>
> *Later we were put together as a special platoon of tank-smashers for quick actions. Ivan pressured us with his infantry while we pushed them back with our Sprenggranaten. Bruns appeared to be satisfied with us. The retreat was called in, but the PAKs remained for the defense. Many Soviet tanks attacked and fifteen were knocked out. I had luck and knocked out my seventeenth T-34. Also the Fahnenjunker from Großborn did their best, the comrades from the Wehrmacht were amazed at the non-Germans. At this time our PAKs were subordinated to the Army's 163. Infanterie-Division.*
>
> *Yes, General Krappe with his brave men, he tried as a Pomeranian to hold together his units and also parts of the Waffen-SS. He was a General who was liked to be seen on the front and had won the Knight's Cross. Yes, Oberst Munzel of the 14. Panzer Division. He was a Knight's Cross winner, and helped us members of the III. Germanisches-Panzerkorps with his Panzers near Friedrichsdorf. Obergefreiter Volmer helped us more as a brave gunner. They were all younger dazzling comrades, and Volmer personally shot the way free for the fleeing civilians. I was not far away and blew the transport wagons. Yes sir, this was the front and besides us enlisted men there were also higher officers and generals that stood by their men. For example there was Generalleutnant Karl Rübel of the 163. Infanterie-Division, who fought in the forest at Friedrichsdorf in March 1945 or General-Leutnant Freiherr Siegmund von Schleinitz who fell during the breakout of Friedrichsdorf. Such Generals,*

who were forward with their men and fought along side them, were held in high regard by their men.

My men and I were on the front as soldiers "for special purposes." We blocked the main streets from the Soviets with our 7.5 cm PAKs. It was a hard battle, some ten thousand women, children and old men, wounded as well, were retreating. We had luck, in this cold we managed a breakthrough.

On March 16th, several Panzers from the SS-Panzer-Regiment 10 under the leadership of Obersturmbannführer Otto Paetsch covered a "Langemarck" retreat. During the heated battles, Paetsch himself was killed. On March 17th, the Soviets barraged Langemarck's positions in Stettin but the men remained put. The next day came a brutal Soviet tank attack, some two hundred tanks were reported to have attacked positions in Altdamm after which they were followed by a wave of Russian infantry. The Russian attack was somehow beat back with Panzerfäuste (German Bazookas) but as usual, that only brought a huge artillery attack. Even this late in the war the fighting was fierce with German units holding onto everything they could. That wasn't much, however, and every battle deteriorated the situation at the front still further. By March 20th, the battle group's strength had been reduced to some two hundred men. The retreat continued on March 19th and by March 20th the men had crossed the Oder river. Schrijnen continued:[7]

The PAK's position was good and slightly elevated, as I prefer it. There we were, behind the barrel looking out over the battlefield. We would also set up dummy positions, beautifully camouflaged with tree branches similar in size to our gun. This would make it harder for Ivan to pick us out of the woodwork. The Russians then began to attack with their bombers which decked us and the dummy positions as well. Then came the artillery, Stalin's Organs. We could only wait and hope that our luck would remain loyal to us. Finally the Soviets came, from a good kilometer away. They came from the forests and climbed out of their foxholes. Our platoon leader, Unterscharführer Stamm, ordered us not to fire too soon. Under the protection of attack planes, the Soviets came forward and approached our old positions which were well-mined and lay some five to six hundred meters before us. The mines started to blow near Stamm, and then Ivan stopped his charge. It was a dangerous situ-

---

[7] Letter to the author from R. Schrijnen dated Dec. 13, 1996.

ation for us all. I then heard the call "FEUER FREI" upon which I began to send the Sprenggranaten in to the Soviet lines. Both of our MGs started up, and the Fallschirmjäger and Stamm's crew joined as well. The grenade launchers plopped their lively punches into the Soviet lines. Sturmgeschütze blast away at the lines as well from behind us. The harvest was rich, Soviet officers and commissars pushed their soldiers forward and they were soon only one hundred meters away, but they began to run out of steam and began to rush back. We shot with all our weapons, it was a bloody finale to a battle that lasted at least forty-five minutes.

An order came at night, we were to retreat. A part of the infantry pulled back, and later the PAK guns followed. The Russians were not to know it. Our wounded and a few of our dead had already been brought to the back, the wounded Ivans stumbled or crawled back, but no one helped them. The Soviet medics still had not arrived, too bad for those boys, even though they were the enemy. Heinrich Himmler was the Heeresgruppe Kommandeur then, but it seems to have went well for the most part, we still had ammunition and rations. We could only praise our artillery, led by Oberst Bruns who was a fine brave man. He stood by his men during the attack and also next to his Germanic volunteers. "Unbelievable," he said about us, how we defended his homeland. An Oberst von Witzleben was a very good infantry regiment commander. Under his command were comrades from the Kriegsmarine. The Volksturm, which consisted of boys under the age of 16 and men as old as 64 had to come to the rear and help dig trenches as well as help and guide the Pomeranians, because there were many columns of them, coming from West Prussia with a Kreisleiter (district leader), an Ortsbauernführer, it appeared as if this man was still very disciplined. The party officials did as the officers told them in their will to continue on. It was a difficult time.

I am sure that Kotlowski and Laperre continued to fight bravely. The Kampfgruppen of the Walloons and Flemings had a good reputation within the III. Germanisches-Panzerkorps. The men of the corps stood like iron on the front, just as their German comrades did. There were no cowards in this corps. Felix Steiner and his divisional and regimental commanders were still ready for the fight. Because they weren't just fighting for Germany, they were fighting to save their homeland and people. It was a cruel fate that stood before their population, also ours in Flanders. One can say what they want about the III. Germanisches-Panzerkorps, but our officers and commanders were loyal and brave like nobody else and they stood alongside their men. I can now speak for the greater German Wehrmacht in Pommerania, and I can state that all actions that I personally took part in 1945 were a sign that they did all they could to protect their homeland. Some of the officers in the Wehrmacht, even Knight's Cross winners, helped to dig trenches right alongside their men. It was also so in the Waffen-SS, that NCOs and officers would help during the building of new positions. I personally stood guard as I had always done before. I wasn't conceited and even though I was an Unterscharführer and I didn't let my men do all the work. When one is a front-line soldier, one remains a comrade above everything else. One could think that in war it should be that way without even having to think about it. But at the same time one had to act and make decisions that could only be made on the front. On the front it was the simple man who personally decided the situation in which others found themselves.

Much had changed after 1944. The large retreats were foreign to us. Our higher leadership knew better how to attack and how to go forward. Despite this we were pushed ever deeper into the Reich in 1945. The enemy had already held the advantage in 1944. There was nothing that we could make excuses for, in Pommerania in March 1945 we could only hold the enemy up. There were indeed successful counter attacks, and at one time we managed to advance 35 km to the east.

Located in Brüssow and Retzin, the remaining portions of the 27. SS-Division began to rebuild with the last remaining units which had been continuously training elsewhere. These men were from the incomplete SS-Grenadier-Regiment 68 which consisted of two battalions and a staff. First Battalion of the regiment consisted of 15 to 17 year old members of the Flemish National Socialist Youth. The other two regiments also received a new contingent of men and the strength of the Division grew to some four thousand men and the fighting portions were now referred to as Kampfgruppe "Schellong." Due to the true conditions at this time, units from Regiment 68 would shortly be distributed amongst the other two remaining regiments, however.

After reorganizing, the men were put into defensive positions along the Oder river. Only two artillery pieces are known to exist at this time. For the first two weeks of April there was little fighting and the men remained in their positions. On April 15th, the Flemings were repositioned and the refreshed PAK unit arrived and was sent to positions in Schwedt-Freienwalde to the south along with Panzers from the 11. SS-Division to block the expected advance on Berlin. Other divisional non-infantry units that were forming in the West arrived that second week in April as well and on the 15th, several Flemish units, along with some of their comrades in the 28. SS-Division and Army Panzerabwehr Abteilung 6 (Assault Guns) were put under the command of Standartenführer Müller and referred to as Gruppe "Müller." At this time a Kampfgruppe "Schellong" also existed, but it is unknown which of the Flemish units belonged to which group. Schrijnen continues:

> *Yes, March came to an end and in April varying orders arrived, we were to go to Berlin or follow the Oder river south to Schwedt on the Oder river.*
>
> *Retreat after retreat, we saw so many sawmills – so many villages were lost. We won back one village but unfortunately when we returned we only found dead old men, women and children. Even old women and very young girls (6-7 years old) had been raped. Smashed babies heads lay also about and these sights hardened us still further. Our tank-hunting commando suffered badly as well. But I continued to have luck, as always, and when I suffered another direct hit and lost my fourth gun, I survived once again. It was then that I was sure that I would survive the war.*
>
> *The Americans bombed the columns of civilians on the retreat as well, even though they knew that they weren't soldiers, only German women and children. During this time we remained loyal and brave and continued to fight, as all our comrades did. We remained bound to our people, we were soldiers and remained soldiers – despite everything that was stacked against us. We were loyal and remained ready to give our lives for what we fought for.*

During this time a poem was found on the corpse of an unknown girl from Pommerania. The title of the poem: "Early Spring in Pommerania."

Vorfrühling in Pommern, ahnende Zeit,
Soldaten im feldgrauen Ehrenkleid.
Trotzige Minen, Stahlhelm, Gewehr,
So sah ich kommen das tapfere Heer.
Deutschen, Flamen, Wallonen.

Vorfrühling in Pommern, vergangene Zeit,
Gräber und Kreuze in Einsamkeit.
Stilles Gedenken, ein Beten vielmehr,
So will ich danken dem tapferen Heer.
Deutschen, Flamen, Wallonen.

Early Spring in Pommerania, a divine time,
Soldiers in field-gray uniforms.
Defiant mines, helmets, rifles,
So I saw coming the brave army.
Germans, Flemings, Walloons.

Early Spring in Pommerania, a foregone time,
Graves and crosses in solitude.
Silent memories, a prayer even more,
So I want to thank the brave army.
Germans, Flemings, Walloons.

In Kampfgruppe "Schellong's" section, several scouting patrols were sent out between the 15th and the 18th of April, but only casualties and missing men were the result. The other men took the time to place mines and other obstacles in the path of the Russians. On April 20th, the Russians formed a bridgehead in the sector of the 4. SS-Polizei-Division. Elsewhere, in Eberswald, "Langemarck's" Sturmgeschütze were supporting other units of the 4. SS-Division in vain, and at last the final obstruction to Berlin was run over by the Russians. The situation at the front continued to deteriorate and the leadership corps lost their ability to properly control the situation. Confusion surmounted and makeshift battle groups continued to fight local battles for the next three weeks. Some men chose to continue to fight, while others were ordered to march to the West and surrender to the Western Allies, to thus avoid Soviet captivity.

The Panzerjäger of Battle Group "Schellong" were still together during this time. They were successful but suffered many casualties and were deployed like the fire department, running here and there, wherever there were problems on the lines. After a while they had no more anti-tank guns and no more trucks. Anton Kotlowski, the company commander for the PAK company, reported:[8]

---

[8] Letter to the author from A. Kotlowski dated May 10, 1997.

*...the Panzerjäger (tank-hunters) became Panzerzerstörer (tank destroy-
ers) and used German Bazookas and Panzerfäuste to knock out tanks. Contact to the rest of the battalion and its staff was often lost. Shortly before
Prenzlau an ordinance officer from the battalion found me and notified me
that I had been promoted to Obersturmführer and had been awarded the German Cross in Gold. He didn't have the badge with him, he was supposed to
pick up the document and the award at battalion headquarters. I had no idea
where that was. We were often lost and I could no longer maintain an orderly
leadership. At this time rank and awards no longer held any meaning. It was
only important to deploy the troops effectively and avoid heavy and unnecessary casualties. In the area of Prenzlau, we were supposed to stop an already
occurring Russian tank and infantry attack along with an army bicycle company which was subordinated to the company. Two NCOs of the bicycle company threatened me with machine pistols while the Kommandeur of the unit, a
Leutnant, took off with his 70 men to the west. The Russians then rolled over
our company. We had heavy casualties but managed to knock out 3 Russian
tanks. I then lost contact with Untersturmführer Laperre who took off to the
north. I had just recommended him for the German Cross in Gold. Kassberger,[9]
who had taken over Hugo Mortier's platoon,[10] took off to the south and fell
into enemy hands and was taken prisoner.*

Jan De Wilde reported:[11]

*Due to the overpowering Russian forces, we were forced (with heavy ca-
sualties in men and equipment) to pull back behind the Oder River. There we
had some time to rest until the 20th of April, when the last Russian offensive
began with an enormous artillery barrage, followed by incredible amounts of
tanks and fighter planes. Many Flemings were killed on the Oder river. We
pulled back, powerless, to Schwerin. Everyone fought bravely to the end, especially Kotlowski, who lost almost all of his PAK guns.*

*Late in April, the word about Hitler's suicide had filtered its way to the front.
Schrijnen recalls:[12]*

---

[9] After two years of being held prisoner, Kassberger escaped and married a Dutch woman. He
also visited with Kotlowski after the war. Letter to the author from A. Kotlowski dated May 10, 1997.
[10] Mortier had been badly wounded again. As in early March 1944, Mortier was shot in the jaw.
[11] Letter to the author from J. De Wilde dated March 10, 1997.
[12] Letter to the author from R. Schrijnen dated July 22, 1997.

Ersatzpanzerjäger, 1945: Pictured here is an example of how the Panzerjäger were equipped and forced to fight. Lacking the necessary PAKs, the tank hunters resorted to fighting only with Panzerfausts.

I heard that the Führer was dead and I couldn't believe it. But no, it was confirmed, Hitler had killed himself. I thought to myself, "Remy, the Führer is dead." I was somewhat disappointed to learn that he had killed himself, as I had hoped that he had been killed with a gun in his hand, fighting on the front, as I had once imagined.

For Remy Schrijnen and the men surrounding him and their gun, they continued as long as possible to aid the masses of refugees in their flight from the advancing Soviets. According to Schrijnen, his gun continued to hold open a path for the refugees even two days after the formal surrender. Schrijnen and his men, now out of ammunition, fled to the West where they hoped to receive better treatment than what they knew they would suffer in Soviet captivity. Schrijnen reports:[13]

There were unimaginable battles in April and early May 1945, heavy attacks. The III. Germanisches-Panzer-Korps remained the bravest corps of the Waffen-SS. At this time every officer, NCO and enlisted man fought next to comrades from the Heer, Kriegsmarine, Luftwaffe, next to Fallschirmjäger and young men from the Heeres-Artillerie-Schule Großborn. Yes, the boys

---

[13] Letter to the author from R. Schrijnen dated Oct. 30, 1995.

Digging in Pommerania in the Spring of 1945: Here a Langemarck soldier digs in before an upcoming battle to defend the German mainland.

were now behind the Oder: Estonians, Latvians, Norwegians, Swedes, Danes, Dutch, Walloons, Flemings and our German comrades in the land of the many small lakes.

On the 10th of May we fired our guns for the last time, doing what we could to help the refugees fleeing to the west. During the evening of the 10th of May we surrendered to the English who promptly handed us over to the Americans. It was then that I destroyed everything I had, my medals, my Soldbuch and anything else I had on my person. I also changed my name to Gustav Wiest, a mountain trooper I had known from Kempten-Allgäu who had been killed in action. In order to camouflage my membership in the Waffen-SS I cut off the blood-group tattoo under my arm and cut the other side to make it appear as if a bullet had gone through it.

Yes, there were so many good men. Retreat after retreat, we had fought these final battles to save women, children, Red Cross nurses and the wounded. These were the last days of the war. Despite this we remained front soldiers, true to our oath, we couldn't bring the gods of war to our side. We went down proud, we knew what would come to us.

After the heavy casualties in Prenzlau, Kotlowski and his men pushed their way to the West. They had no truck, just a couple of bicycles and were partly encircled by the Russians. After knocking out one last T-34, they managed to make their way into American prison in the town of Schwerin an der Oder.

After the War – Internment

And so began the long and bitter end to the war. In Belgium the authorities were waiting for the return of the German "collaborators." Everyone who had volunteered to help the Germans in one way or another was convicted of being a German collaborator. Soldiers from the Wehrmacht, members of the N.S.K.K., volunteer German Red Cross nurses, all were sentenced to prison or in some cases, sentenced by the Belgian court to death. Apparently the exiled Belgian government in England had passed new laws in 1942 and 1943 which made political and military collaboration with Germany, among other things, illegal. Therefore the young "Oostfronter" were tried and convicted in absentia for breaking retroactive laws.

In Flanders and the rest of Belgium, the sentiment towards Germany had changed during the years of war. As was initially noted, the Flemings believed in 1940 that the Germans would be victorious. The Flemish King Leopold had decided to remain in Flanders and there was a calm peace. Over time, however, it became increasingly apparent that the Germans would ultimately lose the war. The shortages of food and material on the front worsened and required that the Germans procure raw material for their armies. Certainly these and many other factors changed the minds of many who were initially not certain which side to support, and many others as well. In 1944, during the Allied invasion of Western Europe, King Leopold had fled to Austria.

During the initial days after the conclusion of the war, Flemish communists and members of the resistance came out of the wood work and terrorized those that had sided with the Germans. The occupying Allied forces did little or nothing to bring order to the situation. Random executions took place and a certain limited anarchy spread throughout the land. At times, six to eight prisoners were stuffed into a prison cell for one person.

After the things settled down, the Belgian court tried those collaborators that survived through the initial confusion. In total, 57,052 people were given a court martial. Of those that went before the court, over thirty-two thousand were tried for military collaboration, almost twenty-four thousand for political collaboration, over four thousand for economic collaboration and almost four thousand were convicted of being informants.[14] Almost three thousand people were given a death sentence and 242 of these convictions were carried out. Over two thousand were given life sentences, but it is unknown how many of these, if any, were carried out. The number of convictions was particularly high, especially considering that in Holland, a country that suffered under German occupation greater than the Belgians, only 42 of a mere 154 death sentences were carried out.

The families of the collaborators also suffered a grim fate and were cast out from society. Houses were broken into and searched – which destroyed them in the process. In every case the volunteers lost their Belgian citizenship and this made it virtually impossible to obtain work. The families of volunteers lost their jobs and what social status they had. While some former volunteer workers were able to escape to Germany, many were sentenced to prison.

---

[14] The number of cases exceeds the total number of people brought before the Belgian court martial because some were tried for more than one form of collaboration.

TER NAGEDACHTENIS

aan

AUGUST CLAES

Geboren te Antwerpen op 23 februari 1922, aldaar als **Oostfronter** op bevel van het Belgisch Gerecht **gefusilleerd** op 14 juli 1945.

ver. uitg. : God. Claes, Hopland 31, Antw.

An Executed Oostfronter: August Claes had served with the Waffen-SS on the Eastern Front. He was executed by the Belgian Court on July 12, 1945 for being a German collaborator. Claes had served as an enlisted man and was 23 years old at the time of his execution. On the left is his obituary and on the right is his gravestone. The gravestone is in the form of a birch tree cross, which was used on the Eastern Front. The symbol is a combination of the Germanic death rune above and the cross of Christ below. Many of the former Oostfronters in Belgium have crosses similar to these.

The veterans of the Waffen-SS who were on the front surrendered to the Americans, but were subsequently handed over to the British and imprisoned in the concentration camp in Neuengamme. From there they were sent back to their homeland and were imprisoned in the former Belgian concentration camp in Beverloo. The camp was taken over and run by an American and the Belgian administration. Anton Kotlowski reported:[15]

> *Just before we landed in American prison I avoided a Russian fighterplane attack on a wide street because I stayed on the street and the plane*

---

[15] Letter to the author from A. Kotlowski dated May 10, 1997.

followed a large group of men that fled into the field. I survived, even though I didn't want to.

Shortly thereafter we surrendered to the Americans and stayed in American prison for eleven days. We were situated in an open field and without food or water. There we experienced the end of the war. Within the eleven days I experienced a wonderful sign of camaraderie. One of the men of my company, I forget his name – how deplorable, searched for me in the crowd of some ten thousand men. He found me and gave me a sugar cube, despite the fact that he was starving himself – something I will never ever forget.

The treatment by the Americans was good. After a few weeks the camp with the soldiers of the Waffen-SS were transferred to the English zone, while the other camps of prisoners were handed over to the Russians. The English picked us up at the train station in Bergedorf. From there they lined us up and set us out on a very fast-paced march, the speed of which was determined by their tanks which followed us. Whoever couldn't maintain the pace was run over by the following tanks. After being whipped, stomped-on and beat up by English officers and soldiers, during which many men lost their teeth, we arrived at our barracks, which didn't have any beds. There were only broken tables and chairs which we had told were removed from the former concentration camps. The English took our American rations away from us. English officers stole the wedding rings from our fingers. I experienced this treatment in six camps from six different troops – each which never followed the rules of the Geneva convention for the handling of prisoners. It was finally in the seventh camp the we received normal treatment.

Jan De Wilde reported:[16]

The time as a POW was one of the most difficult of the entire war. For the first three weeks we were in an open field without food. We fed ourselves with leaves from trees and straw. We drank water from puddles. After three weeks we received tents and something to eat. At one moment the Americans wanted to hand over the SS prisoners to the Russians. But that didn't happen. The American soldiers handled themselves correctly. Since the Americans wanted to pull out of the area, we were all loaded into train cars and were placed under English guard. Two days long without food or water we had to stay in

---

[16] Letter to the author from J. De Wilde dated Aug. 29, 1996.

the wagons without being let out. After two days we were imprisoned in the Neuengamme concentration camp.

The English were cynical. We had to sleep on the bare ground. After a few weeks the so-called elite Belgian troops from the Brigade Piron came to us to get our identities. We were beat up and everything in our possession was stolen from us, wedding rings, wrist-watches, etc. By the end of our stay in Neuengamme I had lost between sixty and seventy pounds. In July we were loaded on to freight train wagons and taken to the Belgian concentration camp in Beverloo. There we were regularly beaten by Belgian soldiers.

Here the rations were better. But many died due to lack of food. The dead looked like skeletons. I was active in the infirmary with two doctors and medics. Everyday we requested medication for the sick, but we were refused. During our time there we always wore the same underwear. We were never given the opportunity to shower or bathe.

On September 25, 1945 I was transported to the prison in Ghent. My mother had supplied me with a suit and some underwear. Already in October 1944 I had been sentenced to death in absentia. Protests were raised against the judgment, but they were refused after three minutes by the war court. The death sentence was confirmed two times and any hope for a dismissal was lost. In 1947 I managed to get a new trial. My Wallonian Gruppenführer, whose life I had saved during the hostilities with Germany in 1940, had come forward with his story that I had saved his life during the fighting on the Leie river. That impressed the court and as a result my death sentence was repealed after two and a half years. I was released during Pfingsten in 1947. I had been interned for 25 months total. During this time I had starved for about a year.

An American Captain Frankfurter who was in Beverloo remains clearly in the memory of those that were imprisoned there. There the veterans were treated with regular beatings and poor living conditions. Many men were packed inside a single room with only a toilet in the corner to relieve themselves. The men were repeatedly humiliated and were fed very little. Remy Schrijnen reported:[17]

After the British handed us over to the Americans in Beverloo, we were greeted with beatings, one after the other. We were beat up daily by guards

---

[17] Letter to the author from R. Schrijnen dated Feb. 15, 1997.

Remy Schrijnen in the Internment Camp at Beverloo, 1947: Shown above is a sketch done by one of Remy's comrades on August 10, 1947 in the Beverloo internment camp. Remy remained in Beverloo until 1950 and as a supporter of general amnesty for himself and his former comrades, was imprisoned again from 1953-1955.

whose task it was to re-educate us. Everything was forbidden, enlisted men were even forbidden from saluting officers. I remember when one of the Americans dropped a piece of chocolate on the ground into the dirt. He ordered me to get down on all fours and pick it up from the ground with my mouth and eat it like a dog. I just stamped the chocolate into the ground. Then blows to the stomach rained upon me. Everyday we were forced to write about the tens and thousands of Jews that we had supposedly killed. As we were beat, we were continually asked how we could have fought on the side of the Germans and were told again and again that that we were war criminals. Ironically, we then heard about how the how the Americans dropped two atom bombs on Japan. We didn't know what atom bombs were then. I have to say, though, that these prison guards weren't front line soldiers.

Remy was finally released from prison in 1950. During his internment he had not contacted his family. Remy's mother had died of cancer in 1940 and he did not want to burden his father with his problems. Attempts to contact his family could have also caused other problems for his family due to Remy's status as German collaborator. After his release, he moved in with his sister Bertha. His father was very disappointed that Remy had not contacted him while in prison. While living with his sister Remy sought work, but could find none due to his status as a German collaborator. Eventually he did find work, first doing odd jobs, then working once again in the coal mines. In the beginning of 1951, about a year after Remy was released from prison, he met Joanna Buseyne in Brussels while visiting a family of one of his comrades. She knew that he was an "Oostfronter" and had just been released from prison. She was twenty-three years old when she met him and had just returned from the French part of Flanders where she worked in a weaving mill. Things went well and they were soon engaged. Joanna was born in 1928 in Menen near Kortrijk on the border of France. The fact that Remy worked in the coal mines and had no rights as a citizen did not bother her in the least, because, as she put it, "for a Fleming it is an honor not be Belgian!"

After getting out of prison Remy was immediately in contact with his old comrades and politics was once again the primary topic of discussion, despite the situation in Belgium. Now the former soldiers and German collaborators had other things to fight for within their homeland, things much more basic in nature, like the right to hold a job and earn a living to support their families. Sometime in 1953 there was a demonstration put on by (among others) the former members of the Waffen-SS. The "Oostfronters," as they were referred to, demonstrated against the repression they suffered within their homeland. The wanted political amnesty for their comrades from the Belgian state. During this demonstration Schrijnen spoke and was subsequently arrested by the political police. He was once again sent to prison in Diksmuide and newly interned as a political prisoner. Joanna Schrijnen reports:[18]

> *Despite Remy's problems with the Belgian government, I found Remy's political beliefs to be good. Surely I would have rather had Remy as a free man, as a Democrat who fights for freedom, but he was put in prison by these so-called democrats which I found incorrect, it was a democracy in name only, a fake democracy.*
>
> *Even my residence was searched, for what I don't know. After the political police got done ripping apart my apartment, they asked if they could wash their hands, I refused them, telling them that they could do that while they were on guard duty. I then got a job as a cashier in a butcher's shop in Brussels, where Remy was released from prison.*

---

[18] Letter to the author from J. Schrijnen-Buseyne dated Feb. 15, 1997.

Joanna Schrijnen. Above left is a picture of Joanna Buseyne-Schrijnen in the 1950s and center at home with Remy in Germany. **Hektor Gijse and Remy Schrijnen**: Right: Hektor Gijse (left) was with Remy during the battles in Ukraine in early 1944. He was a Schütze IV, one of the munitions handlers in the PAK crew. Before the war was over, Gijse was shot in the arm while on guard duty. He refused to leave his post until he was relieved. His wound was so bad that his arm had to be amputated.

On September 22, 1955 Remy Schrijnen and Joanna Buseyne were married in Brussels. Remy remained a man without a state and had no citizenship and was therefore unable to hold a job. He worked as a truck driver until 1962 and then Remy was once again to go to prison since he retained his stance for amnesty for himself and his comrades. After hearing the rumor of the planned arrest, he secretly went to a meeting of the former Knight's Cross winners in Germany where his German comrades convinced him to apply for political asylum there. He was asylum and has lived in the city of Hagen since then. It wasn't until 1991 that Remy was able to return to visit Flanders, which he did to visit the 40th anniversary festivities for St. Maartensfonds, the Flemish veteran's relief organization. In 1992 the statute of limitations for his arrest in Belgium ran out. Since 1955 Remy has been an active member of the Ordengemeinschaft der Ritterkreuzträger (Organization of Knight's Cross Winners) and has attended almost every one of the annual reunions since joining.

The Fate of Convictions: Opinions of those who served and fought for a free Flanders and a Greater Germany

The young Flemish soldiers, feeling repressed in their homeland, went to the front and fought a brutal war for several years. They fought for their beliefs and convictions, their hopes for something better, a better world where they would not

Paul-Albert Kausch in 1981: Pictured here is Paul-Albert Kausch at the age of 70. As is evident in the photo, Kausch went on to win the Oakleaves to his Knight's Cross, which he was awarded during the final days of the war on April 23, 1945. Kausch was notified of the award while leading ad-hoc battle groups in the battle for Berlin. The Germans, their fate sealed long ago by this time, were still a force to be reckoned with and Kausch's Panzer Regiment alone knocked out 487 Russian tanks in those final battles. Kausch was badly wounded during these battles and was taken prisoner by the Soviets on May 2, 1945. From there he had to endure almost eleven years in various Soviet POW camps, namely Tscherepovez, Minsk, Stalingrad and Sverdlovsk. After being released on January 16, 1956, he returned to his native Germany and rebuilt his life. From July 1, 1956 to June 30, 1976, Kausch was an executive purchaser in a world-wide pharmaceutical firm.

be treated as second-class citizens. They were supported by their families, much of the population and even by their church. For a short time they felt that they were heroes, fighting for a noble cause.

But after many tragic battles, the fight had been lost. When the war was over they returned to their country as the vanquished, the defeated. Instead of flowers, they were greeted with stones. They arrived and were granted less than their fathers who had fought in the First World War. Instead of retaining their rights as second-class citizens, they were thrown in jail. Some were executed. Their families and friends were forced to denounce them.

Many of the soldiers who fought in the Second Great War have strong opinions on those violent and often tragic days of their youth. Some regret the war and its destruction and feel that the many young boys who died fighting the Russians on the Eastern Front did so in vain. They did not achieve what they were fighting for. Others have remained convinced that they did the right thing, despite the losses and the fact that they ultimately lost the war. These men are proud to have served, and have no regrets. There were still others who simply wanted to forget the sad and tragic, as well as the good days of the war.

Anton Kotlowski wrote, among other things:[19]

---

[19] Letter to the author from A. Kotlowski dated May 10, 1997.

Veterans of the PAK: Pictured here are from left to right, Fons Van Broeck, Karel De Maeyer, and Hans Wallow. The gentleman on the far right has not been identified. Fons, a motorcycle messenger throughout the war, was interned for 42 months. After being released he became a construction worker and in July 1971 he was married. Karel De Maeyer, who had been with the heavy weapons platoon (5./ "Flandern") since the beginning, and had first served as a Richtschütze for the 1. Geschütz under Unterscharführer Behling in the single PAK platoon. De Maeyer was badly wounded on January 9, 1944 during the battles in Ukraine and never returned to Langemarck. After the war he contributed to the history of the Flemish Waffen-SS units by writing the history of the PAK unit for the book "Vlaanderen in Uniform" by Jan Vincx. Hans Wallow, a German who served as "Spieß," often visited his Flemish comrades after the war and was regularly seen at reunions in Flanders.

No. 1 Gunner and his Commander: Pictured here are Remy Schrijnen at the left and his former Commander, Georg D'Haese at Schrijnen's home in October 1996.

Despite that fact that Himmler did not in any way have command over the Waffen-SS – as the Waffen-SS was completely led by the army – he had ordered the formation of the Totenkopf Division. Some of the officers of this unit came from the SS-TV, or SS-Totenkopf-Verbände. With this chess-move, service in the SS-TV and the SS-Verfügungstruppe (later the Waffen-SS) became one in the same. With that he cheated the SS-Verfügungstruppe units out of official service in the German army.

By making the SS-TV (Totenkopfverbände = guard units of the concentration and work camps) and the Waffen-SS the same, the Waffen-SS was claimed to be a criminal organization in Nürnberg. It is a fact, though, that the "Totenkopf Division" was one of the forty Waffen-SS divisions that fought the best. I can't judge the members of the TV, we had <u>nothing</u> to do with this organization.

What did we know? We knew that there were concentration camps. But people came back from them. What really happened, especially in the concentration camps in the Polish areas, we didn't know about this and neither did the German population.

Perhaps the opening of the archives will bring out the truth. Unfortunately the opening of the archives has been postponed another fifty years.

That is it for this subject. It has nothing to do with the Waffen-SS and especially not with the Flemings. The Israeli Court even confirmed that during the Eichmann Trial.

The soldiers of the Waffen-SS, who survived the murderous war and belong to my circle of acquaintances, are and were, everyone of them without exception, good and decent fellow citizens, who have made something of their lives. They are all entrepreneurs, officials in high positions or leaders in firms.

I fled from English prison on March 1, 1946 and arrived in my homeland of Braunau on March 10th. I first went to the dentist who repaired the holes left in my jaw from the teeth that had been kicked out by the English guards.

I had no occupation, and therefore I had to learn something new. I attended technical courses and during the sixth semester I quit school and got a job with the "Coca-Cola Export Corporation." The American manager there had fought against the Waffen-SS during the war and had known them to be a brave and fair enemy. He hired veterans of the Waffen-SS – the Austrian manager was an Untersturmführer, the administration leader was an Oberscharführer, the leader of production had been Hauptmann in the Divi-

sion "Großdeutschland" and the plant manager was a captain in the Kriegsmarine. I began as an accountant and quickly thereafter I became a depot manager, later the sales manager for Austria, then general manager and finally part-owner. In April of 1988, after forty years, I sold the factory to an Australian Coca-Cola company. Since this time I have been a consultant. It is understandable that I didn't have any time to occupy myself with the problems of the past, especially since I was building a family.

That didn't prevent me from avoiding the interests of the soldiers of the former Waffen-SS. I wrote letters to (Austrian) Bundeskanzler Vranitzky and other Austrian officials on our behalf. I never denied my membership in the Waffen-SS and still have my blood-type tattoo on my left arm.

Unfortunately I have large gaps in my memory about the war years. Names and dates I have mostly forgotten. Through correspondence with Flemish comrades more gaps in my memory have become apparent. What little I remember from a talk with the battalion adjutant in January or March 1945 about a promotion to Obersturmführer and the award of the German Cross in Gold has also been confirmed by these letters. But what should all this mean after a lost war?

Toon Pauli wrote:[20]

The Wallonian part of Belgium is socialistic. The Flemish part is Catholic. In general all Belgians are Catholics. Sermons in the schools and in the Church were always directed at the danger of communism. Rome or Moscow. Many Flemings, certainly those of the Legion,[21] volunteered for Catholic reasons. They were disappointed even during the war. In many Flemish churches no funerals were allowed for killed comrades. After the war the church denied that they had any knowledge that volunteers had volunteered due to their religious beliefs. From then on many comrades gave up the Church and Religion.

As far as whether we were used by the Germans, well that is a question that does not have a generalized answer. Everyone has to decide for themselves. A large majority of the volunteers did feel that they were used. Others will deny this. It is certain that Germany needed soldiers (surely after

---

[20] Letter to the author from T. Pauli dated Dec. 6, 1997.
[21] As opposed to the Sturmbrigade or Division. (Author's note.)

Soviet Occupation: On the left is Anton Kotlowski, who became a manager at Coca-Cola in Austria during the Soviet occupation. To his right is a friend and colleague, Potye, who was with Otto Skorzeny during the famous Ardennes Offensive.

Stalingrad) and that there was little consideration for the motives of the volunteers. "Everything was to be cleared up after the war," they told us. In spite of this, one must say that the volunteers from all countries, with very, very few exceptions, remained true to their oath until the end.

Considering the conditions from before and at the beginning of the war, the vast majority of volunteers, I as well, would make the same decision.

With the exception of the Left, we have a good reputation in Flanders, also because the nationalists remain active in politics. Surely in Flanders we have the respect of our people. Due to that we can allow some things which are not possible in other countries.

Certainly during the first years after the war we were sick of politics. There are those who have retained this attitude even today. The majority first became members of the Volksunion (People's Union) and later Vlaams Blok. There were even three or four volunteers that were elected to parliament.

Hermann Van Gyseghem wrote:[22]

---

[22] Letter to the author from H. Van Gyseghem dated Oct. 5, 1996.

My sister, who was a German Red Cross nurse, received a prison sentence of one year and I received four years, which was really very little. Some of us were shot, and the majority of us received ten or twenty year sentences. With that one can understand that the hate towards the Belgian state remains, above all because Belgium is the only country in Europe that has not granted amnesty to their former soldiers. The European volunteers made sure that the communists were only able to advance to the Elbe river, but no one is allowed to say that. Sad, but we don't let it get us down: the majority of us have been successful in life and have built a good existence. We have beautiful families, I myself have five daughters and thirteen grandchildren. Not a week goes by that we don't gather together.

As far as the past is concerned, I don't regret a thing, above all when one considers how our peoples live today. There are no more values in life, marriages break up and no one has respect for life, buildings or the environment. Politics are corrupt, the judges and the politicians are bound to one or another so-called democratic party. The use of drugs increases every day. So then, when one critically thinks about the past, then one must compare everything today directly with the time period we experienced, the time period from back then, from 1933 to 1945.

Jan De Wilde wrote:[23]

Different sources report that about ten thousand Flemings served with either the Flemish Legion and the Sturmbrigade, later Division, "Langemarck." Of those men and boys, two thousand were killed or missing in action. Other sources claim that it was fifteen thousand, but in those cases the N.S.K.K., the Todt Organization as well as other pro-German organizations must have been included.

It has been approximated that about thirty different nations served within the Waffen-SS, mainly Germans and ethnic Germans, as well as men from Western Europe, Eastern Europe, the Balkans and even Asia. In total there were about a million men. It has been approximated that about four hundred thousand were killed or are missing.

---

[23] Letter to the author from J. De Wilde dated Aug. 29, 1996.

Toon Pauli: Pictured above is Toon Pauli, who is the chairman of the Flemish Veteran's Association, St. Maartensfonds, giving a speech at the 45th anniversary of the organization. Pauli fought with the PAK Kompanie during the battles to Jambol during which he was wounded in the face by shrapnel in March 1944. He also fought with the PAK Kompanie in Panzerjägerabteilung 27. In late April 1945, during the fighting on the Oder River, Pauli was once again wounded by shrapnel, this time losing an eye. By the end of the war he had earned the Infantry Assault badge, the Wound Badge in Black, the Close Combat Clasp in Bronze and the Iron Cross 2nd Class. Pauli ended the war as an Unterscharführer, although he stated that this was unofficial.

In conclusion, one can only be amazed at what such a small part of the German Army performed.

It would be interesting for one to read the book "America's War Politics," written by Curtis Dall (Roosevelt's son-in-law). This book is about Pearl Harbor. The book "The Planned Death," written by James Bacque (a Canadian) is about the starvation of one million German prisoners of war after the end of the war in 1945. The book "Wild Pigs" by the Chinese writer Yung-Chang who lived in China reports on his experiences when about sixty million Chinese were killed at the order of Mao Tse Tung. After the fall of Communism in Russia the Russians admitted that they killed twenty thousand Polish officers in 1940. Lenin and Stalin did the same with about forty million Russians. Tito in Yugoslavia never took prisoners, they were immediately killed by partisans. He also cemented in thousands of German prisoners in caves. With all of these statistics I don't want to claim that the Germans did not commit war crimes, I only want to show that no country escapes wartime completely blemish-free.

Anton Kotlowski and Jan De Wilde in 1996: Pictured here are Anton Kotlowski (left) and Jan De Wilde (right) in a café in Vienna, Austria. After being released from prison, Jan De Wilde found a job as a long-distance truck-driver, a job he held for two years. He then became a supervisor for a construction company. Later he founded a dry-cleaning company in Kotrijk which he sold after twenty years. During this time he took various courses in truck-driving, sales and chemical cleaning. After selling the dry-cleaning company, he studied wine and then found a job selling wine, which he kept for the next four years. De Wilde founded and was active in many Flemish cultural and veterans organizations and was a leading official in many.

> *I myself have become a pacifist and anti-militarist due to my own convictions. I think that it is a joke what politicians and rich capitalists put people through and how former enemies that once murdered each other are now supposed to be allies.*

Georg D'Haese wrote:[24]

> *...You know that I didn't want to be confronted with the events of the war years any more. I will never forget them, but I wanted to preserve both the beautiful and painful memories deep in my heart, and not always have to repeatedly pull them out again. Therefore I have always been, in contrast with others, conservative with my statements about the time of the young soldiers. And now I have to bite into the "sour apple" once again. I answer your letters*

---

[24] Letter to the author from G. D'Haese dated Aug. 20, 1996.

Artist Georg D'Haese: D'Haese was in a field hospital during the final days of the war where he was still recovering from a motorcycle accident. Before the Americans came, he managed to escape with his German girlfriend whom he later married. He remained underground for a few years and then later managed to find a job working for a publisher. He proved himself to be a valuable asset to his firm. After he retired, D'Haese also fulfilled a boyhood dream of becoming an artist. He achieved great success and in 1992 his gallery published a book of his art work.

for our dead. Because to remain silent about the past would be like killing them all over again...

...The front camaraderie was actually a one-time thing, unforgettable and unrestorable, a truly expensive good.

No outsider can understand the beating of hearts in unison, the feeling of fighting together and surviving. Nor can one imagine what it feels like to see death in the eyes of the dying. This camaraderie is not possible in "normal life."

New priorities were set for every soldier in his place, in his situation: the battle for existence, problems with the family, and of asserting one's self amongst others. Efforts to maintain a certain appearance occasionally blurred fiction and truth. Spatial differences as well as differences of opinion (political) weakened contacts with others.

As Goethe once wrote to his lover Charlotte, as she complained that she did not receive enough letters from him during his stay in Italy: "passion requires nearness." With camaraderie it is the same.

Camaraderie nevertheless remained between those of the same opinion and between those who more often than not never made a big deal of their performances or awards. But even here the memories of suffering and tears as well as those of the evils of the war faded away. That is also good.

In conclusion I will write the last lines of a poem with the title "Für unsere Toten, sie liebten ihre Heimat so sehr" ("For our dead, they loved their homeland so very much"), which was found on the body of a killed officer:

Eines nur, Mond und leuchtendes Sonnenlicht,
Eines, Eines sagt unseren Toten nicht.Verschweigt es tief,
Sterne und leiser Wind,
daß sie umsonst gefallen sind!

Only one thing, moon and shining sunlight,
just don't say one thing, not one thing to our dead,
remain deeply silent, stars and soft wind,
that they died for nothing!!

Remy Schrijnen wrote:[25]

For months after I was released from prison I would paint slogans on walls voicing our call to be granted general amnesty for our soldiers. We stuck stickers on sign posts wherever they could be found. It was what little we could do. Then for years I was in jail. I didn't regret what I had done, my convictions have remained firm to this very day. One can think and believe what he wants about the situation in the world today, but I remain ready to fight for something better. But even to this day I have not found any so-called democratic politicians, parties or states to be truly democratic, neither the Americans nor the English. Even here as an outcast in the Federal Republic of Germany I have been left ice-cold. So many incorrect things have been done since the end of the war. When it comes to the real truth about the war and the things that came after it, one has to keep his mouth shut. Is that a democracy? I constantly tell myself that one day the moon and the sun will shine. When we were in prison, Adrian Heusdens, who had been in my PAK crew in Narva, said to me, "Yeah, Remy, freedom will never come for us." He was right.

---

[25] Letter to the author from R. Schrijnen dated Oct. 14, 1997.

Appendices

DOCUMENTS

Generalkommando
I.G. (germ.) ╫ Panzer Korps
IIa

Reichsführer ╫ Persönl...	
Derb. Offz. b. OKH / PN /D 5	
Eingang	2 8. Aug. 1944
Tgb.Nr. 757/44	

V o r s c h l a g

für die .

Nennung im Ehrenblatt des Deutschen Heeres

und

besondere Anerkennungsurkunde des Führers.

f. RK vorgeschlagen

K.Gef.St., den 13. August 1944

Der Kommandierende General

[signature] Steiner.

╫ Obergruppenführer und
General der Waffen-╫.

Z u n a m e	Vorname	Geburts- Ort	Tag	Dienstgrad und Dienststellung	Truppen- teil
Schrynen	Remi	Kümtich Flandern	24.12.21	⁊⁊ Sturmmann Richtschütze	3./5. ⁊⁊ Frw. Sturmbrigade Langemarck

1. Seit wann in letzter Dienststellung: 31. Dezember 1943

2. Dienstverhältnis des Vorgeschlagenen: Res.
   (aktiv, E-Offz., d.Res., z.V.)

3. Beruf des Vorgeschlagenen: Bergmann
   (falls nicht im akt. Dienstverhältnis)

4. Friedenstruppenteil des Vorgeschlagenen:
   (nur bei aktiven Soldaten)

5. Diensteintritt: 4.10.1942

6. Zuständiges Wehrbezirks.Kdo.: 'Ers.Kdo.Flandern der Waffen ⁊⁊
   (nur bei Soldaten des B.) Brüssel

7. Rangdienstalter: 1.8.1943

8. Im gegenwärtigen Kriege verliehene Auszeichnungen:

   Verwundeten Abzeichen in Silber am 17.3.1944,
   Eiserne Kreuz 2.Klasse am 28.5.1944,
   Eiserne Kreuz 1.Klasse am 3.8.1944.

9. Privatanschrift des Vorgeschlagenen Schelldorf/Kempten,
   bzw. der nächsten Angehörigen: Duracherstr. 27
   (Ehefrau, Eltern, Geschwister)

10. Beruf des Vaters: Eisenbahner

Kurze Begründung
und Stellungnahme der Zwischenvorgesetzten

Am 26.7.1944 um 9,00 Uhr vormittags griff der Russe mit drei T 34 längs der Rollbahn Narwa-Reval an. Schrynen schoß mit Entfernung 400 m zwei T 34 ab. Nachmittags 15,00 Uhr griff der Russe nochmals mit Infanterie an, unterstützt durch fünf T 34 und einem Panzer Typ "Stalin". Der Angriff wurde unterstützt durch Artillerie und schwere Granatwerfer. Schrynen schoß wiederum zwei T 34 und den Panzer Typ "Stalin" ab. Ein T 34 wurde beschädigt. Die Basatzung botete aus. Der beschädigte Panzer wurde wahrscheinlich in der Nacht abgeschleppt. Am 27.7.1944 4,00 Uhr morgens ging das Geschütz Schreynen 400 m nördlich der Höhe Kinderheim links der Rollbahn Narwa-Reval in Stellung. Schreynen erkannte eine Bereitstellung von feindlichen elf Panzern. Unter Schutz zwei T 34 rollten sechs T 34 und KW II von NO kommend auf die Rollbahn zu. Auf 700 m schoß Schreynen einen T 34 ab. Die 2 sichernden Panzer beschossen das Geschütz. Schreynen beseitigte eine Ladehemmung, 5 Minuten darauf schoß er einen KW II ab, unmittelbar danach fiel das Geschütz durch einen Volltreffer aus. Sch. wurde in den ergänzenden Mitteilungen zum Wehrmachtbericht erwähnt.

Abschrift.   Zum Akt Nr.

F e r n s c h r e i b e n

H-Berghaus

An   Heeresgruppe Nord / IIa

Der Führer hat am 21.9.44 das Ritterkreuz des
Eisernen Kreuzes verliehen an:

- Waffen-Ostubaf. A p e r a t s , Kdr.ɴ-Gren.
  gef. 15.7.44   Rgt.32
                    15.Waffen-Gren.Div.d.ɴ

Waffen-Hstuf. B u t k u s , Kp.Fhr.im ɴ-Feld-
                                    Ers.Btl.19
                    19.Waffen-Gren.Div.d.ɴ

ɴ-Strm. S c h r y n e n , Gesch.Fhr.3./ɴ-Frw.
                    Sturmbrif."Langemarck"
          Gen.Kdo.III.(germ.)ɴ-Pz.Korps.

Sofort bekanntgeben und Aushändigung der Aus-
zeichnung veranlassen, ausgenommen für Aperats.
Verständigung der Div.und Aushändigung der Aus.
zeichnung an die Hinterbliebenen wird von hier
veranlasst.

                    Verb.Offz.d.Waffen-ɴ
                    b.OKW/PA/P5 1.Staffel
                    Tgb.Nr. 777/44
                         gez. K m e n t
Nachrichtlich: ɴ-Sturmbannführer

ɴ-Ostubaf.Grothmann
RF-ɴ Adjutantur A.u.O.
ɴ-Gruf.u.Gen.Lt.d.W.-ɴ Fegelein
ɴ-FHA. Adjutantur
ɴ-Pers.HA., Adjutantur
ɴ-Ustuf. Dr. Venn

F.d.R.d.A.
ɴ-Obersturmführer

IM NAMEN·DES FÜHRERS
UND
OBERSTEN BEFEHLSHABERS
DER WEHRMACHT
IST DEM

SS-Ober-Schütze   Alfons   V a n   B r o e c k

5./Freiw.-Leg."Flandern"

AM   22. Juni   1942

DIE MEDAILLE
WINTERSCHLACHT IM OSTEN
1941/42
(OSTMEDAILLE)
VERLIEHEN WORDEN.

FÜR DIE RICHTIGKEIT:

Freiw. Legion „Flandern"

und Kommandeur

IM NAMEN DES FÜHRERS
UND OBERSTEN BEFEHLSHABERS
DER WEHRMACHT

VERLEIHE ICH

DEM

ϟϟ-Sturmmann

Alfons van Broeck

5./Freiwilligen Legion "Flandern"

DAS

KRIEGSVERDIENSTKREUZ
2. KLASSE
MIT SCHWERTERN

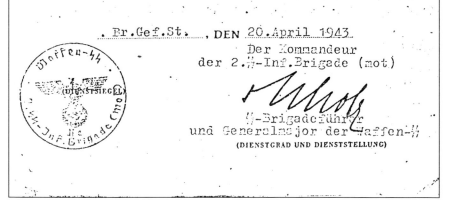

Br.Gef.St. , DEN 20.April 1943
Der Kommandeur
der 2.ϟϟ-Inf.Brigade (mot)

ϟϟ-Brigadeführer
und Generalmajor der Waffen-ϟϟ
(DIENSTGRAD UND DIENSTSTELLUNG)

Im Namen des führers und Obersten Befehlshabers der Wehrmacht

verleihe ich

dem

ϟϟ-Unterscharführer

Joris d ' H a e s e

3./Freiw.Legion "Flandern"

das

Eiserne Kreuz 2.Klasse

Br.Gef.St. ,den 14.Februar 19.43

Der Kommandeur
der 2.ϟϟ-Inf.Brigade (mot)

ϟϟ-Brigadeführer
und Generalmajor der Waffen-ϟϟ
(Dienstgrad und Dienststellung)

258

Beſitzzeugnis

Dem

ϟϟ–Oberschützen Joris D ' H a e s e

[Name, Dienſtgrad]

3./Freiwilligen-Legion "Flandern"

[Truppenteil, Dienſtſtelle]

iſt auf Grund

ſeiner am .... 7. März 1942 .... erlittenen

ein.. maligen Verwundung oder Beſchädigung

das

Verwundetenabzeichen

in .... schwarz ....

verliehen worden.

.... O.U. , den .. 25. Mai .. 19 42

Der Führer der Freiwilligen-Legion
" F l a n d e r n "

[Unterschrift]

ϟϟ–Obersturmbannführer u. Kommandeur.

[Dienſtgrad und Dienſtſtelle]

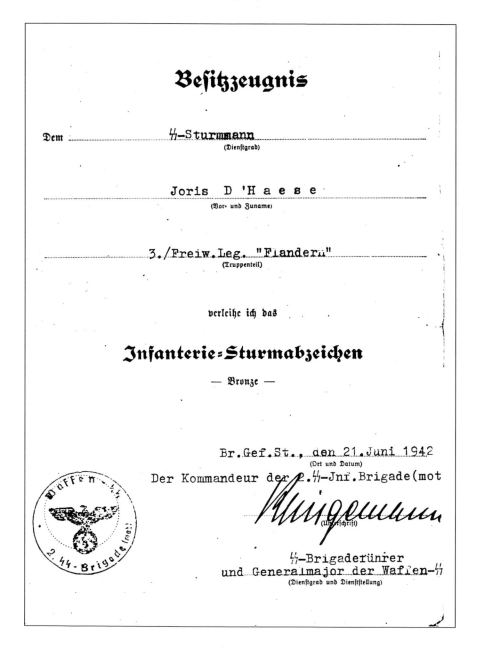

Besitzeugnis

Dem _____ ᚻ-Sturmmann _____
(Dienstgrad)

Joris D 'H a e s e
(Vor- und Zuname)

3./Freiw.Leg. "Flandern"
(Truppenteil)

verleihe ich das

Infanterie-Sturmabzeichen

— Bronze —

Br.Gef.St., den 21.Juni 1942
(Ort und Datum)
Der Kommandeur der 2.ᚻ-Jnf.Brigade(mot

(Unterschrift)

ᚻ-Brigadeführer
und Generalmajor der Waffen-ᚻ
(Dienstgrad und Dienststellung)

IM NAMEN DES FÜHRERS
UND
OBERSTEN BEFEHLSHABERS
DER WEHRMACHT
IST DEM

SS-Sturmmann Joris D ' H a e s e

3./Freiw.-Legion " Flandern "

AM   22. Juni 1942

DIE MEDAILLE
WINTERSCHLACHT IM OSTEN
1941/42
(OSTMEDAILLE)
VERLIEHEN WORDEN.

FÜR DIE RICHTIGKEIT:

Freiw. Legion „Flandern"

SS-Sturmbannführer
und Kommandeur

GLOSSARY

Abteilung	Waffen-SS term for unit of battalion strength
Allgemeine-SS	General-SS
alte Hase	lit.: old rabbit, German "Landser" term for experienced and skilled combat veteran
Armee	army
Artillerie	artillery
Ausbildungs und Ersatz	training and replacement
Bataillon	battalion
Batterie	battery
Brigadeführer	SS rank: major general
De Vlag	Flemish cultural activist society, Duits-Vlaamse Arbeidsgemeenschap (German-Flemish Workers Society)
Ersatz	replacement, substitute
Fahrer	driver
Fallschirmjäger	paratrooper
FLAK	abbreviation for FLieger Abwehr Kanone; anti-aircraft gun
Führer	leader
Führerschule	leadership school
Geschützführer	gun leader, gun captain, responsible for gun's crew
Granatwerfer	mortar
Grenadier	motorized infantry man
Gruppe	group
Gruppenführer	SS rank: lieutenant general, gen. leader of group, same as Geschützführer, but for infantry or other branches of service
Hauptmann	German rank: captain
Hauptscharführer	SS rank: sergeant-major
Hauptsturmführer	SS rank: captain
Heer	Flemish: Mr., German: army
Herr	German: Mr.
Hohlraumgranate	hollow charge anti-tank shell, explodes after impact
Infanterie	infantry
Junkerschule	officer candidate school
Kampfgruppe	battle group
Kanone	cannon
Kommandeur	commander
Kompanie	mil.: company
Kompanie Chef	official company commander, minimum rank: captain or Hauptsturmführer
Kompanie Führer	unofficial or temporary company commander, minimum rank: second lieutenant or Untersturmführer
Korps	corps
Landser	nickname for veteran German combat soldier
Ladeschütze	loader

Lazerett	field hospital
Leutnant	German rank: lieutenant
(mot)	abbreviation for motorized
MG	machine gun
Muni-Schütze	crew member responsible for munitions
Nebelwerfer	smoke grenade launcher
Obergruppenführer	SS rank: general
Oberführer	SS rank: brigadier general
Oberscharführer	SS rank: color sergeant
Oberschütze	SS rank: private first class
Oberst	German rank: colonel
Oberstgruppenführer	SS rank: colonel general
Obersturmbannführer	SS rank: lieutenant colonel
Obersturmführer	SS rank: second lieutenant
Oostfronter	lit.: Eastern Fronter – Flemish term for veteran of the war in Russia
PAK	abbreviation for Panzer Abwehr Kanone; anti-tank gun
Panzer	tank
Panzerbüchse	German "Landser" term for portable Russian tripod-mounted anti-tank weapon
Panzerfaust	German version of bazooka
Panzergranate	anti-tank shell
Panzergrenadier	motorized infantry man in a unit containing tanks
Panzerjäger	lit. tank hunter, gen. anti-tank
Pionier	combat engineer
Ratschbumm	German "Landser" nickname for Russian PAK, named for the sound it made
Richtschütze	no. 1 gunner
Rottenführer	SS rank: senior corporal
Scharführer	SS rank: sergeant
Schütze	SS rank: private, gen. enlisted man
schwer (schw.)	adj.: heavy
Siecherheitsdienst (SD)	security service
SIG	schweres Infanterie Geschütz – heavy infantry cannon
Spieß	position: senior-sergeant, termed "the mother of the troops"
Sprenggranate	anti-personnel shell for anti-tank gun
SS	Schutz-Staffel or protection squad
Stab	staff
Stabscharführer	rank and position: staff sergeant (Spieß)
Standarte	SS term for unit of regimental strength
Standartenführer	SS rank: colonel
Sturmbannführer	SS rank: major
Sturmbrigade	"storm brigade" – fancy term for brigade
Sturmgeschütz	mobile artillery, assault gun
Sturmmann	SS rank: lance-corporal
Strumscharführer	SS rank: warrant officer

Untersturmführer	SS rank: lieutenant
SS-Verfügungstruppe	SS special-purpose troops, precursor to Waffen-SS
VERDINASO	Flemish political movement, VERbond van DIets NAtionaal SOlidaristen or Orginization of Dutch National Socialists.
VNV	conservative Flemish political party, Vlaamsch National Verbond
Volksdeutscher	ethnic German
Volksturm	German people's army, consisting of young boys (< 17 years) and older men (45+ years)
Wehrmacht	former German armed forces, consisted of Heer (army), Marine (navy), Luftwaffe (air force), Waffen-SS (armed SS).
Waffen-SS	armed SS, elite German units, fought under Wehrmacht command
Werfer	rocket launcher
Zug	mil.: platoon
Zugführer	platoon leader

SOURCES

Public Archives:
Bundesarchiv, Abt. VI, Berlin, Germany
Bundesarchiv – Militärarchiv, Freiburg, Germany
Deutsche Dienststelle, Berlin, Germany
United States National Archives, College Park, Virginia, USA

Private Archives:
De Bast, Luc
Etnika V.Z.W.
Van Gyseghem, Hermann
Wangemann, Ekkehard
Yerger, Mark C.

Personal Correspondence:
Anseeuw, Dries (through Toon Pauli): Nov. 1997, Dec. 8, 1997.
Bottu, René (through Luc De Bast): Dec. 1, 1997.
De Wilde, Jan: Feb. 27, 1996, Aug. 6, 1996, Aug. 29, 1996, March 10, 1997, Nov. 20, 1997.
D'Haese, Georg: Jan. 1, 1996, Feb. 13, 1996, April 10, 1996, May 11, 1996, Aug. 20, 1996, Sept. 23, 1996, Nov. 12, 1996, Nov. 29, 1996, Jan. 18, 1997, Jan. 27, 1997, Feb. 9, 1997, March 24, 1997, Aug. 25, 1997, Sept. 17, 1997, Nov. 28, 1997.
Ide, Gaston†: July 6, 1996, Aug. 8, 1996.
Kausch, Paul-Albert: Aug. 7, 1995, Sept. 17, 1995.
Kotlowski, Anton: Feb. 1, 1997, Feb. 2, 1997, May 10, 1997, June 4, 1997, Aug. 5, 1997.
Pauli, Anton (Toon): May 17, 1996, June 11, 1996, June 18, 1996, June 23, 1996, July 27, 1996, Aug. 23, 1996, Oct. 14, 1996, Dec. 16, 1996, Dec. 17, 1996, Dec. 25, 1996, Jan. 27, 1997, Feb. 12, 1997, April 18, 1997, June 16, 1997, Aug. 18, 1997, Sept. 17, 1997, Oct. 20, 1997, Oct. 27, 1997, Nov. 10, 1997, Nov. 17, 1997, Dec. 11, 1997.
Schrijnen, Remy: Feb. 8, 1995, Feb. 28, 1995, March 21, 1995, April 24, 1995, May 1, 1995, Oct. 30, 1995, Oct. 31, 1995, Nov. 10, 1995, Feb. 9, 1996, Mar. 11, 1996, May 13, 1996, May 17, 1996, June 7, 1996, June 12, 1996, June 19, 1996, July 30, 1996, Aug. 10, 1996, Sept. 10, 1996, Sept. 30, 1996, Dec. 13, 1996, Dec. 17, 1996, Feb. 15, 1997, May 16, 1997, June 16, 1997, July 22, 1997, Aug. 28, 1997, Sept. 16, 1997, Oct. 14, 1997, Nov. 28, 1997, Dec. 6, 1997, Dec. 11, 1997.
Van Broeck, Alfons (through Luc De Bast): Aug. 8, 1996.
Van De Wiele-Laperre, Mevr. Lea: June 18, 1996, Aug. 30, 1996.
Van Gyseghem, Hermann: Aug. 21, 1996, Oct. 5, 1996.
Van Ruymbeke, Michael July 11, 1996, Dec. 6, 1997
Wangemann, Ekkehard March 10, 1997, April 8, 1997.

Interviews (conducted on numerous days during the following months):
D'Haese, Georg: Oct. 1996, Oct. 1997.
Schrijnen, Remy: Sept. and Oct. 1996.
Van Broeck, Fons: Oct. 1997.
Pauli, Toon: Sept. 1996, Oct. 1997.

Bibliography:

Angolia, John R., *For Führer and Fatherland – Military Awards of the Third Reich*. R. James Bender Publishing, San Jose, California, USA, fourth printing, 1989.

Bender, Roger James and Taylor, Hugh Page, *Uniforms, Organization and History of the Waffen-SS*, Vol. 2. R. James Bender Publishing, Mountain View, California, first edition, 1971.

Haupt, Werner, *German Anti-Tank Guns – 37mm – 50mm – 75mm – 88mm PAK, 1935-1945*. Schiffer Publishing Ltd., West Chester, PA, USA, 1990.

Klietmann, Dr. K.-G., *Die Waffen-SS – Eine Dokumentation*. Verlag , Der Freiwillige" G.m.b.H., Osnabrück, Germany, 1965.

Krätschmer, Ernst-Günther, *Die Ritterkreuzträger der Waffen-SS*. Verlag K. W. Schütz KG, Preußisch Oldendorf, Germany, 3. Auflage, 1982.

Landwehr, Richard, *Lions of Flanders*,- Flemish Volunteers of the Waffen-SS, 1941-1945. Shelf Books, Bradford, U.K., second edition, 1996.

Littlejohn, David, *Foreign Legions of the Third Reich*, – Vol. 2: *Belgium, Great Britain, Holland, Italy and Spain*. R. James Bender Publishing, San Jose, California, USA, second printing, 1987.

Schulze-Kossens, Richard, *Die Junkerschulen*, Militärischer Führernachwuchs der Waffen-SS. Munin-Verlag G.m.b.H., Osnabrück, Germany, second edition, 1987.

Toelen, Alfred, *Die SS-Freiwilligen-Legion ,,Flandern."* Der Freiwillige Zeitschrift, February 1965.

Toelen, Alfred, *Die 6. SS-Sturmbrigade ,,Langemarck"*. Der Freiwillige Zeitschrift, March 1965.

Toelen, Alfred, *Die 27. SS-Freiwilligen-Panzer-Grenadier-Division ,,Langemarck."* Der Freiwillige Zeitschrift, April 1965.

Van Arendonck, A., *Vlamingen aan het Oostfront* Deel I: Het Vlaams Legioen. Etnika V.Z.W. Antwerpen, Belgium, 1973.

Van Arendonck, A., *Vlamingen aan het Oostfront* Deel II: "Langemarck." Etnika V.Z.W. Antwerpen, Belgium, 1975.

Vincx, Jan, *Archivalia* 1940-1945 Vlamingen aan het Oostfront, Vlamingen op het Thuisfront. Etnika V.Z.W. Antwerpen, Belgium, 1993.

Vincx, Jan and Schotanius, Viktor, *Nederlanse vrijwilligers in Europese krijgsdienst* 1940-1945 – Deel 3: Vrijw. Panstergrenadier Brigade "Nederland," 23e Pantsergrenadier Divisie "Nederland." Etnika V.Z.W. Herentals, Belgium, 1989.

Vincx, Jan, *Vlaanderen in Uniform*, 1940-1945 – Deel 7. Etnika V.Z.W. Antwerpen, Belgium, 1984.

Weidinger, Otto, *Division Das Reich*, Band V: 1943-1945. Munin Verlag GmbH, Osnabrück, Germany, 1982.

Yerger, Mark, *Knights of Steel – Vol. 2, The Structure, Development and Personalities of the 2. SS-Panzer-Division "Das Reich."* privately published, Lancaster, Pennsylvania, USA, 1994.

Photo Credits
Anseeuw, Dries
Bottu, René
Brandt, Allen
Broughton, Scott
Bundesarchiv
De Bast, Luc
De Wilde, Jan
D'Haese, Georg
Fleischer, Heinz
Ide, Gaston†
Kausch, Paul-Albert
Kotlowski, Anton
Neitzke, Erich
Pauli, Toon / Etnika V.Z.W.
Schrijnen, Remy
Van der Wiele-Laperre, Lea
Wangemann, Ekkehard
Yerger, Mark

Index